Oil and British Naval Power

Robin F. Ransom

Abstract

This book analyses the significance of oil to British strategy during 1914 -1923. It shows that by 1923 Britain had a coherent oil policy, which affected naval strategy, diplomatic relations, policy towards the oil industry and post-war aims in the Middle East. Previous works have looked at only part of the picture and have not appreciated the extent to which oil affected all these areas. This work brings all these different facets together into a single study. The most important British user of oil was the Royal Navy, which was replacing coal with oil as its principal fuel even before the First World War, which saw great growth in the use of oil. Aircraft and land vehicles powered by oil fuelled internal combustion engines transformed both warfare and civilian life, but their overall usage of oil was much less than that of the RN. British industry was slower than the RN to adopt oil because coal was cheaper; the RN put the technical advantages of oil ahead of cost.

Britain's power and prestige was based on its naval supremacy; British dominance of naval fuel bunkering was a key factor in this. Britain had substantial reserves of coal, including Welsh steam coal, the best in the world for naval use, but little oil. Britain's oil strategy in 1914 was to build up reserves cheaply in peacetime and to buy on the market in wartime. An oil crisis in 1917 showed that this was flawed and that secure British controlled supplies were needed. The war created an opportunity for Britain to secure substantial oil reserves in the Middle East. Attempts to obtain control of these affected the peace treaties and Britain's post-war relations with its Allies. The USA was then the world's largest producer and was the main supplier to the Allies during the war. It believed, wrongly, that its output would decline in the 1920s and feared that Britain was trying to exclude it from the rest of the world. France also realised that it needed access to safe and reliable supplies of oil.

The largest available potential oilfield was in the Mosul vilayet, part of the Ottoman Empire in 1914, and now part of Iraq. The 1916 Sykes-Picot Agreement allocated about half of Mosul to France, which in 1918 agreed to include all of it in the British mandate territory of Iraq in return for a share of the oil and British support elsewhere. Other disagreements delayed an Anglo-French oil agreement, but one was finally signed at San Remo in 1920. It was followed by the Treaty of Sèvres with the Ottoman Empire, which appeared to give Britain all that it wanted in the Middle East. The resurgence of Turkey under Mustafa Kemal meant that a new treaty had to be negotiated at Lausanne in 1923. Sèvres angered the USA, since it appeared to exclude US oil companies from Iraq. For a period Britain focused on the need to have a large British controlled oil company, but it was eventually realised that control of oil bearing territory was more important than the nationality of companies. This allowed US oil companies to be given a stake in Iraqi oil, improving Anglo-American relations. Britain's need for oil meant that it had to ensure that the Treaty of Lausanne left Mosul as part of the British mandate territory of Iraq. Turkey objected, but the League of Nations ruled in Britain's favour. Britain had other interests in the region, but most of them did not require control over Mosul. Mosul's oil gave Britain secure supplies and revenue that made Iraq viable without British subsidies. By 1923 Britain had devised a coherent strategy of ensuring secure supplies of oil by controlling oil bearing territory.

Table of Contents

Oil Companies

APOC
: Anglo-Persian Oil Company. William D'Arcy obtained a licence to explore for oil in Persia in 1901, going into partnership with Burmah Oil in 1905. Oil was found in 1908 and APOC was formed the next year to develop the discovery. Sir Charles Greenway became Chairman in 1914, the same year that the British government took a majority shareholding and gave APOC a long term contract to supply the RN. Renamed Anglo-Iranian in 1935 and British Petroleum in 1954. British Petroleum was originally a German owned oil distribution and marketing company, which was sequestered by Britain during the First World War. Now known as BP.

Burmah
: British oil company whose oilfields were located mainly in Burma, then part of the British Empire and sometimes spelt Burmah. The Chairman during this period was J. T. Cargill. A subsidiary of BP since 2000.

CFP
: Compagnie Française des Pétroles. Established in 1924 to hold France's stake in the TPC. Owned by French oil companies and banks, but with close links to the French government. Now known as Total.

Mexican Eagle
: Founded in 1909 by Sir Weetman Pearson, an engineer and Liberal MP who became Lord Cowdray in 1910. It operated exclusively in Mexico and was sold to RDS in 1919 and nationalised in 1938.

RDS
: Royal Dutch Shell. Royal Dutch merged with Shell, a British company, in 1907. They split their assets 60 per cent Royal Dutch and 40 per cent Shell, but remained separate holding companies with their own boards of directors and stock market listings until 2007. During this period Shell's chairman was its founder Sir Marcus Samuel, later Lord Bearsted, and Henri Deterding was President of Royal Dutch.

Standard (NJ)
: Standard Oil of New Jersey. Largest of the companies that resulted after Standard Oil was broken up by a US Federal Court in 1911 because it had broken anti-trust laws. Re-named Exxon in 1972 and merged with Mobil to form ExxonMobil in 1998. A. C. Bedford became Chairman in 1917, with Walter Teagle replacing him as President.

Standard (NY)
: Standard Oil of New York. The second largest of the former Standard Oil companies. Re-named Mobil in 1966 and merged with Exxon in 1998. The other former Standard companies operated almost entirely in the Americas at this time.

TPC
: Turkish Petroleum Company. Formed in 1912 to explore for oil in the Ottoman Empire and initially owned 25 per cent by RDS, 25 per cent by Deutsche Bank and 50 per cent by the British controlled National Bank of Turkey. In March 1914 the National Bank of Turkey's stake was transferred to APOC. RDS and APOC each gave up 2.5 per cent of the profits, but not the votes, to

Calouste Gulbenkian, a British citizen of Armenian ancestry who owned 30 per cent of the National Bank of Turkey.

Glossary of Oil Industry Terms

Benzene
At this time a by product of coke, but now mostly produced from petroleum. Added to petrol to improve its octane rating. Use now limited for health reasons.

Bitumen
A black viscous mixture of hydrocarbons, which occurs both naturally and as a residue of refining. Natural sources were used for water-proofing and as adhesives for thousands of years before the development of the oil industry.

Bunker oil
Fuel oil used by ships.

Cannel coal
Type of coal with a high hydrogen component from which paraffin/kerosene can be extracted.

Coal tar
By product of the carbonisation of coal to produce coke.

Creosote oil
Heavy oil distilled from coal tar and suitable for burning in boilers.

Crude oil
Unrefined oil. A classification system using the API Gravity was introduced in 1921. Light crude (API gravity over 31.1°) produces a greater proportion of lighter and more valuable products such as petrol than medium crude (API gravity 22.3° to 31.1°). The output from heavy crudes (API gravity under 22.3°) is mostly suitable only to be burnt in boilers.

Distillation
Separation of the components of a mixture by the difference in boiling points.

Diesel fuel
Refined oil used to power a compression ignition internal combustion engine of the type invented by Rudolf Diesel.

Fuel oil
Technically any oil used to fuel an engine, but here refers to the heavy residue left after the refining process, which is burnt in boilers to power steam engines. Unrefined crude can be burnt in boilers, but it is more economic to use the residue that remains after more valuable products have been extracted from the crude.

Gasoline
See petrol.

Hydrogenation
Process used to produce oil from coal. The Bergius process was patented in 1913 and the Fischer-Tropsch one was developed in the 1920s.

Kerosene
See paraffin.

Lubricating oil
Oil used to lubricate the moving parts of internal combustion engines.

Octane
Properly a hydrocarbon, but popularly used as measure of the quality of petrol; the higher the better.

Paraffin
Refined product used for cooking, heating and, before the introduction of electricity, lighting. Also known as kerosene.

Petrol
Refined oil used to power a spark-ignition internal combustion engine. Also known as gasoline.

Petroleum   Another term for crude oil, from the Latin for rock oil.

Refining   Process of converting crude oil into end-products. Distillation is the first stage, and may be the only one at an unsophisticated refinery.

Shale oil   Oil extracted from oil shale, an organic-rich sedimentary rock.

Toluol   Vital component of explosives, which can be extracted from coal or oil.

Introduction

Oil has affected military and diplomatic strategy since the First World War. A number of books published in the 1920s and 30s argued that Britain and the USA were fighting an undeclared war for control of the world's oil resources. They had titles such as *The World Struggle for Oil, We Fight for Oil, Oil Imperialism, The Secret War, The Oil Trusts and Anglo-American Relations* and *The Oil War*.[1] Their conclusions split broadly along national lines. Frenchmen such as Francis Delaisi and Pierre L'Espagnol De La Tramerye were concerned that their country was being left behind because the French oil industry was dominated by a cartel. It was happy to make monopoly profits importing products from Standard Oil of New Jersey[2], whilst showing no desire to take the risks involved in going out and exploring for oil. Americans, including Ludwell Denny and Frank Hanighan, feared that the British were winning the battle to control the world's oil; they attributed this to the British policy being more coherent that of the Americans rather to any greater perfidy on the part of the British. Anton Mohr, a Dane, believed that the British had a strong lead over the Americans. The British authors E. H. Davenport and Sidney Cooke wished that if only it were true that Britain had as well thought out and successful strategy to control the world's oil as its foreign critics believed. This thesis aims to show that the Britain's oil strategy was far more coherent than Davenport and Cooke realised. It affected many areas, including diplomatic relations, especially with France and the USA, war aims and Middle Eastern policy.

The battle for oil in the 1920s followed the First World War, which showed the importance of oil to modern warfare. At the end of the war Lord Curzon claimed

---

[1] E. H. Davenport, S. R. Cooke, *The Oil Trusts and Anglo-American Relations* (London: Macmillan and Co. Ltd, 1923); F. Delaisi, *Oil: Its Influence on Politics*, trans., C. L. Leese (London: George Allen & Unwin, 1922); L. Denny, *We Fight for Oil* (New York, NY: Alfred A. Knopf, 1928); L. Fischer, *Oil Imperialism: The International Struggle for Petroleum* (Westport, CT: Hyperion Press, 1976; reprint, originally published by G. Allen & Unwin, London, 1926.); F. C. Hanighen, *The Secret War* (Westport, CT: Hyperion Press, 1976; reprint, originally published by the John Day Co., New York, NY, 1934); P. L'Espagnol de la Tramerye, *The World Struggle for Oil*, trans., C. L. Leese (London: G. Allen & Unwin Ltd, 1923); A. Mohr, *The Oil War* (London: Martin Hopkinson & Co. Ltd, 1926).

[2] Standard Oil was split into several companies by a US Federal Court in 1911 because it had broken anti-trust laws. The most important of them was Standard Oil of New Jersey, hereafter referred to as Standard (NJ).

that 'he might say that the Allies floated to victory upon a wave of oil.'[3] This comment has subsequently been widely quoted; one of the objectives of this work is to examine its accuracy.[4] One the authors who quotes Curzon is Daniel Yergin. He argues that oil significantly altered many aspects of life during the twentieth century, not least warfare. Before 1914 armies depended on horses and railways for mobility. During the conflict warfare was transformed by oil fuelled motor vehicles, tanks, aircraft and submarines. An increasing number of surface warships were powered by oil rather than coal. This created a problem for Britain, which was a leader in the adoption of oil for its navy. It had substantial coal reserves; the best coal in the world for maritime use was Welsh steam coal, a type found only in south Wales. Britain had a worldwide network of bunkering facilities.[5] Ian Lessor argues that this dominance of the supply of the world's maritime fuel meant that in the late nineteenth century Britain had a similar position in the world fuel market to that now possessed by Saudi Arabia. Britain supplied the USN with coal at Hong Kong just before the start of the Spanish-American War but refused Russia coal during the Russo-Japanese War.[6] The analogy with Saudi Arabia is not entirely accurate, as the USA was the largest coal producer in the world, but Britain dominated the global export market. In 1913 it exported 100 million out of its total output of 292 million metric tons of coal. Germany exported 35 million of a production of 279 million metric tons; the USA sent only 20 million of its output of 518 million metric tons abroad. No other country exported over 8 million metric tons that year.[7] Britain was in a very strong fuel position in the age of coal but had little oil. Most of the oil that has been subsequently discovered in its Empire could not have been developed with the technology of the day. Oil had become crucial to national security, but Britain lacked secure supplies. During the war most Allied oil came

---

[3] Delaisi, *Oil*, p. 87. The report of the speech in *The Times* of 22 November 1918 quoted Curzon as saying 'we might almost say', making his comment less emphatic, but Leese, the translator of the English language edition of Delaisi's book, stated that he was provided with a copy of the original speech by Curzon. See footnote, p. 86.

[4] For example. G. Jones, *The State and the Emergence of the British Oil Industry* (London: Macmillan, 1981), p. 249; F. Venn, *Oil Diplomacy in the Twentieth Century* (Basingstoke: Macmillan, 1986), p. 35; D. Yergin, *The Prize: The Epic Quest for Oil, Money and Power* (New York, NY: Simon & Schuster, 1991), p. 183.

[5] J. T. Sumida, 'British Naval Operational Logistics, 1914-1918', *Journal of Military History* 57, no. 3 (1993), pp. 460-61.

[6] I. O. Lessor, *Resources and Strategy: Vital Materials in International Conflict, 1600-Present Day* (Basingstoke: Macmillan, 1989), p. 25.

[7] J. H. Ronaldson, *Coal* (London: John Murray, 1920), pp. 6-7., Tables I & II,

from the USA, then easily the largest oil producer in the world. It was not certain that the USA would be either willing or able to supply Britain in a future conflict. It might be unfriendly, and it might not be able to supply British needs even if it were friendly; in the early 1920s US domestic demand was rising, and it was widely believed that its oil output would soon decline.[8]

The modern oil industry is commonly accepted to date from 1859, when Edwin Drake successfully drilled a well in Pennsylvania. A kerosene industry existed in Central Europe, but on a small scale because it was dependent on manual labour until the development of drilling techniques.[9] For many centuries animal and vegetable oils had been used for lighting and heating purposes. In some parts of the world, notably the Middle East but also Central and Eastern Europe, there were natural seepages of oil that were exploited by locals long before the modern oil industry was even dreamt of. Marco Polo reported such activities in Baku in the 13th century; Herodotus wrote of the use of bitumen as cement in Babylon.[10] The development of drilling techniques allowed the growth of the global oil industry in the second half of the nineteenth century. In the early twentieth century navies started to adopt oil in place of coal as their main fuel. The RN was one of the first navies to switch to oil, requiring Britain to adopt an oil policy.

By 1914 Britain had made the first steps towards having an oil policy, but the process had a long way to go. This is a story that has played a part in many histories, including those of the oil industry, Britain and the Middle East, the Mesopotamian Campaign of the First World War, Anglo-American relations and the history of the RN. It has not until now been the central part of a single work. Paul Ashmore gave a conference paper titled 'Ideology and Empire: Securing Britain's Supplies of Oil, C.1918-1929' in 2006. Its emphasis is on the ideology

---

[8] Yergin, *Prize*, p. 194.

[9] Ibid., pp. 23-8.

[10] Herodotus, *The History*, trans., G. Rawlinson (Chicago, IL: University of Chicago, 1990), p. 40. book 1, para. 179; For Polo reference see Jones, *State*, p. 1.

and the way in which attempts to obtain oil from the empire was intended to bring Britain and the Dominions closer together.[11]

There are a number of monographs on Britain and oil: these concentrate on Mesopotamia/Iraq[12], take a longer time period or are more interested in the industry than in politics, diplomacy and military factors. The author who is the most adamant that oil was the central factor in British strategy towards Mesopotamia and later Iraq is Helmut Mejcher. He claims that in 1918 and later there were no objections from other policy makers towards the Admiralty's desire for Middle Eastern oil. Maurice Hankey, the Cabinet Secretary, influenced by Admiral Sir Edmond Slade, the Admiralty's oil expert, pushed for Britain to occupy Mosul and overcame the objections of Arthur Balfour, the Foreign Secretary. Keeping control over the potential oil of Mosul was a key aim of Curzon, Balfour's successor, when negotiating the Treaty of Lausanne in 1923.[13]

Marian Kent makes the case that Britain had an oil policy by the end of the First World War.[14] She does place more emphasis than Mejcher on the other factors that influenced British strategy in the Middle East, such as protection of the route to India and Britain's traditional position in the Persian Gulf. Her *Oil and Empire* studies the attempts of the British Government to secure oil supplies for both military and other economic purposes, the development of a state oil policy and its impact on foreign policy. Persia and Mesopotamia were the most promising areas for Britain to obtain significant quantities of oil. Since Britain gained control of Persian oil just before the start of the First World War, the

---

[11] P. Ashmore, "Ideology and Empire: Securing Britain's Supplies of Oil, C.1918-1929", ESTER and SBR http://www.isb.ruhr-uni-bochum.de/forschung/tagungen/mining/papers.html.de (accessed 28 January 2008).

[12] The Ottoman provinces or vilayets of Basra, Baghdad and Mosul were collectively called Mesopotamia in the West before they were formed into the state of Iraq in 1920.

[13] H. Mejcher, *Imperial Quest for Oil* (London: Ithaca Press, 1976), pp. 377-91; 'Oil and British Policy Towards Mesopotamia, 1914-1918', *Middle Eastern Studies* 8, no. 3 (1972).

[14] M. Kent, 'Asiatic Turkey,' in *British Foreign Policy under Sir Edward Grey*, ed. F. H. Hinsley (Cambridge: Cambridge University Press, 1977), pp. 436-51; 'Constantinople and Asiatic Turkey, 1905-1914,' in *British Foreign Policy under Sir Edward Grey*, ed. F. H. Hinsley (Cambridge: Cambridge University Press, 1977); 'Great Britain and the End of the Ottoman Empire,' in *The Great Powers and the End of the Ottoman Empire*, ed. M. Kent (London: Allen & Unwin, 1984), pp. 172-205; *Moguls and Mandarins: Oil, Imperialism, and the Middle East in British Foreign Policy, 1900-1940* (London: Frank Cass, 1993); *Oil and Empire: British Policy and Mesopotamian Oil, 1900-1920* (London: Macmillan, 1976).

bulk of the work is devoted to the potential oilfields of Mesopotamia; Kent points out that oil was not discovered there until 1927.

Kent and Mejcher concentrate on the Middle East and do not give much consideration to the RN. This thesis will go further and analyse the implications of oil for the British government's naval strategy, diplomatic relations and policy towards oil companies. Until about 1912 the only involvement of the British government with the oil industry was to give its nationals diplomatic support in attempting to win concessions in a foreign country. The RN's need for oil and the government's close relationship with the Anglo-Persian Oil Company meant that the government became involved in APOC's attempts to obtain participation in the Turkish Petroleum Company and the Mesopotamian oil concession. Oil was a major factor in the first years of the war; other considerations played a significant part in military operations in Mesopotamia and early discussions of post-war desiderata in the Ottoman Empire. The first step towards a national oil policy came in 1914 when the government took a 51 percent stake in APOC. There were efforts in 1916 to create a national oil company. These failed, as did other attempts post-war to bring Royal Dutch Shell[15] under British control. The oil supply crisis of 1917 and the growing importance of oil to the war effort meant that an apparatus had to be set up to manage the supply of oil. Post-war the desire for British control over the potential oilfields of Mosul had a major impact on relations with France, since the Sykes-Picot Agreement of 1916 had put Mosul into France's sphere of influence. George E. Gruen points out how many countries were interested in the province of Mosul: as well as Britain and France, Germany and American investors tried to obtain railway oil concessions there. Kemalist Turkey attempted to retain it in 1923. This was largely due to the potentially huge oil reserves that the province contained.[16]

Geoffrey Jones, a business historian whose focus is on the companies, disagrees with Kent's view that Britain had a 'coherent oil policy'[17] after the war. His view

---

[15] The Royal Dutch Shell group was owned 60 per cent by Royal Dutch and 40 per cent by Shell, a British company. Hereafter the group is referred to as RDS. Mentions of Royal Dutch or Shell mean that holding company alone.

[16] G. E. Gruen, 'The Oil Resources of Iraq: Their Role in the Policies of the Great Powers,' in *The Creation of Iraq, 1914-1921*, ed. R. S. Simon, E. H. Tejirian (New York NY: Columbia University Press, 2004), pp. 110-23.

[17] Kent, *Oil*, p. 157.

is that 'British oil policy remained rather vague and vacillating even after the war'[18]; in the early years of the twentieth century British politicians and civil servants distrusted oil companies, especially the largest ones such as Standard (NJ) and RDS. They were concerned both by the potential pricing power of such big concerns and by their foreign ownership. There were few signs of an oil policy before the war as the government pursued a laissez-faire attitude towards industry. It was the oil companies that wanted the government to become more involved with their business and the government that resisted doing so. Only in the Middle East did the British government play a significant role. During the war and afterwards it became more involved, but its attempt to create a large British oil company failed, showing its policy to be ineffective. The US companies were admitted to Iraq and the final terms were agreed by the industry rather than governments since the Foreign Office put Anglo-American relations ahead of oil.[19] Brian McBeth's analysis of British oil policy is not as focused on the Middle East as that of most other writers on the subject. He believed that the Middle Eastern oilfields were not developed quickly enough for Britain's needs, leaving it reliant on US oil. Starting in the late 1920s, attempts were made to reduce this dependency with imports from Venezuela.[20] Correlli Barnett, whilst not writing specifically about oil, believes that one of the reasons for the decline of British power in 1918-40 was the failure to develop the empire's natural resources. Too little effort was devoted to exploration within the empire resulting in a dependence on imports for commodities such as oil. Barnett argues that a lack of technical education meant that the importance of raw materials and industrial capacity in modern strategy was not appreciated.[21]

Yergin notes that Britain had to consider US President Woodrow Wilson's ideals at the same time that it was trying to secure oil supplies. Before the war the Wilson Administration was suspicious of Standard (NJ); anger at the Anglo-French agreement to divide up Iraqi oil and fears of a US shortage of oil cemented the

---

[18] Jones, *State*, p. 249.

[19] G. Jones, 'Admirals and Oilmen: The Relationship between the Royal Navy and the Oil Companies, 1900-1924,' in *Charted and Uncharted Waters: Proceedings of a Conference on the Study of British Maritime History*, ed. S. Palmer, G. Williams (London: National Maritime Museum, 1982); 'British Government and Oil Companies 1912-1924: Search for an Oil Policy', *Historical Journal* 20, no. 3 (1977), pp. 647-72; Jones, *State*.

[20] B. S. McBeth, *British Oil Policy, 1919-1939* (London: Cass, 1985).

[21] C. Barnett, *The Collapse of British Power* (London: Pan, 2002).

reconciliation between the US government and the US oil industry that had begun during the war. Eventually US companies were admitted to Iraq; their technical expertise would speed development, and this eased British diplomatic problems with the pro-business Harding Administration.[22] Fiona Venn is mainly concerned with the impact of oil on international relations and does not go into naval strategy or government policy towards companies. She contends that oil started to become important in international diplomacy before the First World War. She agrees that the war accelerated the growth in its significance. Even without oil Britain would still have wanted to dominate much of Mesopotamia and Persia, but the British occupation of Mosul in 1918 was motivated by its potential oilfields. Oil was a major factor in Britain's post-war strategy in the Middle East. The British desire to obtain control over substantial oil reserves brought them into conflict with the USA, which feared that its production had peaked and that US companies were being excluded from the rest of the world. The situation was exacerbated by mistakes and resentment that resulted from the change in the balance of power between the two countries. She argues that Britain allowed the US companies into Iraq because Britain placed good relations with the USA over the need for control of oil. This brought a temporary halt to the Anglo-American rivalry until it flared up again in the late 1920s.[23] This thesis will show that Britain realised that it was control of oil bearing territory rather than ownership of companies that mattered. Britain retained control over Iraqi oil even after giving US companies a share in it.

William Stivers thinks that British and American interests were aligned, at least once US oil companies were allowed a stake in Iraqi oil. British control of Iraq was important both for its oil and for the defence of India. At the end of the war Britain was over-extended and faced the threat of Turkish nationalism. Withdrawal from Iraq would have been a severe blow to British prestige, but British control was obtained cheaply by establishing a client state. This plan required Iraq to be financially self-sufficient, meaning that was in Britain's interest that the oil concession should benefit Iraq. Britain wanted the Americans to support the British Empire; attempts to persuade them to take on

---

[22] Yergin, *Prize*, pp. 194-96.

[23] F. Venn, 'A Futile Paper Chase: Anglo-American Relations and Middle East Oil, 1918-34', *Diplomacy and Statecraft* 1, no. 2 (1990), pp. 165-84; Venn, *Oil*.

the Armenian mandate failed. US goodwill was obtained by ending both the Anglo-Japanese Treaty and the policy of excluding US oil companies from Iraq. The Americans wanted stability and peace in Iraq, which Britain and its client state provided.[24] Michael Hogan has a similar view, arguing that the USA did not retreat into isolationism after the War. It remained closely intertwined with the world economy. Political involvement was to be avoided but American private businesses were encouraged to collaborate with overseas companies, especially by Herbert Hoover. The Americans needed other countries to be willing to work with them, most of all Britain. It was generally willing to do so because it needed the help of American business and hoped to co-opt the USA into sharing its global burdens. Concentration on Anglo-American rivalry at the start and end of the 1920s ignores the collaboration that took place during the middle of the decade in fields such as cable, radio and oil. Both countries were keen to protect their interests, but their governments were happy to allow many commercial arguments to be settled between private companies.[25] Other histories of the oil industry in the Middle East, such as those by Stephen Longrigg and George Stocking, tend to take a longer time period and devote relatively little space to the period up to 1924. These two authors are more interested in the industry and companies than in government and diplomacy. Stocking suggests that Britain ended up with control over Mesopotamian oil thanks to a combination of luck and planning. Iraqi nationalism was not allowed to obstruct Britain's plans to control the oil. The American companies were admitted after pressure from the State Department and inter-company negotiations; the open door closed behind them.[26]

By far the largest user of oil was the RN. Britain's power and prestige depended on naval supremacy, which required access to secure fuel supplies, making naval strategy key to the analysis of Britain's oil policy. The RN's fuel supplies are the

---

[24] W. Stivers, 'International Politics and Iraqi Oil, 1918-1928: A Study in Anglo-American Diplomacy', *Business History Review* 55, no. 4 (1981), pp. 517-40; *Supremacy and Oil: Iraq, Turkey, and the Anglo-American World Order, 1918-1930* (Ithaca, NY: Cornell University Press, 1982).

[25] M. J. Hogan, 'Informal Entente: Public Policy and Private Management in Anglo-American Petroleum Affairs, 1918-1924', *Business History Review* 48, no. 2 (1974), pp. 187-205; *Informal Entente: The Private Structure of Cooperation in Anglo-American Economic Diplomacy, 1918-1928* (Columbia, SC: University of Missouri Press, 1977).

[26] S. H. Longrigg, *Oil in the Middle East: Its Discovery and Development* (London: Oxford University Press, 1967); G. W. Stocking, *Middle East Oil: A Study in Political and Economic Controversy* (London: Allen Lane, 1971).

subject of David Snyder and Warwick Brown's unpublished PhD theses.[27] Both cover longer time periods and consider naval technology, including comparisons with coal, as much as efforts to obtain oil supplies. Snyder's work is concerned with the USA as well as Britain. He argues that, because of the importance of Britain's coal reserves to its naval supremacy, logistics meant that the switch to oil was a factor in the loss of this hegemony and that oil was not clearly superior to coal. Brown says that the Royal Navy's move to oil meant that it ceased to control its fuel supplies and became dependent on the oil industry for these.

The RN's switch to oil before the First World War and Britain's subsequent need for secure supplies is commented on by the leading naval historians of the RN, such as Eric Grove and Arthur Marder.[28] Jon Sumida has analysed British naval logistics during the First World War, including the need for increasing quantities of oil.[29] Stephen Roskill's work on British naval policy shows the need for oil storage in the 1920s.[30] Details of how it impacted broader British strategy are outside the remit of these works. Naval histories of the war, such as those of Paul Halpern, Richard Hough and Robert Massie, mostly mention the RN's switch to oil and make some comment on tanker losses and oil shortages in 1917.[31] Winston Churchill, who was First Lord of the Admiralty from 1911-15, discusses the RN's switch to oil but says very little about oil during the War in *The World Crisis*.[32] In the British Official Histories efforts to import oil and the importance of stocks and bunkering facilities are covered by C. E. Fayle's volumes on the economic aspects of the naval war.[33] The history of the Ministry of Munitions

---

[27] W. M. Brown, 'The Royal Navy's Fuel Supplies, 1898-1939; the Transition from Coal to Oil' (University of London, 2003); D. A. Snyder, 'Petroleum and Power: Naval Fuel Technology and the Anglo-American Struggle for Core Hegemony, 1889-1922' (Texas A&M University, 2001).

[28] E. Grove, *The Royal Navy since 1815 : A New Short History* (Basingstoke: Palgrave Macmillan, 2005); A. J. Marder, *From the Dreadnought to Scapa Flow; the Royal Navy in the Fisher Era, 1904-1919*, 5 vols. (London: Oxford University Press, 1961-70).

[29] Sumida, 'British'.

[30] S. W. Roskill, *Naval Policy between the Wars: Vol. 1, the Period of Anglo-American Antagonism, 1919-1929* (London: Collins, 1968).

[31] P. G. Halpern, *A Naval History of World War I* (London: UCL Press, 1994); R. A. Hough, *The Great War at Sea, 1914-1918* (Oxford: Oxford University Press, 1983); R. K. Massie, *Castles of Steel: Britain, Germany, and the Winning of the Great War at Sea* (London: Jonathan Cape, 2004); *Dreadnought: Britain, Germany, and the Coming of the Great War* (London: Jonathan Cape, 1992).

[32] W. S. Churchill, *The World Crisis, 1911- 1918*, 2 vols. (London: Odhams Press, 1939).

[33] C. E. Fayle, *Seaborne Trade.*, 3 vols. (London: HMSO, 1920).

describes the administrative aspects and attempts to boost home production.[34] There is no volume bringing together all aspects of oil policy in the manner of D. J. Payton-Smith's work on the Second World War.[35]

The theatre of the land war most associated with oil is Mesopotamia. It was widely and correctly assumed to contain oil and was close to the existing Persian oilfields. In the 1970s the Middle Eastern Centre at St Antony's College, Oxford published a series of monographs including, as well as the book by Helmut Mejcher on oil referred to earlier, two works on British policy towards Mesopotamia/Iraq; one by Stuart Cohen on the period 1903-1914 and another by Peter Sluglett taking the story up to the end of the British Mandate in 1932. Cohen has published journal articles on British strategy towards Mesopotamia before and at the start of the war.[36] A revised edition of Sluglett's book was published in 2007. Cohen shows that Britain had long standing interests in Mesopotamia: defence of the route to India, trade, and a desire for security in the region and good relations with its inhabitants. The importance of these expanded in 1903-14, but all could be discerned earlier. The expeditionary force sent to Mesopotamia in 1914 was intended to protect these interests; Britain then wanted to preserve the existing system and had no plans to take over Mesopotamia. Sluglett agrees that the original reason to send troops to Basra was to protect existing British interests. The objectives expanded into control over Iraq in order to protect the air and land routes to India and to control the oil.

Most writers on this campaign, including A. J. Barker, Lord Carver, Paul Davis, John Galbraith, Matthew Hughes and Ron Wilcox, follow Frederick Moberly's official history in saying that troops of the Indian Army were initially sent to Basra and Abadan for a number of reasons. Protection of the Persian oilfields was one; others included protection of Britain's traditional position in the Persian Gulf and hopes that the Arabs could be persuade to revolt against the

---

[34] *History of the Ministry of Munitions*, 12 vols. (London: HMSO, 1920).

[35] D. J. Payton-Smith, *Oil: A Study of War-Time Policy and Administration* (London: HMSO, 1971).

[36] S. A. Cohen, *British Policy in Mesopotamia, 1903-1914* (London: Ithaca Press, 1976); 'The Genesis of the British Campaign in Mesopotamia, 1914', *Middle Eastern Studies* 12, no. 2 (1976), pp. 19-32; 'Mesopotamia in British Strategy, 1903-1914', *International Journal of Middle Eastern Studies* 9, no. 2 (1978), pp. 171-81; P. Sluglett, *Britain in Iraq, 1914-1932* (London: I. B. Tauris, 2007).

Ottoman Empire. The consensus is that, after the Persian oilfields had been secured in early 1915, oil played little role in the military operations in Mesopotamia until the end of the war when Britain moved to secure Mosul and its potential oilfields. The protection of oil supplies from German and Ottoman forces was a significant reason for the British military presence in Persia and the Caucasus.[37]

This thesis will argue that oil had little direct impact on military strategy during the war, but that the lessons of the war made oil important in war aims from 1918 onwards and in post-war diplomacy. The Allies benefitted from having more oil than the Central Powers, but their supplies were never secure. Britain's pre-war policy of building up stocks in peacetime and buying on the market in wartime was shown to be flawed by an oil crisis in 1917. The war showed that Britain had to control its own supplies in the future; doing so became a post war aim in 1918.

Early English language histories of the whole war, such as those of Basil Liddell Hart and C. R. M. F. Cruttwell, emphasised the Mesopotamian campaign and the importance of the oilfields. The space devoted to what is now regarded as a sideshow has diminished in more recent books. Initially this was in favour of the Western Front orientation exemplified by John Terraine. More recently the emphasis has shifted to the more global approach of David Stevenson and Huw Strachan, which puts oil in the context of various factors affecting the war in the Middle East. Niall Ferguson's *The Pity of War*, a work whose arguments are based to a large extent on economic factors, makes little mention of oil.[38]

---

[37] A. J. Barker, *The Neglected War. Mesopotamia, 1914-1918.* (London: Faber and Faber, 1967); M. Carver, *The National Army Museum Book of the Turkish Front, 1914-1918: The Campaigns at Gallipoli, in Mesopotamia and in Palestine* (London: Sidgwick & Jackson, 2003); P. K. Davis, *Ends and Means: The British Mesopotamian Campaign and Commission* (London Associated University Presses, 1994); J. S. Galbraith, 'No Man's Child: The Campaign in Mesopotamia, 1914-1916', *The International History Review* 6, no. 3 (1984); M. Hughes, *Allenby and British Strategy in the Middle East, 1917-1919* (London: Frank Cass, 1999); F. J. Moberly, *The Campaign in Mesopotamia, 1914-1918*, 4 vols. (London: HMSO, 1923); *Operations in Persia, 1914-1919* (London: HMSO, 1987); R. Wilcox, *Battles on the Tigris* (Barnsley: Pen & Sword Military, 2006).

[38] C. R. M. F. Cruttwell, *A History of the Great War, 1914-1918*, 2nd ed. (London: Granada, 1982); N. Ferguson, *The Pity of War* (London: Allen Lane, 1998); B. H. L. Hart, *History of the First World War* (London: Cassell, 1970); D. Stevenson, *1914-1918: The History of the First World War* (London: Allen Lane, 2004); H. Strachan, *The First World War : A New Illustrated History* (London: Simon & Schuster, 2003); *The First World War: Vol. 1, to Arms* (Oxford: Oxford University Press, 2001); J. Terraine, *The Great War* (London: Hutchison & Co., 1965).

Writers on Britain's strategy and aims during the war do not say very much about oil. V.H. Rothwell points out that Britain went to war with no clear objectives other than the preservation of Belgian independence, French security against aggression and an end to Prussian militarism. It was considered that the Ottoman Empire should suffer for its entry into the war. The initial consideration of British objectives in the Ottoman Empire by the de Bunsen Committee favoured a federal system, with the loss only of Constantinople to Russia and perhaps Basra to Britain; British influence would be extended without annexation. The acceptance that Russia should have Constantinople was a major departure in British foreign policy, which had previously aimed at preservation of the Ottoman Empire as a buffer state against Russia. There were discussions later in the war about a separate peace with the Ottoman Empire with the Arabic speaking parts and Armenia becoming autonomous rather than independent. The Admiralty had been arguing in favour of British control of the potential oil of Mesopotamia since at least 1915, but the India Office had little interest in oil. Not until August 1918, when Hankey convinced the War Cabinet of the importance of Mesopotamian oil, did Lloyd George and Balfour decide that British control over Mesopotamia should be a key war aim.[39]

David French contends that oil was only one of a number of factors driving British strategy towards the Middle East, although in 1918 the British captured Mosul because of the Admiralty's need for its oil.[40] Paul Guinn makes little mention of oil; he argues the principal reason to despatch forces to the Persian Gulf in 1914 was to impress the Turks and Arabs. Guinn believes that the main reason for General Maude's offensive towards Baghdad in 1917 was to increase the British Empire, but makes no mention of oil as a reason for this.[41] Keith Neilson argues that British strategy was driven by imperial considerations that

---

[39] V. H. Rothwell, *British War Aims and Peace Diplomacy, 1914-1918* (Oxford: Clarendon Press, 1971); 'Mesopotamia in British War Aims, 1914-1918', *Historical Journal* 13, no. 2 (1970), pp. 273-94.

[40] D. French, *British Economic and Strategic Planning, 1905-1915* (London: Allen & Unwin, 1982); *British Strategy & War Aims, 1914-16* (London: Allen & Unwin, 1986); *The Strategy of the Lloyd George Coalition, 1916-1918* (Oxford: Clarendon Press, 1995).

[41] P. Guinn, *British Strategy and Politics, 1914 to 1918.* (Oxford: Clarendon, 1965).

included the defence of India and the need to secure oil supplies for the RN; the fate of the empire depended on the navy.[42]

Oil receives little mention in works specifically on the Treaty of Versailles such as those of Antony Lentin and Ruth Henig, and the papers presented at the 75th anniversary conference.[43] It is mentioned a little more by writers covering the whole peace process from 1919-23 but not much; Margaret MacMillan devotes a few pages to it, and Alan Sharp makes only a couple of references.[44] Erik Goldstein argues that Britain wanted to dominate the Eastern Mediterranean. Palestine was a key component of this strategy, but control of Middle Eastern oil is not mentioned.[45] Goldstein has contended that Britain was the most successful of the Great Powers at the Paris Peace Conference because of the great deal of detailed preparation that it undertook, starting whilst the war was still underway. The Petroleum Executive and the Admiralty were responsible for planning how Britain could obtain the oil that it would need in the post-war world.[46]

Most writers on the Middle East argue that Britain ended up with control over Mosul's oil as a fortunate consequence of strategies intended principally to pursue other aims. Michael Dockrill and Douglas Goold say that oil was not the main issue for Britain in the Middle East, but the British were starting to see its significance from 1920.[47] Elie Kedourie says very little about oil in *England and*

---

[42] K. Neilson, '"For Diplomatic, Economic, Strategy and Telegraphic Reasons": British Imperial Defence, the Middle East and India, 1914-1918,' in *Far-Flung Lines: Essays on Imperial Defence in Honour of Donald Mackenzie Schurman*, ed. G. Kennedy, K. Neilson (London: Frank Cass, 1997), pp. 103-23.

[43] M. F. Boemeke et al, *The Treaty of Versailles : A Reassessment after 75 Years* (Cambridge: German Historical Institute and Cambridge University Press, 1998); R. B. Henig, *Versailles and after, 1919-1933* (London: Routledge, 1995); A. Lentin, *The Versailles Peace Settlement : Peacemaking with Germany* (Burford: Davenant Press, 2003).

[44] M. MacMillan, *Peacemakers: The Paris Peace Conference of 1919 and Its Attempt to End War* (London: John Murray, 2001), pp. 392-93, 406-7; A. Sharp, *The Versailles Settlement : Peacemaking after the First World War, 1919-1923*, 2nd ed. (Basingstoke: Palgrave Macmillan, 2008), pp. 189, 195.

[45] E. Goldstein, 'The Eastern Question; the Last Phase,' in *The Paris Peace Conference 1919 : Peace without Victory?*, ed. M. L. Dockrill, J. Fisher (Basingstoke: Palgrave, 2001).

[46] E. Goldstein, 'British Peace Aims and the Eastern Question: The Political Intelligence Department and the Eastern Committee', *Middle Eastern Studies* 23, no. 4 (1987); *Winning the Peace: British Diplomatic Strategy, Peace Planning, and the Paris Peace Conference, 1916-1920* (Oxford: Clarendon, 1991).

[47] M. L. Dockrill, J. D. Goold, *Peace without Promise Britain and the Peace Conferences 1919-23* (London: Batsford Academic and Educational, 1981), p. 176.

the Middle East.[48] Jukka Nevakivi points out that the British had to reconcile the promises that they had made to the French, the Arabs and the Zionists and to consider their own objectives, notably controlling Mesopotamia and its oil, and ensuring that the safety of imperial communications and borders. The only significant area of dispute with the French in 1918-19 was the Middle East, but this threatened to prevent agreement over other, apparently more important, issues in Europe. Eventually the British realised that co-operation with the French was the only way to come to an agreement over Turkey. An old style imperial agreement was concluded in order to meet French wishes, which included Syria and a stake in Mesopotamian oil. [49]

Elizabeth Monroe devotes a chapter of *Britain's Moment in the Middle East* to oil, but starts it by pointing out that 'people forget how lately this asset began to dominate the region's economy and disturb its politics.'[50] She contends that it was luck that put the Middle Eastern oilfields along the British route to India and luck that in 1908 oil was found in Persia adjacent to the British sphere of influence laid in the Anglo-Russian agreement of the previous year. John Darwin's *Britain, Egypt and the Middle East*[51] argues that, whilst the British Government was aware of the possibilities offered by a British controlled oil industry in the Middle East, the establishment of this was a useful by-product of strategies followed for other reasons. In his view almost all the focus of British politicians was on the setting up of lasting and friendly states in Turkey, Iraq and Persia. Balfour and Curzon wanted to transfer Mosul from the French to the British sphere and Curzon wanted to extend Britain's involvement in Persia. Oil was put forward as one of the reasons to do so; Darwin argues this was in order to help win the support of colleagues for measures primarily aimed at the protection of Britain's existing interests.

---

[48] E. Kedourie, *England and the Middle East: The Destruction of the Ottoman Empire, 1914-1921* (London: Mansell, 1987).

[49] J. Nevakivi, *Britain, France and the Arab Middle East, 1914-1920* (London: Athlone Press, 1969); 'Lord Kitchener and the Partition of the Ottoman Empire,' in *Studies in International History: Essays Presented to W. Norton Medlicott*, ed. K. Bourne, D. C. Watt (London: Longmans, 1967)..

[50] E. Monroe, *Britain's Moment in the Middle East, 1914-1971* (London: Chatto & Windus, 1981), p. 95.

[51] J. Darwin, *Britain, Egypt and the Middle East: Imperial Policy in the Aftermath of War, 1918-1922* (London: Macmillan, 1981).

Curzon's impact on British Imperial policy has been examined by John Fisher.[52] His view is that Curzon's principal motivation was to expand the British Empire, but that he was unable to achieve many of his goals in the new era of self-determination. Some of the territories that he wanted to acquire, such as Mosul and the Caucasus, contained oil, but, according to Fisher, this was not Curzon's motivation. Curzon's imperial policy in Mesopotamia and Persia is criticised by Roger Adelson, who argues that it was overtaken by the need to come to an oil agreement with the USA.[53] Briton Cooper Busch's trilogy covers the involvement of Britain and the British government of India in the Middle East from 1894 until the Treaty of Lausanne in 1923. It shows oil playing an increasing role in British Government thinking over this period but argues that it was just one of a number of factors.[54] David Fromkin's *A Peace to End All Peace*[55] shows how the events of the war and the subsequent peace conferences created the modern Middle East. His view is that the British government had to come to arrangements that would allow Britain to rule at little cost to itself; British public opinion would not accept a system that was expensive in either British lives or money. He does not say much about oil; other authors, such as Peter Sluglett, have pointed out that oil contributed much of the revenue of what became Iraq, enabling to British to dominate it at relatively little cost to themselves.[56]

There is no agreement amongst oil industry historians on the question of whether or not Britain had a coherent oil policy during this period. Britain obtained control of the oilfields of Mesopotamia as a result of the war, but it had other interests in this territory, including protection of the land route to India and Britain's position in the Persian Gulf. Oil impacted post war relations

---

[52] J. Fisher, *Curzon and British Imperialism in the Middle East, 1916-19* (London: Cass, 1999); '"On the Glacis of India": Lord Curzon and British Policy in the Caucasus', *Diplomacy and Statecraft* 8, no. 2 (1997); '"The Safety of Our Indian Empire': Lord Curzon and British Predominance in the Arabian Peninsula, 1919', *Middle Eastern Studies* 33, no. 3 (1997); 'Syria and Mesopotamia in British Middle Eastern Policy in 1919', *Middle Eastern Studies* 34, no. 2 (1998).

[53] R. Adelson, *London and the Invention of the Middle East: Money, Power, and War, 1902-22* (New Haven, CT.: Yale University Press, 1995).

[54] B. C. Busch, *Britain and the Persian Gulf, 1894-1914.* (Berkeley, CA: University of California Press, 1967); *Britain, India, and the Arabs, 1914-1921* (Berkeley, CA: University of California Press, 1971); *Mudros to Lausanne: Britain's Frontier in West Asia, 1918-1923* (Albany, NY: State University of New York Press., 1976).

[55] D. Fromkin, *A Peace to End All Peace: Creating the Modern Middle East, 1914-1922* (London: Deutsch, 1989).

[56] Sluglett, *Britain*.

with the USA and France. Writers on British wartime strategy, the peace treaties, and Britain's role in the Middle East mostly emphasis the other factors. Because oil has been looked at from the point of view of the RN, Middle Eastern policy or the industry no previous work has taken all the factors together in order to determine the coherence of British oil strategy. This thesis will seek to determine the importance of oil in such questions and to decide whether or not Britain had a coherent, consistent and successful oil policy in 1914-1923.

1 British Strategy and Oil, 1914-16

By 1914 the growing importance of oil to the RN meant that the British Government had to formulate a policy for the supply of oil. This was based mainly on a desire to build up reserves relatively cheaply in peacetime. The focus was on ownership of oilfields and companies rather than control of territory. Little oil had been found in the British Empire. The largest British oilfield was in Burma; the rising use of oil fuel by the RN meant that as early as 1905 the CID considered it to be vital that the Burmah Company should remain entirely British.[57] The government invested in APOC and gave it a long term contract to supply the RN in order to keep it British. Consideration was given to bringing RDS under British control. Some consideration was given to Mosul's potential oil, but the main impact of oil on military strategy was that measures were taken to protect APOC's Persian oilfields.

1.1 British Oil Strategy in 1914

The RN first experimented with oil in the 1860s. In the 1890s it adopted a policy of experimenting and observing efforts by other navies, commercial ship owners and railways. Significant progress was not made by the RN until the development of pressure spraying in 1902.[58] Subsequent objections to the use of oil were mainly on the grounds of security of supply.[59] From 1905 most destroyers were exclusively oil fuelled; fears over the security of supply meant that cruisers and battleships used oil only as an auxiliary to coal.[60] For the same performance, an oil ship would be smaller than a coal one and require a smaller crew. For the same size, the oil vessel would be faster and better armed and armoured. The

---

[57] NA, ADM 116/3807, 'Burmah Oil Co Ltd: Contract for Supply of Fuel Oil'. Letter dated 10 August 1905, signed by G. T. Clarke.

[58] ADM 1/7676, 'Controller'. N.S. Coal 1849 1903 Request 16 October 1902 by Naval Intelligence Department to Captain Dudley de Chair RN, British Legation at The Hague; ADM 265/27, 'Discussion on Oil Fuel between Prince Louis of Battenburg and H.I.H. Grand Duke Alexander of Russia'; ADM 265/26, 'Experiments in Ships Using Liquid Fuel, 1898-1904'. 'Report on Visit to Royal Italian Navy', S.13313 1902 23 February 1902, Chief Inspector of Machinery J. Melrose to Controller; ADM 265/45, 'History of Oil Fuel in the Royal Navy, 1922-31'. 'Development of the use of oil fuel in H. M. Navy, 4/10/21; ADM 1/10071, 'Use of Petroleum as Liquid Fuel in Ships'.

[59] ADM 1/7676, pp. 1-2. N.S. Coal 1840 1903; C. W. d. I. P. Beresford, *The Memoirs of Admiral Lord Charles Beresford.*, 2 vols. (London: Methuen & Co., 1914). vol. i, p. 483.

[60] ADM 265/28, 'History of Development of Oil Fuel Burning in H.M. Service', pp. 4-5.

last coal burning destroyers, the *Beagle* class of 1908, cost £106,000 each. The later oil fired *Defender* class had a similar performance but cost £86,000 each.[61]

From the *Arethusa* class of 1912 most cruisers ordered for the RN were fuelled exclusively by oil because coal fired cruisers were too slow to work with the newest destroyers and carry out their scouting duties.[62] The world's first exclusively oil fuelled battleships were the *Queen Elizabeth* class. Oil allowed them to be the first dreadnoughts to be armed with 15 inch guns and to be faster than any other battleships without sacrificing protection. The first of the class, HMS *Queen Elizabeth*, was laid down on 21 October 1912, 10 days before the next of her four sister ships, HMS *Warspite*, and a fortnight ahead of the first all oil American battleship, the USS *Nevada*.

1.1.1 The Royal Commission on Fuel and Engines

On 19 January 1912 a Committee on Oil Fuel, chaired by Captain William Pakenham, the Fourth Sea Lord, reported that war reserves should be a year's supply at wartime rates of consumption. There had been no formal Admiralty body dealing with oil since 1906. Britain imported 93 per cent of its fuel oil and demand was rising. As storage was insufficient for existing ships, no change towards more oil should be made in ships of the 1911-12 programme.[63] Despite this, Churchill, who replaced Reginald McKenna as First Lord of the Admiralty in October 1911, wrote after the war that the RN did not use enough oil to make its oil supply a significant issue until the construction of the *Queen Elizabeth* class.[64] Oil had to be found, stored and bought regularly and as inexpensively as possible. Wartime supplies had to be completely secure. The Royal Commission on Fuel and Engines was established to solve these problems, chaired by Admiral Lord 'Jacky' Fisher, First Lord of the Admiralty from 1905-11.[65] In 1886, as Director of Naval Ordnance, he had written a memorandum advocating that the RN should switch from coal to oil, earning himself the nickname of the 'Oil

---

[61] Ibid., pp. 12-15.

[62] Churchill, *Crisis*. vol. i, pp. 107-11.

[63] ADM 265/29, 'Admiralty Committee on Use of Oil Fuel in Navy: Volume 1, Interim Report', 1912, p. 149.

[64] Churchill, *Crisis*, pp. 94-102.

[65] R. S. Churchill, M. Gilbert, eds, *Winston S. Churchill, Companion Documents* (London: Heinemann, 1967-75). vol. ii, part 3, p. 1929.

Maniac'.[66] Eric Grove describes him as possessing 'considerable, if erratic, genius'[67], arguing that he convinced Churchill of the merits of oil.[68]

The Commission favoured the use of oil over coal as the fuel of warships and emphasised the importance of storage of reserves and of supply. Reliable and ample supplies of oil for the Royal Navy could be obtained for the next 15 to 20 years but could not be relied upon under the current system of ad-hoc purchases. The Admiralty was forced to do this because it lacked sufficient storage facilities for reserves. Unlike coal oil did not deteriorate so could be stored for longer. Reserves should be built up over a number of years. In wartime supplies could be disrupted and the price was likely to rise so this policy would be both cheaper and safer. Substantial reserves were required; four years' peace consumption was recommended. Large storage capacity offered the opportunity to take advantage of short term price weakness and a hedge against the risk of the delivery of poor quality oil under contract. The actual quantity to be stored would depend on the extent to which oil was adopted and whether there was a move towards internal combustion engines. Three tons of oil was equivalent to four tons of coal when powering steam turbines but 10 tons of coal if internal combustion engines were adopted. Requirements were rising each year as oil fuelled destroyers, battleships and light cruisers were completed. [69] Oil would be used to power steam turbines. Fisher believed that warships would eventually be powered by internal combustion engines, but the technology was not yet ready.[70]

Few large warships were ever powered by internal combustion engines. Fisher had argued that such vessels would not need funnels so could have a low silhouette but this proved not to be the case, removing one of their potential advantages.[71] When the Washington Treaty restricted the displacement of warships the definition used was the standard displacement, omitting fuel.

---

[66] CC, Esher Papers, ESHR 17/5, 'Some Notes by Sir John Fisher for His Friends', p. 39.

[67] Grove, *Royal Navy*, p. 89.

[68] Ibid., p. 103.

[69] ADM 265/32, 'Royal Commission on Fuel and Engines: Volume 1', 1913, pp. vi-vii..

[70] ADM 265/33, 'Royal Commission on Fuel and Engines: Volume 2', 1913, pp. 8-17..

[71] A. J. Marder, ed. *Fear God and Dread Nought: The Correspondence of Admiral of the Fleet Lord Fisher of Kilverstone*, 3 vols. (London: Jonathan Cape, 1952-59). vol. ii, 'Letter to Lord Esher', 12 September 1912, pp. 477-78..

Diesel engines required less fuel than steam turbines but were heavier so were penalised by the use of this measure.[72]

1.1.2 The Government and the Anglo-Persian Oil Company

APOC, a British company, had discovered oil in Persia. Persia was nominally independent, but was divided into British and Russian zones of influence. APOC's founder, William D'Arcy, had previously had dealings with the Admiralty, which in 1905 had arrange for one of its oil suppliers, Burmah, to invest in his exploration company.[73] APOC lacked the capital required to develop its discovery. The prospect of it paying dividends was too distant for it to be able to raise further funds from private shareholders. It could raise the capital from the government, meaning the Admiralty since the Indian Railways declined to become involved.[74] Alternatively APOC could be taken over by another oil company, probably RDS, which had a better understanding than private investors of the risks and rewards involved. RDS was regarded by many as a foreign company because of its Dutch majority shareholding; the Netherlands was regarded as a country that was potentially pro-German.[75] This fear would prove to be unfounded, but it influenced policy at this stage.

In October 1913 an Admiralty Commission, chaired by Admiral Sir Edmond Slade, formerly DNI and C.-in-C. East Indies, was despatched to investigate the Persian oil industry. Slade and another of its members, John Cadman, Professor of Mining at Birmingham University and Petroleum Adviser to the Colonial Office, would become major figures in British oil policy. Slade would later advocate policies aimed at maintaining British naval supremacy by obtaining control over the world's oil supplies. Phillips O'Brien has described him as 'probably the most anti-American sailor in the Admiralty.'[76]

---

[72] Brown, 'Royal Navy', pp. 244-45.

[73] Jones, *State*, pp. 128-41; Yergin, *Prize*, pp. 134-49.

[74] M. Jack, 'The Purchase of the British Government's Shares in the British Petroleum Company, 1912-1914', *Past & Present* 39 (1968), pp. 156-57.

[75] Ibid., pp. 149-50.

[76] P. P. O'Brien, *British and American Naval Power: Politics and Policy, 1900-1936* (Westport, CT: Praeger, 1998), p. 38.

The final report concluded that APOC's concession would be capable of supplying a substantial proportion of the Royal Navy's oil needs for a long time. It was vital to keep the concession and the company in British hands. The RN's needs could be met from the existing fields in northern Persia. There was also a possibility of further discoveries in the south. The recommendation that the Admiralty should invest the capital needed by APOC to develop the fields and remain independent was accepted. A supply contract giving the RN oil on advantageous terms whilst still allowing the company a reasonable return was signed. The government provided £2,200,000 in shares and debentures in return for 51 per cent of the ordinary shares and the right to appoint two directors.[77]

The question of oil fuel supply for the RN was debated in the House of Commons when the Naval Estimates were considered on 17 July 1913. Churchill laid down the principles on which the Admiralty's oil supply policy was based: supplies should be widely spread geographically, sources should be kept open and independent competition maintained and where possible sources should be under British control with secure transport. Ernest Pretyman, a Conservative who had chaired the Admiralty Oil Fuel Committee until the change of government in 1905, agreed with these, but did not see how they could be maintained if the Admiralty was to be reliant on a single large oilfield.[78] A further debate took place on 17 June 1914 on the Admiralty's intention to invest in APOC. Churchill argued that whilst the RN controlled the seas, Britain would be able to import oil even if the enemy declared it to be contraband. The riskiest period would be early in a war; storage of reserves was being provided against shortages of supply in this period. Points made in the debate included concerns over the lack of security of the Persian oilfields; allegations of price fixing by financiers; calls for the money spent in Britain on the shale oil industry and on developing means of extracting oil from coal; and concerns over the impact on the Welsh coal industry of a switch by navies to oil. The motion was carried easily.[79]

---

[77] PP, *Agreement with the Anglo-Persian Oil Company, Limited, with an Explanatory Memorandum, and the Report of the Commission of Experts on Their Local Investigations*, HMSO 1914 [7419]. pp. 3-7.

[78] *Parliamentary Debates, Fifth Series, House of Commons*, vol. lv, pp. 1490-73.

[79] *Parliamentary Debates, Fifth Series, House of Commons*, vol. lxiii, pp. 1131-251.

1.2 Mesopotamian Oil

APOC was interested in the potential oil of Mesopotamia. The oilfields of the remainder of the Middle East were yet to be discovered, but it was widely believed that there was oil in the Mosul vilayet. As well as the proximity to the Persian oilfields, the frequent occurrences of oil seepages showed that this was almost certainly a rich oil province. Travellers in the region, including Captain F. R. Maunsell, a British artillery officer, and the Frenchman M. de Morgan, commented on this. Bitumen had been used in that part of the world since ancient times; there was a legend that the coating of pitch on Noah's Ark came from Hit. There had been no attempt to test the reserves by modern means; attempts to exploit them had been confined to crude ones by local inhabitants.[80]

In 1912, the Turkish Petroleum Company was formed by RDS, Deutsche Bank and the British owned National Bank of Turkey to obtain the rights to explore for oil in this region. This alarmed APOC whose Persian oil would lose much of its value if a large discovery was made across the border. It convinced the British government that it needed to be involved in the TPC. Anglo-German government negotiations concluded with an agreement of 19 March 1914 that split TPC's shareholding 25 per cent Deutsche Bank, 25 per cent RDS and 50 per cent APOC. RDS and APOC each gave up 2.5 per cent of the profits, but not the votes, to Calouste Gulbenkian, a British citizen of Armenian ancestry who had brokered the original deal to set up TPC; he owned 30 per cent of the National Bank of Turkey.[81] On 28 June 1914 the Grand Vizier wrote to Britain and Germany indicating that the Ottoman Empire intended to grant the TPC a concession. The outbreak of war meant that no contract was ever signed. The question of whether or not TPC had a valid concession would be a major issue after the war.[82]

---

[80] F. R. Maunsell, 'The Mesopotamian Petroleum Field', *Geographical Journal* 9, no. 5 (1897), pp. 528-32.

[81] Jones, *State*, pp. 149-55; Yergin, *Prize*, pp. 185-88.

[82] B. Shwadran, *The Middle East, Oil and the Great Powers*. (London: Atlantic Press, 1956), pp. 196-7, 214.

1.3 Britain and the Ottoman Empire in 1914

Its proximity to India meant that Mesopotamia was of major strategic interest to Britain, which also had significant commercial interests there. Before the war Britain was pursuing its traditional policy of maintaining the territorial integrity of the Ottoman Empire whilst hoping that it would reform itself. The agreements made with Germany and the Ottoman Empire in 1914 were aimed at halting German encroachment into British interests and at strengthening the Ottoman economy.[83] Britain tried to keep the Ottoman Empire neutral in the early months of the war via a series of ambassadorial talks and notes, including offers to guarantee the territory of the Ottoman Empire, but these efforts failed.[84] Hostilities began formally on 5 November 1914. Britain had no war aims in the Ottoman Empire and took some time to develop any. The maintenance of the status quo was no longer an option. Britain's position in the Persian Gulf meant that it would have to participate in whatever arrangements were made for the future of the Ottoman Empire.

1.4 Development of British War Aims in the Middle East

By the end of 1914 stalemate had been reached on the Western Front, most German warships outside European waters had been destroyed and the Russian offensives towards Germany had failed. British attention turned to the possibilities of using Britain's naval power to win the war by operations in other parts of the world. Operations in the Baltic and the Balkans and landings in Syria were suggested. The option taken was an attempt to force the Dardanelles.[85] Hankey argued that opening the Dardanelles would enable Russia to receive the supplies that it needed in order to launch an offensive. The Balkan countries might enter the war on the Allied side and a line of communications up the Danube would be opened. Russian wheat supplies would end of the threat of British food shortages. The revenue from these would allow Russia to pay for its

---

[83] NA, CAB 27/1, British Desiderata in Asiatic Turkey, 1915, p. 1.

[84] PP, *Events Leading to the Rupture of Relations with Turkey*, HMSO 1914 [Cd. 7628].

[85] CAB 24/1, G6 'The Dardanelles and Balkans Operations', A. J. Balfour, 24 February 1915; Guinn, *British*; CAB 24/1, G10 'After the Dardanelles. The Next Steps', M. P. A. Hankey, 1 March 1915; CAB 24/1, G8 'Attack on the Dardanelles', 2 February 1915; CAB 24/1, G2 Suggestions as to the Military Position, D. Lloyd George, 1 January 1915.

imports of war supplies and interest on its loans from France. Hankey did not mention the possibility that Russian oil could be exported through the Dardanelles, both earning it revenue and giving Britain another source of supply.[86] In 1913 Russia exported 670,000 tons out of its total production of 8,370,000 tons; Britain took 130,000 tons, 7.7 per cent of its needs.[87] Russian oil was exported via two pipelines to Black Sea ports, one from Baku to Batum and the other from Maikop to Tuapse. Persia, Mesopotamia and their oilfields were not mentioned as reasons for the operations.

1.4.1 Alexandretta and Mesopotamia

The only mention of oil in papers written before the attack on the Dardanelles was by Fisher, again First Sea Lord. He proposed a complex operation against the Ottoman and Austro-Hungarian Empires. It included attack on Alexandretta (now Iskenderun), a port in the north-eastern corner of the Mediterranean, because of its rail connection to Mesopotamia and its oilfields. A force of obsolete British pre-Dreadnought battleships would force the Dardanelles.[88] In November 1914 Indian Army troops had invaded Mesopotamia from the Persian Gulf and captured the town of Basra. If Britain held Mesopotamia it had to be linked by railway to the Mediterranean; Alexandretta was one of the prime candidates for the Mediterranean terminus of the railway.

Lord Kitchener, the Secretary of State for War, pointed out that an Allied victory in the war would mean that Russia would control Constantinople and France would control Syria, affecting the strategic position of Egypt. The possibility of future conflict with either or both of Russia and France had to be considered. If Britain controlled Mesopotamia it would be necessary to hold Alexandretta, which would otherwise be a risky outpost of no value. Reinforcements from Britain could reach Mesopotamia a fortnight quicker by rail from Alexandretta than by sea via the Suez Canal, Red Sea and Persian Gulf. Holding Alexandretta would mean that the peacetime garrison in of Mesopotamia could be smaller

---

[86] CAB 24/1 G8, Hankey.

[87] CAB 24/59, G.T. 5267 'Petroleum Situation in the British Empire', E. J. W. Slade, 29 July 1918, pp. 2-3.

[88] Churchill, Gilbert, eds, *Companions.* vol. iii, part 1, 'Fisher to Churchill, 3 January 1915', pp. 367-68, map on p. 1596; Guinn, *British*, pp. 44-54; CAB 24/1 G2, Lloyd George.

than would otherwise be the case. Alexandretta would threaten the flank of a Russian advance. If Britain did not take over Mesopotamia the Russians would, threatening Britain's position in the Persian Gulf. Mesopotamia possessed great agricultural potential through the development of irrigation schemes. It would provide an outlet for the surplus population of India. It protected Britain's Persian oil interests and the land route from the Mediterranean to the Persian Gulf. Only a small hinterland around Alexandretta need be occupied. This was readily defensible, as was Mesopotamia, thanks to its mountainous northern frontier, provided that the Tigris and Euphrates were secure. The potential wealth and population of the region should mean that its defence would be a burden on Britain for only a short period of time. It was preferable that a Turkish or Armenian state would provide a buffer to Russia, but a frontier with Russia was better than Franco-Russian domination of the land route from the Mediterranean to the Persian Gulf.[89]

The Admiralty argued in favour of Alexandretta and stressed oil as one of the reasons why. Two papers were submitted to the Cabinet on the subject. One, written by Admiral Sir Henry Jackson, was mainly concerned with the merits of Alexandretta, a large natural harbour, as a British base. British plans for Mesopotamia and possession of the Persian oilfields meant that Britain would need a Mediterranean port on the Baghdad Railway. Alexandretta was the most suitable; Beirut was a possible alternative, but the railway would have to be extended to it. Possession of Alexandretta by another power would threaten British communications and would require the construction of a fortified base on Cyprus; there would be no return on the cost of this.[90] The other focused more on Mesopotamia and the land link to it. The question of a land link from the Mediterranean to the Euphrates had been considered since around 1830. The likely end of the Ottoman Empire, leading to Russian annexation of Constantinople and British acquisition of Lower Mesopotamia, changed the situation. Britain was entitled to compensation for its role in the war. It was necessary to restore Mesopotamia to its former wealth and also to link it to the Mediterranean as a counter balance to Russia's new strength in that key region. The Admiralty had an extra and vital interest; the need to have an oil supply in

---

[89] CAB 24/1, G12 'Alexandretta and Mesopotamia', Kitchener, 16 March 1915.

[90] CAB 24/1, G15 'Alexandretta. Its Importance as a Future Base', H. B. Jackson, 15 March 1915.

the region. Russia would have the supplies of the Black Sea available at Constantinople so Britain must be able to access those of Mesopotamia at Alexandretta.[91] The naval historian Julian Corbett was involved in the preparation of this paper. He wrote to Fisher expressing his concern that he had not emphasised oil enough in the paper. Oil was replacing coal as the principal fuel of warships, and the Mediterranean was again becoming a vital area of the world. An opportunity had arisen for Britain to obtain control of great reserves of oil close to this region. This should not be passed up. Corbett's papers contain two drafts of this letter; it is not clear which version he sent to Fisher. In one he attributes the renewed importance of the Mediterranean to the forthcoming breakup of the Ottoman Empire, in the other to the impending acquisition of Constantinople by Russia. He says in both that the opportunity to obtain supplies of oil in the Middle East is 'a gift of god'.[92]

Haifa was favoured over Alexandretta as the Mediterranean outlet for the British oil pipeline. General Sir Charles Callwell, the DMO, persuaded the de Bunsen Committee, set up in April 1915 to consider British war aims in the Middle East, that the route from Alexandretta to Mesopotamia would have to go through French territory. Haifa was almost as good in other respects and could be linked to Mesopotamia by a railway through British territory. The only disadvantage was that this railway would not be commercially viable.[93]

1.4.2 The De Bunsen Committee

The de Bunsen Committee was the first formal body established to study British war aims in the Ottoman Empire. Its official title was the Committee on British Desiderata in Turkish Asia but it is generally known after its Chairman Sir Maurice de Bunsen, Ambassador to Vienna until the outbreak of war. It reported on 30 June 1915. British desiderata had to take into account the desires of its Allies, who might be its rivals in the future.[94] Britain had nine aims in the region. Three could be left for now. The Moslem Holy Places had to be under Moslem

---

[91] CAB 24/1, G13 'Alexandretta and Mesopotamia', Admiralty, 17 March 1915.

[92] NMM, Corbett Papers, CBT/7/5, 'Official Admiralty Memoranda Written During the War Including Alexandretta and Mesopotamia', 'Corbett to Fisher', 17 February 1915.

[93] CAB 27/1, pp. 45-6.

[94] Ibid., p. 4.

rule; this, along with the future of the Caliphate, was important for Indian Moslem sentiment. Solutions to the problems of Armenia and of Palestine and the Christian Holy Places were needed. Britain would have had an interest in these issues even if it had not had any other involvement in the Ottoman Empire. Before the war Britain had aimed to maintain the Ottoman Empire. Its impending demise meant that Britain had to stake a claim for part of it to protect the interests laid out in the other six points. These were:

1. A clear and lasting acceptance of Britain's position in the Persian Gulf.
2. The elimination of discrimination against British trade and either maintenance of current markets or compensation for their loss.
3. The carrying out of promises made to various Arab leaders and the people of Basra.
4. Industries in which Britain was interested to be developed. Oil was one of those mentioned along with river navigation and irrigation schemes.
5. Irrigation schemes to grow corn supply and perhaps lead to immigration from India.
6. Continuation of Britain's strategic position in the Eastern Mediterranean and the Persian Gulf with as little increase as possible in defence expenditure and responsibilities.[95]

British business interests in Turkish Asia were mostly located in the Basra, Baghdad and Mosul vilayets. Britain had already decided to annex the Basra vilayet and could not return it to the Ottomans because of promises made to the local population and their leaders. It would valueless if another power controlled Baghdad. Mosul was needed in order to have a defensible frontier in the hills. Baghdad would protect the existing oilfields just across the border with Persia. The acquisition of Mosul's oil by a rival power would harm British interests. Mosul could supply water supply for irrigation schemes to restore Mesopotamia as a granary that could supply Britain. Russia was to have Constantinople. Greece would receive the Smyrna vilayet if it entered the war.

---

[95] Ibid., p. 5.

Figure 1-1: De Bunsen Committee Proposals

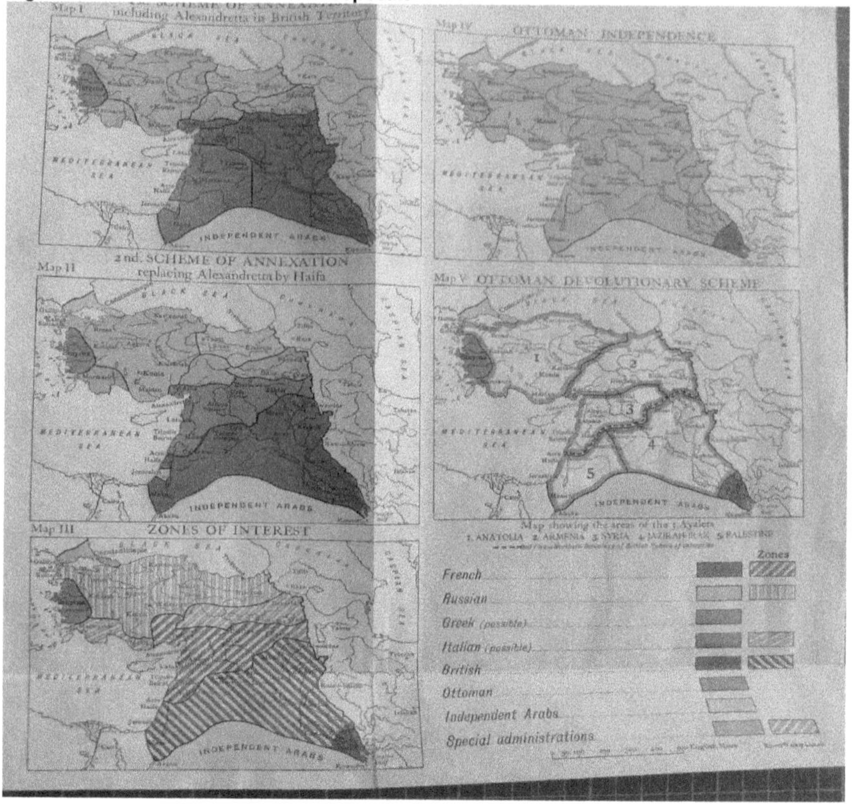

Source: CAB 27/1, Map, No. V.

The Committee laid out four possible schemes, as shown in the map above:

A. Partition. Turkey would be restricted to Anatolia, with the rest of the Ottoman Empire being divided amongst European powers. Britain would need a railway to the Mediterranean in order to transport military reinforcements. Haifa was preferred to Alexandretta as the terminus because the latter would be too close to French and Russian territory to be secure; two maps were provided, one with each option.

B. Zones of Interest: The Ottoman Empire would continue but other powers would have zones of interest. A British railway link to the Mediterranean would not be needed as any line would now be built for commercial reasons, not strategic ones.

C. Maintenance of an independent Ottoman Empire: The Ottoman Empire would lose its European territory and Constantinople to Russia, the Basra vilayet to Britain and perhaps Smyrna to Greece. Various Arab Sheikhdoms would be granted independence in order to comply with promises made to them by Britain. The Armenian reform measures agreed before the war but then suspended would be adopted.

D. Decentralised Administration: The Ottoman Empire was divided ethnographically and historically into five provinces: Anatolia, Armenia, Syria, Palestine and one roughly equivalent to Mesopotamia, termed Irak-Jazirah. The intention of removing Constantinople, the centre of government, allowed the possibility of setting up a decentralised form of government. The French sphere of interest was roughly the same as Syria and the British one corresponded to Palestine plus Irak-Jazirah.

Decentralisation was preferred. It was in line with the political theories of the Allies and the desires of the Arabs and Armenians. It avoided the problems of the others; potential conflicts between powers, construction of new naval bases, Turkish resentment, problems with Indian Muslims and possible exclusion of Britain from other powers' spheres. If it proved to be unworkable then the nucleus of independent states would have been established. The main problems were persuading the Turks and the Allies to agree to it and setting up the provincial governments. [96]

At the Committee's second meeting on 13 April 1915 Admiral Jackson said that the Admiralty believed that Britain should not take over more territory than it had to. Oil made it vital for Britain to control the Baghdad and Basra vilayets. On his suggestion Slade attended the next meeting two days later to explain the importance of oil. [97] De Bunsen started that meeting by saying that Mesopotamia contained substantial oil resources and that Britain's commitments to APOC meant that it was vital to know what should be done to protect these interests. Slade's view was that protecting the interests of the Persian Concession was paramount. Asiatic Turkey contained a great deal of oil:

> A strip of oil-bearing regions was known to run from the southern
> extremity of Arabia along the west coast of the Persian Gulf, through
> the valley of the Tigris and Euphrates, and so on to the northern coast
> of Asia Minor almost to its European end. There was also known to be
> a valuable oil district in Palestine to the south of Haifa...it would be
> sufficient, however, from our point of view if we secured the vilayet
> of Mosul, as that district contained some very rich oil-bearing lands

---

[96] Ibid., pp. 6-26.

[97] Ibid., p. 46.

> connecting with the Persian oil fields, which it was essential we
> should control to prevent undue competition with the Anglo-Persian
> Concession. It would of course be necessary to connect the fields by a
> pipe line with the Mediterranean...Haifa would do quite well as the
> terminus port. [98]

Much of this oil had not then been discovered, but most now has been, apart from in Palestine. De Bunsen summed up by saying that Slade's opinions on Britain's 'requirements in regard to oil practically coincided with the views that the committee had taken in regard to the inclusion of the Mosul vilayet in the territory to be acquired by us.'[99]

Oil was playing a part in Britain's war aims. Britain had interests in Mesopotamia and the Persian Gulf and wanted to protect the land route to India. Consequently, it would have wanted some form of control over the Basra vilayet even if there had been no oil in Persia or Mesopotamia. This could have been annexation, a protectorate or a sphere of influence. The Committee concluded that to control the Basra vilayet it was necessary to also control the Baghdad vilayet. Oil was a clear reason for Britain's interest in the Mosul vilayet. It cannot be said that oil was now a main determinant of British policy, and it is unclear how much impact the Committee's deliberations had on the Government; it is not mentioned at all in Hankey's diary and there are only a couple of passing references to it in his *Supreme Command*.[100] However, the first attempt to devise British war aims in the Middle East had concluded that oil was one of Britain's interests in the region.

1.4.3 The Sykes-Picot Agreement

In May 1916 Britain and France signed an agreement, with Russian consent, to partition much of the Ottoman Empire into five areas. It was named after the chief negotiators, Sir Mark Sykes, who had been a member of the de Bunsen Committee, and François Georges Picot. Each country would have a zone that it directly controlled and another that would be within its sphere of influence but ruled by the Arabs. Palestine was to be under international rule. Britain's

---

[98] Ibid., p. 47.

[99] Ibid.

[100] CC, Hankey Papers, HNKY 1/1, 'Diary: Vol. 1, 4 March 1915 - 20 April 1917'; M. P. A. Hankey, *The Supreme Command, 1914-1918*. (London: George Allen and Unwin, 1961), pp. 389, 531.

directly controlled area included the vilayets of Basra and Baghdad. The town of Mosul was in the French sphere of influence; this has led to a historiography that says that Sykes-Picot gave France the potential oil of Mesopotamia. Kent argues that this was because Britain did not have a clear oil policy in 1916[101], whilst Mejcher says relatively little about Sykes-Picot but implies that it gave France all of Mosul.[102] Jones accepts that Sykes-Picot gave France the oil of Mosul; this is less of a problem for him since he does not believe that Britain had a coherent oil policy in this period. He does point out that Sykes-Picot stated that previous British rights to oil in the French zones would be respected] but questions whether the Grand Vizier's letter of 28 June 1914 really gave the British oil exploration rights.[103] Yergin considers it to be a careless error that was opposed by many British officials who subsequently expended much time and effort to correct it.[104] David Fromkin argues that Britain surrendered the oil of Mosul.[105] Most other Middle Eastern historians tend not to regard the oil of Mosul as an issue until after the war.

Edward Fitzgerald has shown that Sykes-Picot gave only about half of the Mosul vilayet to France.[106] France was allocated the northern part of the vilayet, including the city of Mosul, and Britain the southern section, including Kirkuk. The talks were initiated by Britain after it had made promises to Sharif Hussein of Mecca in order to persuade him to launch an Arab revolt against Ottoman rule. Sir Edward Grey proposed bilateral negotiations to forestall the risk that the French would suspect that there was a threat to their interests in Syria behind the promises made to Hussein.[107] Pre-war reports meant that the French Foreign Ministry was well aware of the potential oil of Mosul.[108] Control of the region did not become a French aim until the British invitation to talks made the

---

[101] Kent, *Oil*, p. 122.

[102] Mejcher, *Imperial*, pp. 28-29.

[103] Jones, *State*, pp. 194-95.

[104] Yergin, *Prize*, p. 188.

[105] D. Fromkin, 'Britain, France, and the Diplomatic Agreements,' in *The Creation of Iraq, 1914-1921*, ed. R. S. Simon, E. H. Tejirian (New York NY: Columbia University Press, 2004), pp. 143-45.

[106] E. P. Fitzgerald, 'France's Middle-Eastern Ambitions, the Sykes-Picot Negotiations, and the Oil-Fields of Mosul, 1915-1918', *Journal of Modern History* 66, no. 4 (1994), pp. 717-18.

[107] Ibid., p. 707.

[108] Ibid., pp. 700-2.

French realise that they were in a position to demand more territory.[109] They were partly successful because Britain wanted the French to have the northern part of Mosul vilayet but insisted on the area round Kirkuk being in the British zone. It was expected that eastern Anatolia would be Russian controlled after the war and Britain wanted a buffer zone between its zone and the Russian one.[110] By 1919 Mosul's oil had become a major issue. Balfour, then Foreign Secretary, commented that it was Kitchener, by then dead, who had wanted a French buffer zone between British and Russian territory for reasons of security. Balfour, who was First Lord of the Admiralty at the time of Sykes-Picot, said that it could now be seen that this was a mistake, but that he had agreed with the decision at the time.[111]

Figure 1-2: Sykes-Picot Agreement

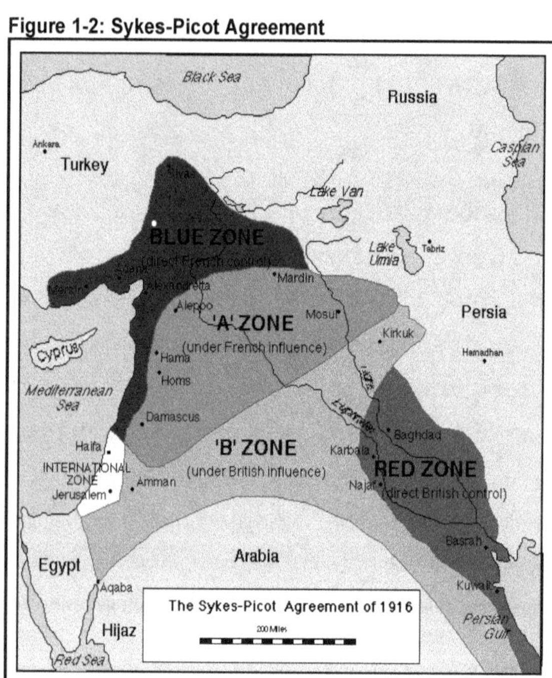

<<http://www.clas.ufl.edu/users/oren/INR4204Middleeast.html>> accessed 11 January 2010.

---

[109] Ibid., pp. 710-13.

[110] Ibid., pp. 714-16.

[111] NAS, Lothian Papers, GD40/1/39, 'Middle East - 11 Aug. 1919 - 12 Dec. 1919', 1919. 'Some difficulties to be borne in mind with any Syrian negotiations': Memorandum by A. J. Balfour, 9 September 1919, pp. 373-74.

1.5 Oil and the Mesopotamian Campaign

In 1914 responsibility for military intelligence and planning in Asia was divided between the War Office in London and the Indian Army in India. Persia, the Persian Gulf and Basra were Indian responsibilities. The rest of Mesopotamia was within the War Office zone but was not given great attention. The presence of a military department at the India Office in London increased the confusion.[112] There were no pre-war plans for a war in Mesopotamia, although in 1911-12 poor relations with the Ottomans led to the formation of a committee of senior officers to consider what recommendations the Indian government might make for protection of the British position in the Persian Gulf. Relations with the Ottomans improved so the issue was left until January 1914 when the question of the defence of the APOC oilfields arose. In July the India Office asked for the Indian government's opinion on the subject. It had not replied by the outbreak of war. As it became likely that the Ottoman Empire would enter the war on the German side operations against it were considered. The General Staff argued that Russia would be able to cope with any Ottoman offensive. At this stage concentrating forces in the West was favoured and operations against the Dardanelles were at first ruled out. The main issues in Mesopotamia were an indirect threat to Egypt and the Suez Canal by an Arab rising against Britain; disruption to the Persian oil supplies; protection of the existing British position in the Persian Gulf; and the risk of a Jihad leading to a rising on the North West Frontier of India and perhaps within India itself.[113]

1.5.1 The Despatch of IEF D

In August 1914 rising tension with the Ottoman Empire meant that measures to protect British interests in the Persian Gulf were contemplated. Slade, a former C.-in-C. East Indies, was at the Admiralty and represented its views on the subject. He argued that the current situation was unsatisfactory but that prompt action would remove the threat to British interests, including the oil refinery at Abadan. He wanted an expeditionary force to be readied at Karachi in order to

---

[112] PP, *Mesopotamia Commission. Report of the Commission Appointed by Act of Parliament to Enquire into the Operations of War in Mesopotamia, Together with a Separate Report by Commander J. Wedgwood, D.S.O., M.P., and Appendices*, HMSO 1917 [Cd. 8610]. p. 102.

[113] Moberly, *Mesopotamia*. vol. i, pp. 70-74.

be despatched to the Gulf at short notice. Part of it should be moved to a position in the Persian Gulf where it could move to the Shatt-al-Arab and protect the refinery within 48 hours. Two gunboats should move to the Shatt al Arab in order to stop any attempt at blocking it and prevent the Ottomans using it for military transport.[114] These proposals were made on 23 August 1914 and sent to the India Office two days later. On 30 August Slade wrote another memo arguing that there was a need for 'prompt action.'[115] The Foreign Office had accepted his proposal but General Sir Edmund Barrow and Sir Arthur Hirtzel of the India Office had told him that they could not do anything without a Cabinet order because so many troops had been sent abroad from India. Slade insisted that troops must be sent:

> It is...of urgent importance that the troops indicated should be sent at once in order to safeguard our supply of oil...This question of defence has nothing to do with the investment of Government capital in the Company...It is necessary in order to ensure the due supply of oil required for the Fleet.
>
> I might also emphasis the political importance of acting strongly in this region. Turkey is very vital here and it is considered that a settlement of many outstanding differences may thus be arrived at. Mesopotamia is a very rich oil field over which we ought to obtain unquestioned control.'[116]

Churchill disagreed with Slade, writing on this minute that:

> There is little likelihood of any troops being available for this purpose. Indian forces must be used at the decisive point. We shall have to buy our oil from elsewhere.[117]

Churchill's reluctance to protect the Persian oil installations appears surprising given his role in the government's purchase of shares in APOC, but it is consistent with his pre-war opinion. In a 1913 Cabinet memorandum on naval oil supplies he assumed 'that in time of war money would be no object.'[118] The objective of

---

[114] ADM 137/6, 'Persian Gulf, Part 1, 30 July - 31 October 1914', 1914. Memo by Sir Edmond Slade, pp. 28f-g.

[115] Ibid. 'Situation in the Persian Gulf. Need for Prompt Action.' Memo by VA Sir Edmond J. W. Slade, 30 August 1914, p. 34.

[116] Ibid.

[117] Ibid.

[118] CAB 37/115/39, 'Oil Fuel Supply for H.M. Navy', 1913, p. 5.

the APOC contract was to build up an oil reserve of six months' wartime naval oil consumption relatively cheaply in peacetime.

Sir Louis Mallet, the Ambassador to Constantinople, argued in favour of co-operation with an Arab movement led by friendly chiefs, such as Ibn Saud and the Sheikh of Kuwait. The capture of Baghdad should be the initial move and would be much better than attacking the Dardanelles.[119] Slade agreed, claiming that Ibn Saud and the Sheikh of Kuwait were very pro-British and would revolt against the Ottomans at the merest suggestion of British support. This would, without much difficulty give Britain control of Mesopotamia with its 'enormous grain growing lands...besides extremely valuable oilfields.'[120] The loss of Mesopotamia would be a major blow to both to the Ottoman Empire and Germany. Germany had substantial interests in the area and had been trying to supplant Britain and India there. Barrow, the Military Secretary to the India Office, also favoured co-operation with the Arabs, which he thought would end any risk of a Jihad and thus protect India, Egypt and Mesopotamia. He saw oil as an excuse for this operation, an intriguing reversal of the now widely held belief that everything in the Middle East is about oil. On 26 September he wrote on a memo arguing in favour of a landing:

> at Mohammerah or at Abadan Island, ostensibly to protect the oil installation, but in reality to notify the Turks that we mean business and to the Arabs that we were ready to support them.[121]

1.5.2 Early Manoeuvres by IEF D

Three Indian Expeditionary Forces had been organised; A to France and Egypt and two to East Africa, B to act defensively and C offensively. The increasing tension with the Ottoman Empire meant that IEF D was formed by detaching part of IEF A. This initially consisted of a brigade of the Sixth (Poona) Division of the Indian Army, later to be followed by the rest of the division. On 5 October Lord Crewe, the Secretary of State for India, gave the following instructions to the Indian Government:

---

[119] ADM 137/6. Telegram no. 692 from Sir L. Mallet (Constantinople), 4 September 1914, p. 42c.

[120] Ibid. Memo by Sir Edmond Slade, 5 September 1914, p. 42d.

[121] Moberly, *Mesopotamia*. vol. i, p. 87.

> The intention is to occupy Abadan, with the Force under orders,
> protect the oil-tanks and pipe-line, cover the landing of
> reinforcements, in the event of such being necessary, and show the
> Arabs that our intention is to support then against the Turks.[122]

The force reached Bahrain on 23 October. Its commander, General Delamain, was ordered to carry out the objectives above. He was to land at Abadan Island, which was Persian and contained APOC's refinery, but not to take any hostile action against the Ottomans before the outbreak of war.[123] On 31 October Delamain was warned that war was imminent. His force landed at Fao on 6 November, the day after the formal commencement of hostilities. By 10 November he had carried out his instructions.[124] Four days later the rest of the Sixth Division arrived. Its commander, General Sir Arthur Barrett, had instructions to take Basra. This was achieved by 22 November with relatively light casualties. Sir Percy Cox, the Political Agent on the scene, wanted to announce that the British occupation would be permanent. He was over-ruled on the grounds that it would contradict the agreement between the Allies that such arrangements should not be finalised until the end of the war. Barrow proposed taking Qurna. This gave a strong military position, control of the navigable waterway to the Gulf, possession of all the agricultural lands, completely protected Persian Arabistan, had a moral effect on the Arabs and enabled control of the telegraph. Crewe agreed, but was against further advances. Qurna was taken on 9 December.[125]

In early 1915 it was found that further advances were required in order to secure the existing position. Ottoman forces attacked from Amara on the Tigris towards the oil pipe-line and from Nasiriyah on the Euphrates towards Basra. The former force was believed to be heading for Ahwaz in Persia on the Karun River and the oil pipeline was cut by saboteurs.[126] The oilfields were protected by the local Bakhtiari tribesmen, but the Sheikh of Mohammerah was concerned that his Arab tribesmen might join the Ottomans if British reinforcements were not sent. The

---

[122] PP, *Cd. 8610.* p. 12.

[123] Ibid., p. 13.

[124] Moberly, *Mesopotamia*, pp. 100-10.

[125] PP, *Cd. 8610.* pp. 14-15.

[126] Barker, *Neglected*, pp. 65-66.

British forces present were too weak to defend the 130 mile pipeline.[127] The Indian Government was initially reluctant to reduce the garrison of India but built the forces in Mesopotamia up to two infantry divisions and a cavalry brigade. Sir John Nixon took command on 9 April 1915. His force was designated as a corps by the Government of India but did not have all the equipment, especially transport and medical services, of a corps.[128] His main objective was to control the Basra vilayet. He was to protect APOC's facilities and to prepare a plan to capture Baghdad. He should respect the neutrality of Persia subject to pressing political or military reasons.[129] Throughout the war both sides found that pressing military and political reasons justified breaches of Persian neutrality.[130]

On 12 April the Ottoman attack towards Basra was defeated at Barjisiya.[131] IEF D had completed the assignment given to it by the British Government except that the oil pipeline was not yet secure. This was the main concern in London. On 19 April Crewe cabled Hardinge urging operations to protect the pipeline as 'Admiralty most anxious for early repair pipeline as oil question becoming serious.'[132] On the same day Nixon requested more cavalry. Hardinge rejected this plea. Crewe informed Hardinge on 24 April that the British Government would not authorise any further advances and that throughout 'the summer we must confine ourselves to the defence of oil interests in Arabistan and of the Basra vilayet.'[133] An advance to Amara might be allowed if it increased the security of the oilfields but reinforcements would not be sent. In London Crewe did not appear to realise that Nixon's orders from India were to plan for the occupation of all of the Basra vilayet, including both Amara and Nasiriyah. 'In Mesopotamia a safe game must be played'[134] was Crewe's conclusion.

---

[127] Moberly, *Mesopotamia*. vol. i, pp. 173-74.

[128] PP, *Cd. 8610*. p. 15.

[129] Ibid., p. 16..

[130] N. S. Fatemi, *Oil Diplomacy: Powderkeg in Iran* (New York, NY: Whittier Books, 1954), pp. 62-63.

[131] PP, *Cd. 8610*. p. 15.

[132] Moberly, *Mesopotamia*. vol. i, p. 222.

[133] PP, *Cd. 8610*. p. 17.

[134] Ibid.

Figure 1-3: The Mesopotamian Campaign, 1914-1915

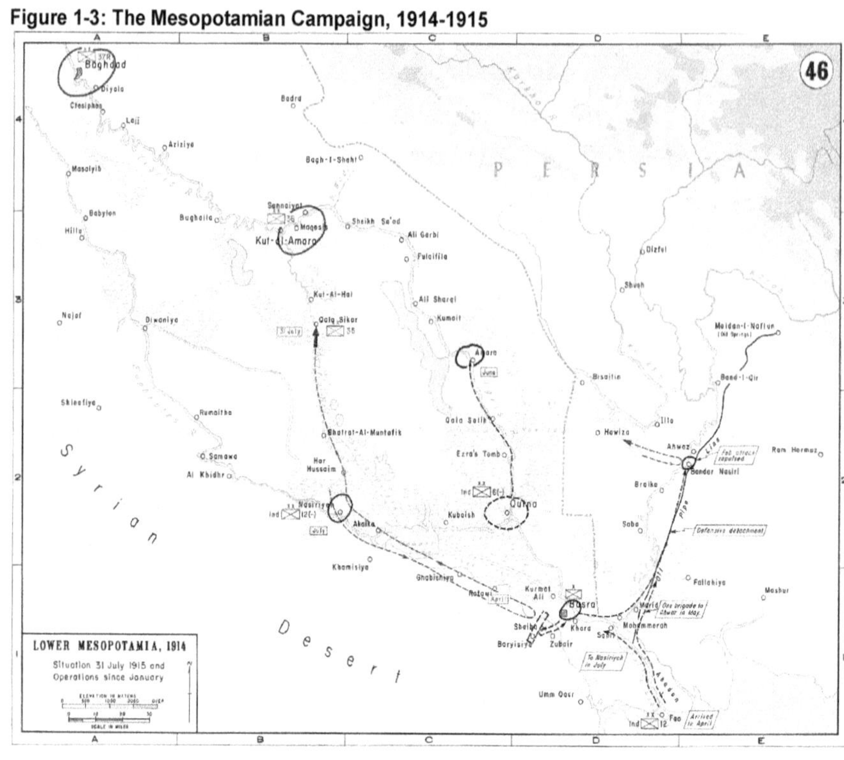

<<http://www.dean.usma.edu/history/web03/atlases/WorldWarOne/WWOneJPG/WWOne46.jpg>> Accessed 11 January 2010

1.5.3 The 1915-16 Offensive

Nixon intended to attack Ahwaz to secure the pipeline and Amara to stop the enemy threatening Ahwaz.[135] The offensives towards Ahwaz and Amara started on 31 May and succeeded by 3 June.[136] Austen Chamberlain, who replaced Crewe as Secretary of State for India when the Coalition Government was formed in May 1915, continued his predecessor's line of urging caution and simply defending the oilfields, pipeline and the Basra vilayet. No reinforcements would be sent. Nixon and Hardinge wanted to take Nasiriyah in order to protect Basra and then Kut-al-Amara in order to safeguard Nasiriyah and Amara.[137] The oilfields and pipelines were not threatened after Nasiriyah and Amara were captured.[138] There are better explanations than oil for the attempt to take Baghdad; the

---

[135] Moberly, *Mesopotamia*.vol. i, pp. 236-37.

[136] Ibid. vol. i, p. 265.

[137] Ibid. vol. i, pp. 303-4.

[138] Ibid. vol. i, pp. 307-8.

need for a victory somewhere after defeats elsewhere; over confidence by local commanders; and momentum created by a series of easy victories early in the campaign. Oil receives little mention in the reports of either an Inter-Departmental Committee set up to consider whether or not to advance on Baghdad or the Mesopotamia Commission, set up later to analyse the reasons for the failure.[139] General Sir Charles Townshend, who commanded the Sixth Division in its offensive towards Baghdad, argued in his memoirs that this operation should not have taken place. Basra vilayet and the oilfields should have been defended by a force based at Basra, with outposts at Qurna, Nasiriyah and Ahwaz.[140] He protested to Nixon about the decision to attack Baghdad on the grounds that his force was too weak to do so. Even if it succeeded the Ottoman success at Gallipoli meant that they could send reinforcements and retake Baghdad. Townshend blamed the decision to go ahead on the politicians.[141] Heavy casualties at the Battle of Ctesiphon in late November and the poor supply situation meant that IEF D had to withdraw.[142]

Barrow successfully argued after the Battle of Ctesiphon in favour of a retreat to Kut-al-Amara. It was a strong defensive position and had 'the further political advantage that it covers the whole of the Basra vilayet and indirectly protects the Anglo-Persian oilfield from Turkish attack.'[143] General Sir William Robertson, the CIGS, argued that remaining at Kut was better than falling back on Amara. A withdrawal from Kut would risk a Turkish attack on Persia and Afghanistan. Loss of the oilfields was one possible negative consequence, but the threat to India of a Jihad was a greater one.[144] The Persian oilfields were a factor in British military strategy, but other considerations were more important. The Admiralty remained concerned over the security of the oilfields. Negotiations between APOC and the Bakhtiari tribes in December meant that defence of the oilfields

---

[139] PP, *Cd. 8610.* pp. 20-30; CAB 24/1, G28 'Report of an Inter-Departmental Committee on the Strategical Situation in Mesopotamia', Secretary, 16 October 1915.

[140] C. V. F. Townshend, *My Campaign in Mesopotamia* (London: T. Butterworth Ltd, 1920), pp. 35-36.

[141] Ibid., pp. 124-29.

[142] PP, *Cd. 8610.* p. 29.

[143] CAB 24/1, G44 'An Appreciation of the Situation in Mesopotamia', E. G. Barrow, 29 November 1915, p. 3.

[144] CAB 24/1, G51 'The Situation in Mesopotamia', C.I.G.S., 31 January 1916.

was ensured without the need to send more British troops.[145] Kut fell on 29 April 1916.

1.5.4 The Capture of Baghdad

The mismanagement of the campaign meant that the Mesopotamian theatre was now under the control of Robertson and the War Office in London. On 22 August 1916 he informed the War Committee that it was necessary to keep the unsuccessful relief force opposite Kut as a withdrawal would enable the Ottomans to follow up their success against Russian forces in Persia.[146] The same month British reinforcements had to be sent to Ahwaz as some of the Bakhtiaris had turned hostile. Protection of the oilfields, which the Admiralty had often urged, had become even more significant because of the need for oil by the local forces.[147] The next month Robertson argued for a withdrawal from the positions opposite Kut. British forces in Mesopotamia were too weak to take Baghdad and were unnecessarily strong for defensive operations. Falling back would release troops to deal with the Bakhtiaris and other troublesome tribes. Objectors to this proposal included General Sir Frederick Maude, the new theatre commander. General Sir Charles Monro, the C.-in-C. India, was asked for his views. Monro visited Basra and reported that Robertson's proposed positions would not command the rivers or the oilfields as well as the current ones. There would be no saving in troop numbers because unrest amongst Mesopotamian and south Persian tribes would increase, thus requiring more troops.[148] On 30 September, Maude had been ordered:

> 'to protect the Oil Fields and Pipe Lines in the vicinity of the Karun River, to maintain our occupation and control of the Basra Vilayet, and to deny hostile access to the Persian Gulf and Southern Persia.[149]

Maude argued that to do nothing would be a poor strategy. He reorganised his force and greatly improved the supply and medical services that had proved entirely inadequate in the earlier offensive. He was permitted to launch an

---

[145] Moberly, *Mesopotamia.* vol. ii, pp. 150-54.

[146] Ibid. vol. iii, pp. 38-39.

[147] Ibid. vol. iii, p. 23.

[148] Ibid. vol. iii, pp. 45-50

[149] C.I.G.S. to C-in-C. India, 30 September 1916. Quoted in Barker, *Neglected*, p. 321.

offensive. It began on 13 December. He adopted a slow and methodical approach.[150] Baghdad was taken on 11 March 1917; General Baratov's Russian offensive from the north left Mosul in an exposed position, but the Allies had not yet taken all of Mesopotamia.[151] The General Staff argued that the capture of Baghdad had ended the risk of an Ottoman attack in Persia and any threat to India. The defeat of their army on the Tigris had required the Ottomans to withdraw from Persia and the Russians had, at British request, taken the offensive against the retreating enemy. The British objectives in Mesopotamia were to set up adequate administration and supply arrangements around Baghdad, to defeat enemy forces from the lower Euphrates and to co-operate with the Russians in removing Ottoman forces from Mesopotamia.[152]

Over the next six months Maude consolidated the British position. The loss of Baghdad was a severe blow to German ambitions in the Middle East and an offensive by a joint German-Ottoman force called *Yilderim* was intended to retake it and threaten Persia. It did not because British successes in Palestine resulted in *Yilderim* being employed there instead.[153] Maude died of cholera on 18 November and Robertson gave cautious instructions to his successor General Sir William Marshall. These were mostly the same as those given to Maude: Marshall was to protect the oilfields and pipelines, maintain British influence in the Baghdad vilayet, co-operate with the Arabs and Baratov but conduct no aggressive offensives. A new order was that Marshall should contemplate how reduce his force. The Mesopotamian campaign had succeeded in all its objectives, which did not then include the capture of the Mosul vilayet. The main campaign against the Ottoman Empire would now be in Palestine.[154] Protection of the oilfields was always a consideration in the Mesopotamian campaign. It became a less significant issue when offensive operations towards Baghdad rather than defensive ones around Basra were being undertaken. Mesopotamia was now a quiet theatre. Offensive operations would resume near the end of the war. Oil would be the major factor behind them.

---

[150] Ibid., pp. 322-24.

[151] Ibid., p. 384.

[152] CAB 24/8, G.T. 229 'A General Review of the Situation in All Theatres of War', General Staff, 20 March 1917, p. 1.

[153] Barker, *Neglected*, pp. 411-15.

[154] Ibid., pp. 431-40.

1.6 The National Oil Company

In 1916 long term oil policy focused more on attempts to establish a large, British controlled company than on plans to obtain control over oil bearing territory. The first government memorandum to deal explicitly with oil policy was written by the Board of Trade in August 1916. It was responded to by a series of Admiralty memoranda, mostly from Slade.

1.6.1 The 1916 Oil Company Merger Proposals

In August 1916 Lewis Harcourt, the First Commissioner of Works and temporarily in charge of the Board of Trade, stated that:

> The war has made clear that it is imperatively necessary for His Majesty's Government to take immediate and effective action to safeguard the future oil supplies of the British Empire...The problem of supply is...no longer merely a commercial question; it is an Imperial question of the first magnitude.'[155]

Ronald Ferrier's history of BP argues that this 'is an important document for it recognised for the first time the importance of the national oil supply situation.'[156] It insisted that oilfields in the British Empire should be British controlled. Foreign owners might delay development of these in favour of their interests elsewhere in the world. Since these could supply only a fraction of Britain's needs, Britain had to get control of as much foreign oil as possible. It would be some time before Persian and Mesopotamian oil could make a difference; the only effective way to solve the current problem was to bring RDS under British control. An Imperial Oil Company should be formed by merging Anglo-Saxon, a subsidiary of RDS, with Burmah. The new company would own all RDS's interests except those in Dutch territory and Romania; its shareholding would split 51 per cent British, 49 per cent Dutch. Shell and Royal Dutch would each have three directors and Burmah two; the Shell and Burmah directors would have to be British subjects. This would establish a British company that

---

[155] ADM 1/8537/240, 'Oil Situation', 1918, p. 1.

[156] R. W. Ferrier, *The History of the British Petroleum Company: Vol.1, the Developing Years, 1901-1932* (Cambridge: Cambridge University Press, 1982), p. 243.

controlled both substantial oil production and a major distribution network. Measures would be taken to safeguard the British consumer.[157]

The idea of a Shell-Burmah merger to create a large oil company with a British majority had been proposed by Shell in 1915. It suggested including APOC, but APOC's chairman, Charles Greenway, favoured an amalgamation with Lord Cowdray's Mexican Eagle. Cowdray thought that a large national oil company would be good for Britain but was reluctant to be involved himself. He thought that government capital and directors brought problems and that people with significant shareholdings in them ran companies better than hired managers. The government was reluctant to include Mexican Eagle in any national oil company because of potential diplomatic problems with the USA. Civil servants foresaw problems working with Cowdray.[158]

Slade produced three memoranda in reply to the one from the Board of Trade, all dated 24 August 1916 but circulated to the Cabinet by Balfour, then First Lord of the Admiralty, on 6 September.[159] Balfour referred to Slade's papers in his Cabinet memorandum of 18 August. He argued that the Admiralty could get as much oil as it required 'provided..[t]hey can carry it; and...[t]hey can pay for it. The shortage in the present war is one not of oil but of tonnage.'[160] He raised a number of questions, mostly dealing with the risk of a monopoly raising prices and the government's potential role. He asked: '[c]an we afford to *be* responsible for the policy of a huge combine dealing with a prime necessity of modern life? Can we afford to *seem* responsible if in fact we are powerless [Balfour's italics]?'[161]

Slade's memoranda were circulated by the Admiralty but did not reflect the Balfour's sceptical opinions. Slade was a government director of APOC at the time. He became Vice-Chairman on 15 December; on 8 January 1917 he resigned

---

[157] ADM 1/8537/240.

[158] Jones, *State*, pp. 189-95.

[159] CAB 37/154/16, 1916. Slade's memoranda on 'Strategic Importance of the Control of Petroleum' and 'Petroleum Supplies and Distribution', but not his 'Observations on the Board of Trade Memorandum on Oil', are also in CAB 23/6, 'War Cabinet Papers 379-437', 1 April - 28 June 1918.

[160] CAB 37/154/3, 1916. 'Admiralty Interests', A. J. Balfour, 18 August 1918.

[161] Ibid.

as a government director but was immediately re-appointed to the board.[162] Although representing the government on the board, he supported the company's growth plans and lobbied on its behalf. He had access to government information about RDS's activities.[163] According to Ferrier the initial two government directors received no formal instructions from the government on their responsibilities and concentrated on their areas of interest and expertise; defence and security for Slade and business for Lord Inchcape.[164]

Geoffrey Jones points out the ambiguities in Slade's position after 1914. He was supposed to represent the government on APOC's board but lobbied on its behalf whilst still holding positions on Admiralty committees.[165] Nicholas Lambert, commenting on Slade's earlier time as DNI, argues that he had a straightforward and simplistic view of life that led him to object to political machinations; he could not see why the army and navy should be rivals when competing for budgets.[166] If this analysis, based on a study of his diary, is accurate then it may be that Slade thought that what was good for APOC was good for the country and did not understand how controversial his views were. His dual role at the Admiralty and at APOC did mean that APOC found it easier than Shell to have its views heard in government circles.

Slade agreed with the Board of Trade that oil was of great importance and that foreign interests must not be allowed to control British supplies. He disagreed with their proposal. Much of RDS's oil was unsuitable for British needs. Russia and California were badly located to supply the RN. Mexican oil was of too poor quality to be used as naval fuel. The combined network of all the wholly British oil companies was superior to that of RDS in the British Empire. The Shell directors of the Imperial Oil Company would probably vote with the Royal Dutch ones, creating a six to two majority against Burmah and reducing, not increasing, British control of oil supplies. The British Empire could become self-sufficient in oil if the Persian field was considered to be British. The proposal

---

[162] Ferrier, *History*. Appendix 8.4, p. 650.

[163] Jones, *State*, pp. 183-84.

[164] Ferrier, *History*, p. 297.

[165] Jones, *State*, p. 183.

[166] N. A. Lambert, *Sir John Fisher's Naval Revolution* (Columbia, SC: University of South Carolina Press, 1999), p. 173.

would help RDS towards what Slade regarded as its goal of dividing up the world oil market with Standard (NJ). He suggested that his:

> 'very grave objections can be overcome, and at the same time much greater advantages in the direction of petroleum for the nation can be attained, by forming a National Oil Company...with the Anglo-Persian, Burmah, and other purely British companies as a nucleus.'[167]

Slade explained how the move from coal to oil as the principal fuel of ships altered Britain's strategic position:

> It is evident that in the present war the control we have been able to exercise on neutral shipping and the check that has thereby been placed in free imports into countries adjacent to the enemy of goods required by him, has been in a great measure due to the power of limiting the supply of bunker fuel in case of necessity. It is therefore of vital importance to the country that we should retain as large a measure of control in the future as possible.
>
> ...
>
> It is therefore necessary to see that the geographical distribution of our oil resources is such that we retain as large an amount of control as possible. It is also of prime importance that no foreign interests, whether for monopolistic trade or political reasons, shall have any power of hampering either the development of our own resources or shall control in any way the distribution of oil.[168]

He argued that the Admiralty proposal of a merger between APOC, Burmah and perhaps other British companies would produce a company with a greater and wider spread of oil production than the Board of Trade's suggestion of an amalgamation of Shell and Burmah. Table 1-1 shows his figures:

---

[167]CAB 37/154/16. 'Observations on the Board of Trade Memorandum on Oil', E. J. W. Slade, 24 August 1916, p. 6.

[168] Ibid., p. 1.

Table 1-1 British oil production under merger schemes, tons

	Eastern Hemisphere	Western Hemisphere	Total
Board of Trade Scheme	1,030,000	900,000	1,930,000
Possible later additions	1,400,000	40,000	1,440,000
Total	2,430,000	940,000	3,370,000
Admiralty scheme	2,400,000	1,600,000	4,000,000
Possible later additions	100,000		100,000
Total	2,500,000	1,600,000	4,100,000

Source: CAB 37/154/16., 'Strategic Importance of the Control of Petroleum', E. J. W. Slade, 24 August 1916, p. 3.

Slade's third memorandum, 'Petroleum Supplies and Distribution'[169], argued that British control of distribution as well as production was needed. The government had sequestered British Petroleum, a German controlled company that distributed oil in Britain for RDS and various German owned companies. A new board should be appointed; BP should become the distribution company throughout the British Empire for both British and foreign controlled oil. It would be state owned until a public share issue could be arranged. The new BP would have 4,740,000 tons of oil compared with a current demand of 5,000,000 in the British Empire, half of it in Britain; Standard (NJ) provided nearly half of the Empire's supplies and 800,000 tons to Britain.[170] His scheme would mean that British demand was met from British controlled supplies and was distributed by a British company. This would remove the threat of a monopoly forcing up prices. He did not consider the counter-balancing market power of a very large consumer such as the RN.

By October the Admiralty had withdrawn its objections to the merger of Burmah and Shell subject to a number of conditions; existing contracts between APOC and RDS should be re-drawn; a new deal should be agreed between them for oil bunkering in Asia; the Burmah shareholding in APOC should be transferred to trustees; and BP should be sold to APOC. The Board of Trade had accepted all these except for the last, claiming that it would result in the government being involved in the commercial distribution of oil. The Admiralty now argued that APOC could survive and prosper on its own provided that it was free from foreign interference and had the necessary refineries and transport and distribution

---

[169] Ibid. 'Petroleum Supplies and Distribution'

[170] Ibid., pp. 3-4.

networks.[171] A Cabinet meeting on 1 November 1916 approved the Board of Trade proposal, subject to the Admiralty's caveat.[172] The next day Slade wrote to Pretyman, who was now at the Board of Trade, indicating that APOC was satisfied with this. The wording of this letter implied that Slade was representing APOC rather than the Admiralty in it.[173] The proposals were unattractive to RDS and Burmah, and no merger took place. The one corporate transaction that did occur was the one objected to by the Board of Trade; the acquisition of BP by APOC.[174] This gave it a distribution company and, many years later, a new corporate name.

1.6.2 Royal Dutch Shell and the British Government

APOC had a commercial rivalry with RDS. Many, including Slade, clearly distrusted the latter because it was partially foreign even though its actions did little to justify this. In January 1915 it dismantled its Rotterdam toluol extraction plant and re-erected it in Somerset, later building another in Britain. Toluol was a vital ingredient of explosives. Before the war Britain had extracted it from coal, but output was insufficient for wartime needs. The two RDS plants provided 80 per cent of Britain's requirements.[175] During the war RDS chartered its tankers to the British Government at favourable rates.[176] Its wartime actions favoured the Allies. Shell's British management acted patriotically; one of the sons of its founder, Marcus Samuel, was killed in action.[177] Both parts of the group put their national interests first, but the Dutch favoured the Allies for rational and pragmatic business reasons.[178] Initially some Dutch executives wanted to be strictly neutral. Henri Deterding, the President of Royal Dutch, preferred the Allies; his colleagues realised that this was in the company's

---

[171] ADM 1/8537/240. 'Progress of the Negotiations with Regard to the Burmah-Shell Amalgamation', A. J. Balfour, 19 October 1916.

[172] PA, Bonar Law Papers, BL/60/9/2, 'Other Cabinet Papers: Oil'. Note of the Proceedings at the Cabinet on Oil, 1 November 1916.

[173] Ibid. Slade to Pretyman, 2 November 1916.

[174] Ferrier, *History*, pp. 246-47.

[175] Yergin, *Prize*, pp. 174-75.

[176] T. A. B. Corley, *A History of the Burmah Oil Company, 1886-1924* (London: Heinemann, 1983), pp. 233-34.

[177] Yergin, *Prize*, pp. 174-75.

[178] J. Jonker et al, *A History of Royal Dutch Shell*, 4 vols. (Oxford: Oxford University Press, 2007). vol. i, p. 221.

interests. Some oil did reach the Central Powers from RDS's Swedish and Romanian subsidiaries, whose managements ignored the wishes of the centre. Over the war the size of its contribution to the Allied cause meant that official suspicion of it diminished, albeit more slowly at the Admiralty than at other departments. The War Office appointed Robert Waley Cohen, a senior Shell executive, as its Petroleum Adviser in April 1917.[179]

1.7 Chapter Summary

In 1914 British oil policy was to buy oil cheaply on long term contracts in order to provide reserves. These would be needed early in a war; it was assumed that further supplies could be bought on the market during wartime, a point made by two First Lords, Churchill and Balfour. Since 1900 the RN had moved from being behind several European navies in the adoption of oil to being ahead of even the USN, which had access to the world's largest oil industry.[180] Other navies had mostly confined the use of oil to torpedo craft and as an auxiliary in cruisers and battleships. The importance of the control of oil bearing territory rather than oil companies had not yet been realised; efforts were made to bring RDS, wrongly feared to be pro-German, under British control. The potential of Mosul's oil was known, but in 1914 Britain had no war aims in the Middle East beyond preservation of its existing position. Corbett pointed out in 1915 that the war had given Britain an unexpected opportunity to obtain control of Mosul's oil. The entry of the Ottoman Empire into the war required Britain to consider its position and the de Bunsen Committee was the first step in this process. It put forward the Mosul's oil as a British interest, albeit just one of several. The Sykes-Picot Agreement then gave part, but not all, of Mosul and its oil to France. The desire to control all of Mosul would influence post war British policy and military strategy in the final month of the war. Britain had an oil policy in 1916. It did not touch many other aspects of strategy and was too focused on the ownership of companies rather than control of oilfields.

---

[179] Jones, *State*, pp. 187-89.

[180] See J. A. Denovo, 'Petroleum and the United States Navy before World War I', *Mississippi Valley Historical Review* 41, no. 4 (1955), pp. 641-56.

2 Wartime Oil Supplies

Throughout the war the oil position of the Allies was stronger than that of the Central Powers. Austria-Hungary produced oil in Galicia, but Germany imported 90 per cent of its 1913 consumption of 1.4 million tons, mostly from the USA, Dutch East Indies, Romania and Russia.[181] In 1914 the only large producer on the Allied side was Russia whose production peaked at over 10 million tons in 1916 but collapsed after the revolution. Closure of the Dardanelles prevented exports from Russia and Romania after September 1914[182], but the Allies were still in a stronger position than their enemies. They were able to import oil because the USA was willing to sell oil to anybody who could pay for and transport it. British control of the seas enabled the Allies to import American oil, although the efforts of the U-boats meant that this was in doubt for a while. The Allies, unlike the Central Powers, were able to increase their use of oil during the war. Importing and distributing oil did create problems for the Allies from 1917 onwards. Britain and France both had oil crises in 1917. These were overcome but made both countries realise that they needed secure oil supplies.

During the war Germany and Austria-Hungary never had available more than the 2 million tons that they jointly consumed in 1913. Germany's wartime oil supplies were only 85 per cent of peacetime consumption and only two-thirds of lube requirements were met. About a third of German oil consumption came from substitutes by 1918 and Germany may have produced over 2 million tons of synthetic oil during the war. French analysis of German aviation fuel in 1917 concluded that it was superior to that of Allies, possibly because of the addition of benzene.[183] About 60 per cent of the Central Powers' oil came from Galicia.[184] Their other source was Romania.

---

[181] Jonker et al, *History.* vol. i, p. 173.

[182] Ibid., p. 163.

[183] Ibid., pp. 173-77.

[184] A. F. Frank, *Oil Empire: Visions of Prosperity in Austrian Galicia* (Cambridge, MA: Harvard University Press, 2005), p. 173.

2.1 Oil and Land and Air Warfare

Many of the technological advances during the war involved oil fuelled weapons such as tanks and aircraft. The Allies' oil supplies gave them an increasing advantage. In 1914 troops moved by train to railheads and then marched to the front line. Supplies generally travelled from the railheads to the front lines by horse transport. Moving a German Corps required 240 trains. Transporting only the combat elements needed 120 trains and would have required 18,000 motor vehicles. The German Army had only 4,000 motor vehicles in 1914.[185] Half of them carried beer in peacetime; civilian ownership had been subsidised since 1907.[186] The German motor industry was only the third largest in Europe in 1914, behind those of France and Britain.[187] German horse drawn ammunition columns could not keep the right wing of the 1914 Western offensive supplied, leaving its ammunition supply dependent on the small number of lorries available. These had to be driven hard, meaning that 60 per cent were unserviceable by the Battle of the Marne in September; petrol was in short supply.[188] The most famous contribution of the internal combustion engine to the 1914 campaign came when French reinforcements were rushed to the Battle of the Marne by 600 Parisian taxis.[189] The Paris taxi fleet could not carry enough men to make a difference to a battle of the scale of the Marne; the importance of this event is in its symbolism, both of French determination to resist the invader and of the future use of motor transport in war. The British also used public transport for military purposes in 1914, commandeering a number of London buses. The trench warfare that developed soon after the Marne had little role for measures such as the improvised use of taxis and buses for military transport.

Set piece trench warfare required the movement of huge amounts of supplies. These were normally moved by train to railheads about 10-12 miles from the trenches. Horse drawn transports were used for the last five miles because of

---

[185] M. Van Creveld, *Supplying War: Logistics from Wallenstein to Patton* (Cambridge: Cambridge University Press, 1977), pp. 136-37.

[186] Strachan, *To Arms*, p. 240.

[187] J. M. Laux, 'Trucks in the West During the First World War', *Journal of Transport History* Third Series, 6, no. 2 (1985), p. 65.

[188] Van Creveld, *Supplying War*, pp. 125-27.

[189] Laux, 'Trucks', p. 65.

the poor state of roads that were under constant enemy shelling, but motor vehicles or light railways were used for the distance in between.[190] The quantity of supplies needed rose greatly over the war and motor vehicles could be built more quickly than horses could be bred. A British Army division required 20 wagon loads of food and horse fodder and 7 of other items per day in 1914. In 1916 it needed 50 wagons in total, 30 carrying non-food supplies. Verdun had to be supplied by motor vehicles because the narrow *Voie Sacrée* could not have coped with the same volume of supplies carried in horse wagons. There were 1,230 British, 2,750 French and 600 US aircraft on the Western Front by the end of the war, using 31,000 tons of fuel per month. The 2,600 British and 3,800 French tanks consumed 42,000 tons of fuel each month.[191] In 1914 the British Army possessed 807 lorries, 20 cars and vans and 15 motor cycles. Only 80 of the lorries were directly owned; the others were peacetime civilian vehicles subsidised by the War Office. By the end of the war the British military had 57,000 lorries, 23,000 cars and vans, 7,000 motor ambulances and 35,000 motor cycles.[192] The French Army had 54,000 trucks on the Western Front, the French Air Force 14,000 motor vehicles and the US Army 33,000 trucks plus 13,000 cars and ambulances. Italy was well provided with motor transport; Fiat was the world's largest truck manufacturer, enabling Italy to supply 17,000 trucks to its Allies.[193]

Germany had only 45 tanks and 40,000 trucks in 1918; use of the latter was heavily restricted because of shortages of oil. In 1917 it had 2,270 aircraft in France with 11,000 tons of oil per month to fuel them. The number of aircraft had risen to 3,600 aircraft by the start of the March 1918 offensive, but monthly fuel supplies had fallen to 7,000 tons and were less than 5,000 tons by June. Allied air superiority was greater than the numbers of aircraft suggested since Allied aircraft could fly more sorties. Shortage of lubricating oil meant that the Germans had to take radial engined aircraft, including the Fokker Triplane, out of service. Germany had to make more use of horses and railways; pressure on

---

[190] J. Singleton, 'Britain's Military Use of Horses 1914-1918', *Past and Present* 139, no. 1 (1993), p. 190.

[191] Jonker et al, *History*. vol. i, pp. 163-65

[192] *Statistics of the Military Effort of the British Empire During the Great War, 1914-1920* (Uckfield: Naval and Military Press, 1999), p. 877.

[193] Laux, 'Trucks', p. 67. Other sources differ because of different date and definitions of the type of vehicle.

the railways led to restrictions on German ability to transport their large coal reserves.[194] The German navy switched to oil for their torpedo boats in 1908 but did not build any larger all oil warship. Oil was used as a supplementary to coal in light from 1907 and dreadnoughts from 1909. Technical problems prevented the fitting of diesel cruising engines to dreadnoughts.[195] German ship designers thought that side coal bunkers offered extra protection, but the lack of guaranteed oil supplies was a significant factor.[196] An oil fired ship could be more heavily armoured than an otherwise identical coal burning vessel; coal bunkers only offered protection when full.

General Erich Ludendorff admitted in *The Nation at War*[197] that shortages of oil were a major problem for him. Obtaining oil, as well as food supplies, was a reason for the German invasion of Romania, but the Allies successfully sabotaged the Romanian oilfields. By 1918 the growth in demand for oil and German shortages forced Ludendorff to turn to Transcaucasia for supplies.

2.2 U-Boats and Oil

The submarine was one of the war weapons made possible by oil. There had previously been man powered submarines. The *Turtle* unsuccessfully attacked HMS *Eagle* in 1776 during the American War of Independence. The CSS *Hunley* sank the USS *Housatonic* in 1864 during the American Civil War. The submarine did not become a viable weapon until the invention of the internal combustion engine. Submarines used these on the surface and battery powered engines when submerged; the limited range of the latter meant that they spent most of their time on the surface, and were really submersible torpedo boats. Early submarines used petrol engines, but diesel ones were more suitable. Fisher was quick to realise the submarine's potential, and in 1913 wrote a paper titled 'The Oil Engine and the Submarine.'[198] It stated several times that '[t]he submarine is

---

[194] Jonker et al, *History*, p. 177.

[195] H. H. Herwig, *'Luxury' Fleet: The Imperial German Navy, 1888-1918* (London: Allen & Unwin, 1980), pp. 60-71.

[196] Ibid., pp. 82-83.

[197] E. Ludendorff, *The Nation at War*, trans., A. S. Rappoport (London: Hutchison & Co., 1936), pp. 78-79.

[198] CC, Fisher Papers, FISR 5/19, 'The Oil Engine and the Submarine', 1913.

the coming type of war vessel for sea fighting.'[199] He argued that it would not be possible for submarines to capture merchantmen: they had no men to spare for prize crews or space to take prisoners on board the submarine. They would have to sink merchantmen without warning. Submarines could defend a coastline, making it much hard to launch amphibious invasions, but they would make it easier to cut an enemy's seaborne trade. This meant that starvation rather than invasion was now the main threat to Britain. The navy's oil supplies could be cut off as well as the nation's food imports. [200] Adoption of the submarine was to Britain's advantage, since its geographical position meant:

> that while the development of submarine warfare will render us absolutely safe from overseas attack, it cannot possibly cripple our trade to anything like the extent to which it can be made to cripple that of our enemy.[201]

Churchill and Admiral Battenberg, the First Sea Lord, both thought that Fisher's arguments were weakened by the suggestion, which proved to be correct, that the enemy would use submarines to sink merchant ships without warning.[202]

The U-boat became the German Navy's main weapon in both the World Wars of the twentieth century, and Rudolf Diesel was German, but Germany was initially slow to adopt the submarine. Admiral Alfred von Tirpitz, the architect of the German Navy, favoured battleships and had little time for either cruiser warfare or submarines. The first U-boat was not completed until late 1906. Diesel engines were not introduced until 1910. French submarines had used diesel engines from 1904. The switch to the diesel engine meant that the U-boat was considered a potentially decisive weapon for the first time, but against the enemy battle fleet, not merchant shipping.[203]

In 1914 Germany possessed only 24 operational boats. Four were used for training and 16 were under construction. Only 10 of the operational boats had diesel engines; the others used Körting heavy fuel oil engines that produced a

---

[199] Ibid. This phrase appears twice on p. 1 and again on pp. 7 and 12

[200] Ibid., pp. 9-13.

[201] Ibid., p. 13.

[202] R. H. Gibson, M. Prendergast, *The German Submarine War, 1914-1918.* (London: Constable, 1931), p. 24.

[203] Herwig, *'Luxury'*, pp. 38-39, 86-87.

great deal of smoke and sparks. This made them very visible on the surface and required ventilation pipes; stowing these slowed diving.[204] Before the war Kapitänleutnant Blum of the German Navy had estimated that 222 U-boats would be needed to successfully carry out a war against British commerce under international law. On 8 October 1914 the commander of Germany's U-boats, Korvettenkapitän Bauer, urged that German U-boats should attack British commerce. Germany did not announce unrestricted submarine warfare in the waters around the British Isles until 4 February 1915. It had only 37 U-boats. A maximum of 25 were available at any one time, with only a third of them in the operational area. This campaign lasted until 18 September; losses were low as a proportion of British shipping, but rose after June despite some restrictions introduced to placate the USA after the sinking of the *Lusitania* on 7 May. By the end of the campaign, which came as a relief to the British, losses were greater than new construction.[205] The Germans did not have enough U-boats at this stage and were concerned about neutral opinion.

On 1 February 1917 they had 105 available and more under construction; their strength rose to 129 by the start of June and did not fall below 120 for the remainder of the year. Admiral Henning von Holtzendorff, the Chief of the Admiralty Staff of the Imperial German Navy, believed that this was enough to defeat Britain in five months by a campaign of unrestricted submarine warfare; the time scale was crucial because the German calculations depended on victory before the next harvest. His arguments were based mostly on the opportunity to starve Britain by cutting off its food supplies; he mentioned blocking imports of wood, which would cut coal output because it was used for pit props, and of iron ore, which would reduce the production of steel and thus munitions. He said nothing about oil. He accepted that the USA would probably join the Allies, but believed that Britain would have to sue for peace before the Americans could make a significant contribution. [206]

---

[204] V. E. Tarrant, *The U-Boat Offensive, 1914-1945* (London: Arms and Armour, 1989), p. 7.

[205] Halpern, *Naval*, pp. 291-303.

[206] D. Steffen, 'The Holtzendorff Memorandum of 22 December 1916 and Germany's Declaration of Unrestricted U-Boat Warfare', *Journal of Military History* 68, no. 1 (2004), pp. 215-24.

2.3 Efforts to Deny Oil to the Enemy

Romania entered the war on the Allied side in August 1916. It was invaded by German and Austrian troops the next month. In late October a British report stated that the Central Powers' oil supply was restricted, but their oil problems would be almost completely solved if they obtained the Romanian oilfields.[207] By then the Germans had captured a large amount of oil stocks and were close to capturing the oilfields and refineries. When the Romanians appeared reluctant to destroy their most important industry the British sent a small group to destroy both it and Romania's grain stock.[208] It was led by Colonel John Norton-Griffiths, a mining engineer who had pioneered mine warfare on the Western Front.[209] He arrived in Romania in mid November 1916, soon realising that the Romanian Army was too weak to stop the enemy from taking the oilfields or the grain growing region. He decided that to be certain of destroying the oil he must supervise the action in person and delegate destruction of corn. He thought that this had to be done ahead of the advancing enemy, running the risk that facilities would be destroyed unnecessarily. The Romanians, more optimistic than him about the course of the campaign, at first hesitated to carry out any destruction and then wanted only to burn stocks and remove key parts from refineries and wells.

Norton-Griffiths recruited a small number of British oil engineers and some locals and wrecked oil refineries and wells at 14 locations over ten days. His team claimed to have destroyed 210 million gallons of oil, over 800,000 tons.[210] The enemy was deprived of Romanian oil for five months and 1917 output was less than 30 per cent of the 1915 level. Concentrating on the most productive wells meant that by November 1918 less than half the wells operating in July 1916

---

[207] CAB 24/2, G89 'The Economic Position in the Central Powers', W. G. M. Müller, 26 October 1916, p. 2.

[208] Yergin, *Prize*, pp. 179-81.

[209] For a positive view of Norton-Griffiths see T. Bridgland, A. Morgan, *Tunnel-Master and Arsonist of the Great War: The Norton-Griffiths Story* (Barnsley: Leo Cooper, 2003). For a more critical one see his entry in the ODNB.

[210] CAB 24/6, G.T. 25 'Report on the Destruction of Roumanian Oilfields', J. Norton-Griffiths, 22 January 1917.

were back in production but 75 per cent of output had been restored.[211] The Central Powers never had quite enough oil.

One potential source of oil for them was the oilfields of Grozny and Baku in the Caucasus. On 25 June 1918 Curzon, a member of the War Cabinet and Chairman of the Eastern Committee, told the Imperial War Cabinet that the Treaty of Brest-Litovsk had been followed by a treaty with the Ukrainian government that had given the Germans large supplies of cereal. The Germans could next gain control of the Black Sea and access to the great natural resources of the Caucasus. These included the Baku and Grozny oilfields that produced 20 per cent of global oil, more than enough to supply German needs. A rivalry between Germany and the Ottoman Empire was developing since both wanted the oil of Baku for themselves. If either took Baku then it would probably also capture the Caspian Fleet, enabling it to control the Caspian and threaten Turkestan and Northern Persia.[212] Two days later the Foreign Office PID wrote that it was highly important to prevent the enemy from occupying Baku. The oil wells were believed to be intact and Baku was important for communications; it was a port on the Caspian Sea and was linked to the Trans-Caspian Railway.[213] A month earlier the PID had published a memorandum putting forward similar views to those of Curzon and arguing that the significance of the oilfields of Grozny and Baku 'could hardly be overestimated.'[214] As well as the oil, capture of Baku and the Trans-Caspian Railway would give a direct route towards the borders of Afghanistan.

A small British Military Mission under General Lionel Dunsterville, initially comprising only a dozen officers, had already been sent to the Caucasus. It left Baghdad on 27 January 1918 and arrived in Enzeli on 17 February but was unable to move onto Baku and its final destination of Tiflis. Dunsterville's force, named Dunsterforce, was reinforced by several infantry companies and some armoured cars and light artillery. In late July he was ordered to help the Centro-Caspian Government defend Baku against the Ottomans. The first British elements

---

[211] M. Pearton, *Oil and the Romanian State* (Oxford: Clarendon Press, 1971), pp. 82-85.

[212] CAB 23/43, 'Imperial War Cabinet Shorthand Notes', 1918, pp. 4-7. 25 June 1918

[213] CAB 24/57, G.T. 5068 'Political Developments in Russian Central Asia since the Revolution', P.I.D., 27 June 1918, p. 8.

[214] CAB 24/52, G.T. 4609 'Memorandum on the Caucasus', 18 May 1918, p. 2.

reached Baku on 4 August; the rest of Dunsterforce and its commander arrived 13 days later. It was not strong enough to hold Baku and was forced to withdraw on 14 September, without destroying the oil facilities. Dunsterville blamed the locals for the fall of Baku because they did not give Dunsterforce enough help. Artin Arslanian argues that Dunsterville was to blame. He had lobbied his superiors to send his force to Baku, although it was inadequate for the purpose. He promised the locals British reinforcements that were never going to be sent.[215] Baku was occupied by the British for only 42 days but Yergin argues that this made a difference at a vital stage of the war.[216] This is doubtful. Having the oil of Baku much earlier could have made a difference to the cause of the Central Powers. Taking it in early August rather than mid September could not have prevented the signing of armistices by Ottoman Empire on 30 October and Germany on 11 November.

2.4 Oil and Diversions into Sideshows

Britain deployed a large number of troops away from the Western Front. Most of the General Staff wanted to concentrate on the main theatre of operations, namely the Western Front. Others, such as Hankey and Lloyd George, argued that operations elsewhere would use Britain's naval strength and avoid the heavy casualties of the Western Front.

On 1 November 1918, the total strength of the British Empire Expeditionary Forces was 3,226,879, of which 408,138 were in Mesopotamia. This appears to be a very large proportion for a secondary theatre, but the supply problems of Mesopotamia meant that labour units and native followers comprised a large proportion of the force there. Excluding these, Mesopotamia accounted for 222,399 out of 2,668,737 soldiers in overseas Expeditionary Forces.[217] Sir George Buchanan, an engineer who was recruited to help solve the supply and logistics problems of the campaign, argued that the initial objectives of protecting the

---

[215] A. H. Arslanian, 'Dunsterville's Adventures: A Reappraisal', *International Journal of Middle Eastern Studies* 12, no. 2 (1980), pp. 199-216; L. C. Dunsterville, *The Adventures of Dunsterforce* (London: E. Arnold, 1920); 'From Baghdad to the Caspian in 1918', *Geographical Journal* 57, no. 3 (1921), pp. 153-66.

[216] Yergin, *Prize*, p. 182.

[217] *Statistics of the Military Effort of the British Empire During the Great War, 1914-1920*, pp. 62-63.

existing oilfields and the Shatt-el-Arab River could have been achieved at a lower cost in both lives and money.[218] This is true, but the expansion of the campaign from its origins was largely not because of oil. A smaller and more defensive campaign would not have resulted in Britain occupying Mosul and its potential oil at the end of the war.

2.5 The 1917 Oil Crisis

British oil stocks fell to crisis levels in the Spring of 1917. On 31 January 1917, Germany announced that it would carry out unrestricted submarine warfare. Significant numbers of tankers were sunk, reducing oil imports at a time when the rising number of oil fired warships and greater use of motor vehicle, tanks and aircraft was increasing demand for oil. Anti-U-boat warfare placed extra demands on oil burning escort vessels. Britain had some home production of oil, mostly from the Scottish shale industry, but this accounted for only a small proportion of the total demand, as shown in Table 2-1 below. Demand rose sharply in 1916 and 1917.

Table 2-1 British oil production, imports and consumption, tons

Year	Output of oil shale	Crude oil produced	Imports	Total	Exports	Consumption
1911	3,206,576	293,660				
1912	3,284,956	294,699	1,653,333	1,948,032	26,846	1,921,186
1913	3,369,321	289,683	1,952,427	2,242,110	16,505	2,225,605
1914	3,388,869	285,464	2,586,850	2,872,314	20,444	2,851,870
1915	3,187,592	263,083	2,354,079	2,617,162	46,079	2,571,083
1916	3,102,036	247,471	3,159,195	3,406,666	27,907	3,378,759
1917	3,200,883	249,598	4,187,569	4,437,167	20,800	4,416,367

Source: POWE 33/13 ' Negotiations regarding petroleum policy of His Majesty's Government Vol. 1 reports and proceedings of Petroleum Imperial Policy Committee', pp. 109, 111.

The first measures to control the demand for petroleum products were taken in early 1916. Until the middle of 1917 there was no process to co-ordinate the work of several committees whose responsibilities overlapped responsibilities. Walter Long, the Colonial Secretary, was then given overall authority over the supply and demand of petroleum products.

---

[218] G. C. Buchanan, *The Tragedy of Mesopotamia* (Edinburgh: William Blackwood & Sons, 1938), pp. 260-61.

2.6 Early Administrative Arrangements

An Inter-Departmental Oil Committee met at the Colonial Office to consider oil exploration within the Empire, mostly in the Crown Colonies, but until 1917 there was no body with overall responsibility for oil policy. On 29 February 1916 representatives of the Admiralty, Board of Trade, Munitions Ministry and the War Office met to consider petrol supply. A further meeting on 25 March agreed that measures should be taken to ensure that petrol supplies for vital purposes were adequate. In late April a Petrol Control Committee was established under President of Board of Trade. It issued two reports in 1916 and was re-organised in June 1917 when the Petrol Control Department of the Board of Trade was set up with Sir Evan Jones as Controller.[219]

A Committee for the Regulation of Petroleum Supplies was established in the summer of 1916 by the Munitions Ministry. It set up an Advisory Committee of importers. The supply issue related almost totally to tanker tonnage. Co-operation with the Petrol Control Committee was deemed to be vital, but it was unwilling to give information that might result in the Admiralty removing tankers from petrol supply. By 11 January 1917 the shortage of tankers was becoming more significant and the Committee for the Regulation of Petroleum Supplies proposed various measures. Their recommendations were partly implemented by the formation of a number of committees. The Munitions Petroleum Supplies Department was set up in February 1917 to ensure that munitions manufacturers and other vital industrial companies received sufficient supplies of petroleum products. It included a Petroleum Research Department under Sir Boverton Redwood, charged with developing oil supplies within Britain. It was for a while transferred to Admiralty control.[220]

On 18 February Hankey informed the War Cabinet of the seriousness of the situation.[221] Earlier in the month Sir Albert Stanley, the President of the Board of Trade, had pointed out that UK petrol stocks were declining because demand exceeded imports. Shortages of shipping meant that imports in 1917 were likely

---

[219] *Munitions*, pp. 138-41. vol vii, part iii, pp. 138-41

[220] Ibid., p. 144.

[221] CAB 24/6, G.T. 40 'Consumption of Petrol', Secretary, 18 February 1917.

to be lower than in 1916. Civilian consumption of 10,000,000 gallons per month could be reduced to 8,000,000. Any further cuts would severely disrupt the life and commerce of the country. Military use at home had to be restricted; the War Office and the Admiralty were both taking measures to economise on the use of petrol. A meeting of representatives of the Admiralty, Board of Trade, War Office and Munitions Ministry had taken place at the Admiralty on 15 February. It decided that all the departments and committees dealing with oil needed to co-operate. The intention was to prevent over-lapping work; departments would not have to have the approval of the proposed committee before taking action. Pretyman, the Civil Lord of the Admiralty, was proposed as chairman. The Board of Trade did not want the committee to deal with post war issues, but Pretyman thought that it would be impossible for it to ignore them. The Admiralty, Board of Trade, Munitions Ministry, War Office, Colonial Office and Controller of Shipping were to be represented permanently, with representatives of the India Office and Foreign Office attending when required.[222] Cadman and Redwood were appointed as technical advisers.[223] The committee was established with the following terms of references:

> To consider all questions of petroleum products and make such arrangements as will secure the best means of providing the necessary supplies and their allocation for military, naval and civil requirements, and to co-ordinate and determine the policy of departmental and other Committees dealing with various sections of the subject, subject to the usual procedure in regard to obtaining the sanction of the Treasury and Cabinet to important matters of expenditure or policy.[224]

The committee set up a Pool Board, consisting of representatives of the six main oil distributors. The government would purchase its petroleum products from the Pool Board rather individual companies. The details of the organisation and management of the supply, import and distribution of petroleum products would be left to the Pool Board under the supervision of the Board of Trade.[225]

---

[222] CAB 24/6, G.T. 51 'Petroleum Products', I.-D. Committee, 23 February 1917.

[223] *Munitions.* vol. vii, part iii, p. 145

[224] CAB 24/7, G.T. 107 'Terms of Reference to Inter-Departmental Committee on Petroleum Products', Secretary, March 1917.

[225] *Munitions*, pp. 146-47.

The establishment of various committees with overlapping responsibilities created confusion; nobody had overall responsibility for oil matters. On 8 May Stanley wrote to the Cabinet warning that sinkings of tank steamers by U-boats and rising demand by the Army in France had led to a fall in stocks of motor spirits, which were now less than a month's supply. He urged that 'some member of the War Cabinet should be appointed to take the matter in hand.'[226] Three days later Pretyman followed up Stanley's memo by suggesting that the Interdepartmental Petroleum Committee might present its views on the situation to a Cabinet Minister. It had some problems in dealing with the current position because petrol distribution was the responsibility of the Petrol Control Committee of the Board of Trade; the Pool Board could not limit petrol supplies without its consent.[227]

2.7 Walter Long and the Petroleum Committee

Long was told by the Prime Minister to look into the issue. Geoffrey Jones describes Long as being 'a depressing choice, indicative of the low priority given to oil.'[228] Long admitted to knowing nothing about oil, but as Colonial Secretary he was impartial on the subject, unlike the ministers for the oil consuming departments.[229] Cadman was the Colonial Office's petroleum adviser and Long relied on his great knowledge of the oil industry.[230] Long produced a report on 11 June in which he wrote that: 'I find everything in great confusion, and there can be no doubt that the situation must be full of anxiety for some time.'[231] His solution was to replace the existing arrangements with the following structure:

1. Four bodies would be set up:
   1. An inter-departmental committee, now including the Board of Agriculture, which would collect information and co-ordinate action but have no executive functions.

---

[226] CAB 24/12, G.T. 675 'Motor Spirit', A. H. Stanley, 8 May 1917.

[227] CAB 24/13, G.T. 707 'The Oil Situation', E. G. Pretyman, 11 May 1917.

[228] Jones, *State*, p. 195.

[229] Brown, 'Royal Navy', p. 152.

[230] Jones, *State*, pp. 195-96.

[231] CAB 24/16, G.T. 1006 'Control of Petrol & Petroleum Products', W. H. Long, 11 June 1917, p. 1.

2. The Petrol Committee under the Board of Trade to regulate civil and industrial use of petrol.

3. The Pool Board, a voluntary body of oil companies under a government appointed chairman, intended to economise man-power and material. It would be under the Board of Trade instead of the Munitions Ministry.

4. A Production Department, under the Munitions Ministry, to encourage home production.

2. A Committee of the Chairmen of these four bodies, chaired by the Colonial Secretary, would discuss and sort out problems.

3. The Colonial Secretary would have the final say in all matters, apart from interference with the requirements of the fighting departments, which he would refer to the War Cabinet.[232]

On 13 June, the War Cabinet approved his recommendations.[233] A Petrol Committee was established and met for the first time on 3 July. The attendees at the first meeting were:

Walter H. Long (Chairman);
E. G. Pretyman (Chairman of the Inter-departmental Petroleum Committee);
Sir Evan Jones (Petrol Controller);
Sir Walter Egerton (Chairman of the Pool Board);
Rear Admiral H. Tothill (Fourth Sea Lord);
Mr Kemball Cook (Shipping Control Dept);
Mr M. Waller (Director of Naval Stores, the Admiralty);
G. B. A. Grindle (Colonial Office);
Professor J. Cadman.

Others, most frequently Sir Frederick Black, Director of Contracts at the Admiralty, attended meetings as appropriate. [234]

In August 1917 a Petroleum Executive was set up in order to make certain that all services had adequate supplies of oil, to look after issues of general policy and to co-ordinate the various Government departments interested in oil. Cadman was appointed its Director, reporting to Long.[235] They hoped to develop

---

[232] Ibid.

[233] CAB 23/3, 'War Cabinet Papers 154-226', 5 June - 30 August 1917. 13 June 1917, War Cabinet 162, paragraph 1.

[234] NA, POWE 33/5, 'Petroleum Committee: Minutes of Meetings 1-28', 1917-18.

[235] POWE 33/150, 'Petroleum Executive: Report on Policy and Activities', 1918.

it into a Ministry of Petroleum, but doing so would require other departments to surrender control over their interests in oil.[236]

2.7.1 Stocks and Demand

Admiral Sir John Jellicoe, the First Sea Lord, informed the War Cabinet on 24 May that naval oil stocks amounted to less than three month's supply. Five large tankers had been sunk during the last month. The cruising of the Grand Fleet had consequently been restricted.[237] In early June Tothill said in a memorandum that: '[t]he situation as regards oil is critical. Under present circumstances, oilers must be considered the most valuable vessels afloat. They should be convoyed.'[238] On 30 June he warned the War Cabinet that stocks of naval oil fuel had fallen because of delays in the completion of tankers, losses of tankers, greater activity by oil burning vessels and an increase in the number of warships burning oil. Further supplies of oil had been requested from the USA, but had not yet been received. Long was in contact with Lord Northcliffe, Head of the British War Mission to the USA, over this issue. In Britain the construction and repair of tankers had been speeded up. The speed of oil-burning warships had been restricted, 'except in the gravest emergency and except in the Southern part of the North Sea.'[239] Fleet movements were to be as restricted as much as possible. Tankers were to be convoyed both on route to and from Britain and on coastal passage and to be escorted in the submarine area. The number of tankers with the Fleet was to be reduced to the minimum possible number. Oil fuel was being imported from America in the double bottoms of cargo ships. Home production was being increased; this could have only a small impact in the immediate future.[240]

Three tables were attached. Statement A showed that at the current rates of loss and oil use naval stocks would run out in January 1918. Statement B

---

[236] Jones, *State*, p. 196.

[237] CAB 23/2, 'War Cabinet Papers 83-153', 1 March - 30 May 1917. War Cabinet 145, 24 May 1917, paragraph 5.

[238] NA, MT 25/2, 'Convoys - Assembly Points for Tankers from American and Eastern Ports', 1917. Fourth Sea Lord to Assistant Chief of Naval Staff and First Sea Lord, Oil Situation, Convoy of Oilers, 6 June 1917.

[239] CAB 24/18, G.T. 1233 'Oil Fuel Situation', H. Tothill, 30 June 1917, p. 2.

[240] Ibid.

assumed a 30,000 ton per month fall in consumption; stocks would be run down, but would last past June 1918. Statement C made the same demand forecast as B along with higher supply because of a fall in tanker losses; stocks would fall until the end of 1917 and then be rebuilt. Table 2-2 shows Tothill's three scenarios and the actual outcome. A memorandum from Sir Joseph Maclay, the Shipping Controller, in late May stated that naval oil stocks were 747,000 tons on 1 May so they had fallen by over 20 per cent in May and June. Maclay pointed out that stocks of other petroleum products were also low. The increase in demand for petrol by the BEF had required the number of tankers engaged transporting petrol to France to be increased from two to six since the start of the year. This had resulted in a fall in stocks at home from six weeks' supply (60,000 tons) to around a month since the start of May. Reserves of kerosene and gas oil were equal to about only one month's supply. The decision that heavy fuel stocks should be six months' consumption was taken whilst the USA was neutral. Maclay suggested that, since the USA was in the war, Admiralty stocks should not be increased above four months until commercial ones had reached two months. Even then it would take some time to re-build stocks. Admiralty reserves of four months' supply meant 1,000,000 tons, 250,000 more than the total on 1 May; increasing commercial stocks to two months would require an extra 150,000 tons. Building reserves up to this level would take five months for the Admiralty stocks and four months for the commercial ones assuming that the Americans agreed to a British request for more tankers. They probably would not because the US Government did not have the ability to requisition tankers; US companies were reluctant to transfer their tankers to a risky route. [241]

---

[241] CAB 24/14, G.T. 895 'Building of Tank Steamers', J. Maclay, May 1917. The exact date of the memo is not given, but the number shows that it was written in the last 3 or 4 days of May.

Table 2-2 Forecast and actual month end naval oil reserves, tons.

Month	Statement A	Statement B	Statement C:	Actual
Jun-17	593,000	593,000	593,000	593,000
Jul-17	472,000	502,000	512,000	614,000
Aug-17	358,000	418,000	528,000	655,000
Sep-17	275,000	365,000	665,000	700,000
Oct-17	189,000	309,000	889,000	839,000
Nov-17	104,000	254,000	1,204,000	
Dec-17	33,000	213,000	1,605,000	
Jan-18		175,000	2,081,000	
Feb-18		145,000	2,631,000	
Mar-18		110,000	3,242,000	
Apr-18		102,000	3,946,000	
May-18		92,000	4,714,000	
Jun-18		78,000	5,544,000	

Sources: CAB 24/18 G.T. 1233 'Oil Fuel Situation', Fourth Sea Lord, 30/6/1917,
CAB 24/28 G.T. 2246, 'Naval Oil Fuel Situation', M. P. A. Hankey, 10/10/1917,
CAB 24/30 G.T. 2455, 'Oil Fuel Situation', M. P. A. Hankey, 30/10/1917.

Stocks never fell to the level of even Statement C because action was taken to alleviate the situation. Until the end of October, when the position had improved, Tothill kept the War Cabinet informed of the level of naval oil stocks.

The target level of naval oil stocks was disputed. After the war Churchill wrote that Fisher's Royal Commission had advocated a reserve of four years' war consumption, which was far more than could be afforded, and that Jellicoe, then Second Sea Lord, wanted substantial increases in stocks.[242] The Royal Commission actually recommended four years' peace consumption. The Pakenham Committee used war consumption but proposed stocks of only one year. The 1913 standard was four month's war consumption for ships burning only oil and three months' oil for those using both oil and coal. This was increased to having storage in Britain for six month' war consumption; Churchill admitted that this was less than proposed by either the Pakenham Committee or the Royal Commission, and was 'the minimum compatible with safety.'[243] He argued that Britain would have to control the seas in order to import food, so would also be able to import oil, and that cost did not matter in wartime.[244] He

---

[242] Churchill, *Crisis*. vol ii, pp. 136-7

[243] CAB 37/115/39, p. 6.

[244] Ibid., p. 5.

later wrote that the 'conclusions stood the test of war.'[245] Jellicoe's papers contain a document in which he criticises the refusal of Churchill and the rest of the Cabinet to accept the level of reserves proposed by the Sea Lords in 1913. In 1917, following tanker losses, this culminated in the need to restrict the speed of oil fired warships except in emergency.[246] Jellicoe later wrote that in 1917 reserves fell to only 8 weeks.[247]

In August Long reported to the Cabinet that he had adopted a policy of having a minimum of two months' supply for all departments, which was not really enough for national security. The Admiralty was always prioritised. Total demand for all petroleum products for the Admiralty, War Office and civil use was just under 500,000 tons per months. Stock should be at least three times this level, but were currently just under two months' demand. Stocks of some commodities were even lower; there was only enough kerosene for a month and petrol for six weeks. Kerosene was very important because it was heavily used by the working classes for cooking. Measures were being taken to raise these stocks. He explained that:

> [t]he task of evolving order out of chaos and of increasing the supplies [had] been an extremely anxious and difficult one and [he was] deeply indebted to Professor Cadman...for invaluable assistance. [He was]...greatly indebted to all the Departments for their ready and cordial acceptance of the new conditions and for their loyal co-operation."[248]

A number of measures had improved the position. Shipping oil in the double bottoms of cargo ships and liners and in barrels meant that ships other than tankers could transport oil. Conditions in the USA had been improved. The handling of tankers had been re-arranged in order to make more available for use in the Atlantic. Attempts were being made to increase domestic output from existing sources, including the Scottish shale industry, gas works and tar oil. New sources were being developed, including distillation of cannel coal, developing

---

[245] Churchill, *Crisis*. vol. i, p. 137.

[246] BL, Jellicoe Papers, MSS. 49041: vol. liii 'Replies to Criticism in Printed Works'. f. 62.

[247] J. R. Jellicoe, *The Crisis of the Naval War* (London: Cassell and Company, 1920), p. 147.

[248] CAB 24/23, G.T. 1756 'The Petroleum Position', W. Long, 18 August 1917, p. 2.

new shale deposits, low temperature distillation of coal and exploration for oilfields.[249]

These measures had alleviated the situation, but British oil reserves were still too low for comfort. In late September a request from the Admiralty that four American dreadnoughts be sent to reinforce the Grand Fleet specified that they should be coal-burners.[250] In October Long wrote that '[t]he oil position has materially improved, although it is not yet in a condition to relieve me of anxiety.'[251] Much of the improvement was because of the use of double bottoms of cargo ships to carry fuel oil. Imports by this method had now reached 85,000 tons per month. It allowed ships other than tankers to carry oil, but at the expense of other cargoes. Long argued that it was necessary to continue to use this method until stocks had reached a satisfactory level.

2.7.2 Tanker Construction

The main problem was transporting oil from the USA. In May Maclay's Cabinet memorandum said that tanker losses were responsible for the low level of oil stocks. Even with US help it would take a long time to re-build stocks. Only 20 tankers were under construction in British shipyards; all of these would be completed by the end of the year. A policy for the construction of Standard cargo ships had already been adopted; a similar one was required for tankers. As well as trade tankers to import oil, the Admiralty required more tankers to work with the fleet. Specialist tankers, designed to safely carry light oil of a very low flash point, could carry only oil. If oil demand and losses later fell, building a large number of these instead of cargo ships might result in there being too many tankers and too few cargo ships. Cargo ships could be converted to carry heavy fuel oil in two to four months. The flash point of heavy fuel oil was over 175° so a ship that was to carry only this type of fuel did not need to take such major safety precautions as one that was capable of transporting light oils of a very low flash point. If various small changes were made early in their

---

[249] Ibid.

[250] BL, Balfour Papers, MSS. 49709: vol. xxvi 'Correspondence'. Secret. Extract from memorandum from the Naval Staff dated 27th September 1917, f. 175

[251] CAB 24/29, G.T. 2320 'Memorandum with Regard to the Oil Position', W. H. Long, 15 October 1917, p. 1.

construction the decision on whether a ship was to be a tanker or a cargo ship could be delayed until two months before completion. Construction of such a vessel would take only eight months versus 12 for a specialist tanker. It could later be converted back into a cargo ship. The advantages of building the Standard type of cargo ship were retained, and the ship would not look like a tanker. Using converted cargo ship to carry heavy fuel oil for the RN would enable Admiralty tankers to be used instead for the conveyance of light oils. Eighteen Standard ships should be converted, by November at the latest, to replace the expected losses of three tankers per month. Additionally 12 of the ships under construction in the USA and Japan should be converted, and the preliminary work to ease conversion to a tanker should take place on six of the standard ships being built each month.[252]

2.7.3 Bread or Oil?

Restrictions on oil imports affected food supplies in two ways. The first was that importing oil in double bottoms of cargo ships meant that ships not designed to carry oil could transport it. It did not increase the cargo capacity of the ship so there was a trade off between oil and other goods such as food. On 13 August Maclay told the First Lord of the Admiralty and Hankey that imports from the USA and Canada had fallen by about 1,250,000 tons per annum because of the need to carry oil in the double bottoms of liners and cargo ships. To replace losses 480,000 tons of tankers were being constructed annually, a fifth of the total merchant ship construction programme. The absence of the cargo ships that otherwise would have been built meant a fall of 1,750,000 tons of imports over twelve months. These figures were for naval oil only: another 250,000 of capacity must be allocated to double bottom imports to maintain commercial stocks and 240,000 tons of construction used to replace sunk commercial tankers.[253]

The shortage of oil also impacted domestic food production because of attempts to increase output by replacing farm animals with motorised tractors. On 17 July Rowland Prothero, the President of the Board of Agriculture, wrote to Long

---

[252] CAB 24/14 G.T. 895, Maclay.

[253] CAB 24/23, G.T. 1704 'Effect on General Tonnage of Anticipated Demands for Oil Fuel for the Navy', J. P. Maclay, 13 August 1917.

regarding a letter sent by Cadman to the Board of Agriculture asking it to consider cutting its demands for petrol for tractors. Prothero wanted to help as much as possible but could not do so without reducing a ploughing programme that had been approved by the Cabinet. If insufficient petrol was available to carry out this out then he felt that it was up to the Cabinet rather than himself to reconsider the situation.[254] Long explained that Cadman was acting on his authority; he was responsible to the Cabinet for all issues regarding oil.[255]

In November Prothero warned the War Cabinet that insufficient fuel had allocated to the motor tractors ordered as part of a programme to increase agricultural output in England and Wales. He argued that food production should be given the same status as the armed forces and munitions output, giving it priority over other civilian and industrial uses. The Cabinet should make sure that more oil was imported and that enough of it was allocated to food production. Otherwise the part of the ploughing programme to be carried out by motor tractors would have to be abandoned. In that case the Cabinet must give the order or the Board of Agriculture would lose all credibility with farmers.[256] Long explained that oil stocks still were dangerously low despite the importation of 100,000 tons per month in double bottoms. Doing so reduced the imports of food and other essentials so all new tankers would have to be used to replace the use of double bottoms. The Ministry of Shipping estimated that overall imports must be reduced by 8,000,000 tons per annum (666,000 tons per month), showing that the use of double bottoms must end as soon as a safety margin of oil stocks was secured. Demand for petroleum products from the Armed Forces was rising; almost all new warships burnt oil. The required level of naval stocks was rising each month. Prothero's requests placed demands on tanker tonnage that Long would do his 'utmost to meet, but which it is impossible to guarantee in the existing conditions of the Admiralty and War Office stocks.'[257] Adoption of Prothero's proposal to treat agriculture the same as the armed forces would contradict the Cabinet's ruling, and would return to the situation that the

---

[254] POWE 33/3, 'Petroleum Supplies: Correspondence, Reports, Memoranda and Minutes of Meetings, File 3', 1917. No. 99, Prothero to Long, 17 July 1917.

[255] Ibid. No. 99, Long to Prothero, 19 July 1917.

[256] CAB 24/33, G.T. 2767 'Food Production. Board of Agriculture, England and Wales', R. E. Prothero, 24 November 1917.

[257] CAB 24/36, G.T. 3021 'Food Production. Memorandum with Reference to Memorandum by Mr Prothero to the War Cabinet. Date 24th November', W. H. Long, 13 December 1917, p. 3.

current structure was intended to avoid. Shipping resources were already operating at maximum effort.

In December Maclay told the Petroleum Committee that Britain was 'faced with a very serious deficit in the tonnage now required to be allotted to Government services. The wheat position is particularly grave.'[258] By the end of January, wheat stocks would be only 15-16 weeks demand, a very low level since half was held by the farmers. Wheat was available in the USA; the problem was finding ships to transport it. Maclay said there was a shortage of 40 ships, and it was 'of the utmost importance that every possible step be taken to reduce this deficit.'[259] He suggested that half the deficit could be covered by abandoning the use of double bottoms for oil for a month. J. A. Salter, the Director of Shipping Requisition, attended the 12th meeting of the committee on 12 December 1917. He explained that the main problem was the failure of the French and Italian harvests, meaning that imports had to be diverted from Britain to those countries. The meeting concluded that a telegram should be sent to Sir Frederick Black in New York urging that the Americans release more tonnage for the North Atlantic route. Stopping use of double bottoms was discussed. Long insisted that naval fuel had to be prioritised. At the 17 December meeting of his committee, attended by Commander Paul Foley and L. I. Thomas of the US Mission, Long stated that:

> A shortage of food meant probably a further measure of self-denial on the part of the inhabitants of this country but a shortage of fuel involved the inability of the Navy to protect our shores, and to protect the shipping of ourselves and our allies.[260]

On 20 February 1918 he told the committee:

> 'that in the event of a bread shortage we could substitute potatoes and other articles of food but in the event of a serious oil shortage there was no other substitute which we could successfully employ.'[261]

---

[258] POWE 33/5. 12th Meeting, 12 December 1917, p. 6.

[259] Ibid. 12th Meeting, 12 December 1917, p. 6.

[260] Ibid. 13th Meeting, 17 December 1917, p. 3.

[261] Ibid. 18th Meeting, 20 February 1918, p. 5.

Tanker shortages continued to the end of the war. In October 1918 Long told the War Cabinet that in the first half of 1918 tanker capacity had been 155,788 tons short of the required level. This figure had been reduced to 116,387 tons by 31 July 1918. This meant that it was impossible to build stocks in Europe to the agreed minimum safety level. The only source of additional tankers was the USA. The Allied Maritime Transport Council had proposed that, if the USA supplied enough tanker tonnage to allow the ending of the use of double bottoms, the USA would be given all the tonnage made available for other supplies. The US had allocated a further 102,000 tons during the final four months of 1918; the dates of arrival of tankers meant that this was equivalent to a monthly average of only 45,498 tons over the second half of the year. There was still a deficit of 70,889 tons carrying capacity; this meant that reserves could not be build to the minimum level and double bottoms had to be used to carry oil, limiting other imports from the USA.[262] Table 2-3 shows that total British stocks of all petroleum products did not exceed Long's minimum safe levels until September 1918:

Table 2-3 Stock and consumption of all petroleum products including British Army in France, tons.

Month	Consumption	Minimum safe stocks	Actual stocks	Deficiency	Surplus
Jun-17	397,055		951,575		
Jul-17	382,693		937,328		
Aug-17	391,748		974,149		
Sep-17	397,887		974,441		
Oct-17	418,829		1,150,044		
Nov-17	419,427		1,175,571		
Dec-17	394,147		1,284,839		
Jan-18	424,734	1,608,050	1,448,820	159,230	
Feb-18	415,793	1,573,550	1,500,943	72,607	
Mar-18	435,270	1,624,550	1,421,031	203,519	
Apr-18	463,468	1,675,550	1,463,532	212,018	
May-18	438,436	1,681,550	1,521,568	159,982	
Jun-18	478,177	1,720,550	1,539,121	181,429	
Jul-18	469,530	1,750,550	1,619,983	130,567	
Aug-18	507,579	1,729,550	1,590,000	139,550	
Sep-18	441,251	1,726,550	1,760,707		34,157
Oct-18	487,191	1,729,550	1,813,711		84,161

Source: POWE 33/150: Petroleum Executive: report on policy and activities 1918.

---

[262] CAB 24/66, G.T. 5916 'Allied Petroleum Tank Tonnage Position. Memorandum by the Petroleum Executive', W. H. Long, 5 October 1918.

Long's refusal to give up the use of double bottoms in favour of food supplies was justified by the failure of the U-boat campaign to starve Britain out. Grain imports were prioritised over other shipments; grain stocks held by the government and millers, but excluding those of bakers and retailers, rose from five and a half weeks supply at the end of March to fourteen weeks four months later. The Germans emphasised tonnage losses, but the U-boat campaign did not inflict enough damage on the grain supply, and it brought the USA into the war.[263] The Germans had anticipated the latter but greatly under-estimated its impact. The British were able to have adequate supplies of both oil and bread.

2.7.4 Re-consideration of Coal Fired Warships

The RN remained the most important user of oil. Reversion to coal as a fuel for warships was considered. Maclay's 13 August memorandum urged that building either coal fired ships or ones that could burn either oil or coal should be considered. Sir Eustace D'Eyncourt, the DNC, had looked into this in June and concluded that it would be very difficult to convert existing oil burning ships to coal. Oil boilers were much bigger than coal ones. Oil bunkers were in the wrong parts of the ship to be used for coal. One of the advantages of oil was that, unlike coal, it could be stored in parts of the ship that were awkward to for sailors to access. Oil was often carried low down, so there would be stability issues if the position of the fuel storage was changed. Ships that had been designed from the outset as oil burners would have to be completely rebuilt. Those completed as entirely oil fired, but designed to burn both coal and oil, would be difficult to convert to use coal and would have their fuel storage significantly reduced. New ships would have to be either slower or larger if they reverted to coal and would have bigger crews and shorter ranges than oil burners. D'Eyncourt thought that it was feasible to build a coal burning 22 knot destroyer for anti-submarine work, but it would be too slow to work with the Grand Fleet. Converting enough ships to burn coal to make a significant difference to oil usage would take the country's entire warship construction capacity for a year. He suggested that a substantial saving could instead be

---

[263] A. Offer, *The First World War: An Agrarian Interpretation* (Oxford: Clarendon, 1989), p. 366.

made by ordering oil burning warships to use reduced power except when it was crucial to achieve maximum speed.[264]

The RN did construct small coal fired warships, such as convoy sloops, gunboats and minesweepers, during the war; several monitors, slow ships intended for coastal bombardment, used coal. Some of the battleships and cruisers that were under construction in British shipyards for foreign navies, and were taken over by the RN, burnt a mixture of oil and coal. All destroyers, battle cruisers and battleships ordered for the RN during the war burnt exclusively oil, as did all cruisers with the exception of the five ships of the *Hawkins* class. They were designed to hunt down commerce raiders, probably operating in remote areas where oil might not be available. One of the class was lost accidentally and the others converted to oil in the 1920s.[265]

2.7.5 Home Production

British dependence on oil imports could be reduced by raising home production. Potential ways of achieving this included increasing the amount of oil that was produced from shale and cannel coal, using creosote produced from coal tar as a substitute for oil and encouraging domestic drilling. Cannel coal contains a high proportion of hydrogen. James Young patented a method to extract paraffin, also known as kerosene, from it in 1850. Oil shale is a form of rock, from which kerogen can be extracted; it can be converted into crude oil by heating it in a large retort, but the process is more elaborate and costly than conventional oil drilling. Creosote produced from coal tar can substitute for heavy fuel oil.

In October 1917 Redwood's Petroleum Research Department produced a report recommending that production of oil from cannel coal should be increased. The Munitions Ministry thought that this was impracticable because of shortages of labour, materials and suitable minerals, and the time that it would take to construct the necessary retorts and supporting infrastructure.[266] In March 1918

---

[264] ADM 1/8640/70, 'Re-Conversion of Oil-Burning Warships to Coal-Burning, 1917, 1918, 1921'. S01538/17, 27 June 1917, DNC to Third Lord.

[265] For technical details of warships R. Chesneau, *Conway's All the World's Fighting Ships, 1922-1946* (London: Conway Maritime Press, 1980); R. Gray, *Conway's All the World's Fighting Ships, 1906-1921* (London: Conway Maritime Press, 1985).

[266] *Munitions.* vol. vii. part iii, p. 149-50.

the Ministry appointed a committee under Lord Crewe to look into the domestic production of oil. It reported in July that the Petroleum Research Department's recommendation that oil be produced by the carbonisation of cannel coal and similar substances was impracticable; it was based on over-optimistic assumptions. The alternative of producing fuel oil from cannel coal and similar substances at gasworks should be pursued. There were a number of other potential sources of supply; drilling for oil in Britain; developing the Scottish shale oil industry; using dehydrated tar by employing suitable solvents; increasing the amount of coal carbonised into oil, which might transform 20,000,000 tons of coal into 1,000,000 to 1,250,000 tons of fuel oil; development of the Kimmeridge shale of England, which had not yet been exploited successfully; using Britain's extensive deposits of peat, which was being considered by the Fuel Research Board; and increasing oil storage capacity in the UK, which could only be provided in peacetime.[267]

The Scottish shale industry's output was almost at its maximum possible level by the middle of 1917. A new refining process, called Scheme G, was proposed; it would increase the output of fuel oil but would reduce that of some other products.[268] In November Long's committee considered this issue. The shale companies were very cautious, and were reluctant to carry out Scheme G because they would risk losing their existing markets in lubricating and batching oils. The possible solutions were to give them a 10 year contract to supply the Admiralty, or to take their operations under Government control. The committee preferred the former.[269] The proposed price was too high for the Admiralty. It suggested that the Munitions Ministry take control of the industry; it was reluctant to do so. Scheme G would add only 40,000 tons of fuel oil to the existing output of 55,000 tons per annum; the Admiralty took 35,000 tons. In April 1918 it was decided that this was too little to justify the cost and disruption of Scheme G, including the loss of domestic supplies of batching oil to the jute industry. The Scottish shale industry was important enough that in May Long ordered that no men should be removed from it if this would cut production. Efforts to use deposits in England came to nothing because English

---

[267] CAB 24/57, G.T. 5058 'Production of Fuel Oil from Home Sources. Report of Ministry of Munitions Committee with Covering Note by Mr Churchill', W. S. Churchill, 8 July 1918.

[268] *Munitions.* vol. vii, part iii, p. 153.

[269] POWE 33/5. 10th Meeting, 21 November 1917, pp. 5-6.

shale was less suitable than that in Scotland, and there was a shortage of manpower and machinery.[270]

Another domestic source of oil was the use of creosote produced from coal tar. In June 1917 the export of tar oil was restricted, mainly to save on shipping tonnage. The Admiralty and Munitions Ministry agreed to buy the former exports. The agreed price was less than commercial customers were prepared to pay; use of creosote as an industrial fuel increased. The Admiralty received only the equivalent of 80,000 tons per annum rather than an expected 150,000 tons. A series of Orders restricted the uses of tar oils, increasing the supply for the Admiralty. The substitution of tar oil for petroleum by other users also released 50,000 tons of the latter for the Admiralty.[271]

Table 2-4 Production and consumption of creosote, tons

	1913	July 1917, annualised	1918
Production	330,000	360,000	396,000
Reduction in stocks			29,000
Exports	172,000	40,000	9,117
Civil consumption	158,000	240,000	216,565
Admiralty consumption		80,000	199,340

Source: *History of the Ministry of Munitions*, 12 vols. (London: HMSO, 1920), vol vii, part iii, p. 151.

The Crewe Committee suggested that carbonisation of coal might produce 1,000,000 to 1,250,000 tons of fuel oil per annum. Around the same time, another committee chaired by R. W. Barnett MP, with Slade as Vice Chairman, was set up to look into the production of oil from cannel coal and allied minerals. It detailed the technical aspects of the process, concluding that 400,000 tons of fuel oil could be produced from cannel coal. Much of the raw material would be waste that had either not been brought to the surface or else thrown onto spoil heaps.[272] Britain did not make any major attempts to convert its substantial coal reserves into oil. In the early 1920s it was cheaper to import oil than to carbonise coal into oil.

---

[270] *Munitions*. vol. vii, part iii, pp. 153-54.

[271] Ibid. vol. vii, part iii, pp. 150-52.

[272] CAB 24/60, G.T. 5311 'Committee on the Production of Oil from Cannel Coal and Allied Minerals. Interim Report', R. W. Barnett, 24 July 1918.

Attempts were made to encourage conventional oil exploration in the British Isles. A system of drilling licences was regarded as being less wasteful than one of linking ownership of land and the oil under it. In 1917 a Petroleum Production Bill was presented to Parliament; it proposed that, rather than owning any oil under his land, a landowner would receive royalties. Sir Eric Geddes, the First Lord of the Admiralty and a businessman before the war, pointed out to Long that there were a number of difficulties with this. Landowners would regard it as a loss of their property. Labour objected to the principle of landowners receiving anything at all. Oil companies would not invest unless they knew what the royalties were for longer than the duration of the war.[273] The last point was also made by Sir Alfred Mond, the First Commissioner of Works, another minister with pre-war business experience.[274] The Government lost a vote on an amendment on the bill in October 1917. Since attempting to pass it might be a lengthy and controversial process, it was proposed instead to make a regulation under the Defence of the Realm Act.[275] As DORA regulations applied only to wartime this did not address the problem that the companies were unwilling to drill unless they knew what the situation would be after the war. A new bill was presented in July 1918, allowing landowners to receive compensation for use of their land. Oil companies would act as contractors for the Government, and the costs and proceeds of oil would be paid into a Petroleum Account; Parliament would decide on its distribution after the war.[276] The bill was passed by the House of Commons but was still with the Lords at the end of the war.[277] The inescapable problem with attempts to encourage domestic oil exploration was that the British Isles does not have much onshore oil. North Sea oil could not have been discovered or exploited with the technology of the first half of the twentieth century.

---

[273] Geddes Papers, ADM 116/1805, A/159 'Petroleum Bill', 27 October 1917.

[274] CAB 24/30, G.T. 2424 'Petroleum Production Bill. Report of Committee', A. Mond, October 1917.

[275] CAB 24/35, G.T. 2975 'Petroleum Production Bill. Report of Committee', G. Cave, 13 December 1917.

[276] CAB 24/57, G.T. 5087 'Petroleum Production Bill', 10 July 1918.

[277] *Munitions.* vol. vii, part iii, p. 155.

2.8 Chapter Summary

During the war the Allies had more oil than the Central Powers. The USA was the world's dominant oil producer. Before its entry into the war it was willing to supply oil to anybody who could pay for and transport it. British financial resources and control of the seas meant that the Allies met these criteria. Austria-Hungary had oil but not enough to make up the imports that Germany lost as a result of the war and the British naval blockade. The Central Powers had to make decisions about oil allocation. They were never able to make as much use as the British and Americans of oil fuel for warships, despite its clear advantages. They were unable to make as much use of motor vehicles as the Allies, and their aircraft could fly fewer sorties than Allies ones in 1918.

As the war progressed the belligerents became more dependent on oil. In 1914 Britain sent troops to Mesopotamia to defend its Persian oilfields. Germany, short of oil, tried to obtain control of the oilfields of Romania and the Caucasus. Britain attempted to deny Germany these supplies. The Allied assumption that oil could be bought in the market, mostly from the USA, led to an oil crisis for Britain in April 1917 because of rising demand for oil and increased sinkings of tankers by U-boats. Later in the year France found itself in a similar crisis.

Long was not an obvious choice to sort the situation out, but he had the political strength to insist on tough but necessary measures, such as favouring the navy over other users. He had the sense to rely on Cadman for technical issues. Long has received relatively little attention from historians; those who have written about him have not paid much attention to his role in overcoming the oil crisis. The most recent work on Long's political career is Richard Murphy's unpublished 1984 doctoral thesis. [278] It points out the lack of previous works on Long's career and their limitations; his own memoirs were largely based on often incorrect memories; the 1936 biography by Sir Charles Petre is uncritical; and Roderick Clifford's 1970 doctoral thesis was written from the papers of Long's rivals since most of his papers were then unavailable to researchers.[279] These works say little

---

[278] R. Murphy, 'Walter Long and the Conservative Party, 1905-1921' (University of Bristol, 1984), pp. 314-15.

[279] Ibid., pp. v-vi.

about oil. Long's memoirs devote more space to his role in eradicating rabies when President of the Board of Agriculture in the 1890s than to oil. Petrie and Murphy give oil only brief coverage.[280] Murphy's comments are based largely on a journal article by Geoffrey Jones that argues that Long, although not clever, was able to work well with professional advisers, in this case Cadman.[281] Jones's later book argues that the appointment of Long indicated that that oil was being given a low priority but credits Long and Cadman with successfully re-organising the administration of oil matters.[282]

Long deserves great credit for his role in overcoming the oil crisis. His initial report to Lloyd George identified the urgent need for action and to have one person in charge. Once given those powers he used them effectively to ensure that oil supplies were directed to the most important users. He recognised that naval supplies had to be given the highest priority; without oil, the RN could not escort other supplies, including food, to the British Isles. Long relied on professional advisers, notably Cadman, but should be praised for appointing the right men and backing them. Cadman had the technical knowledge, but it required Long's political expertise and authority to insist that oil was more important than food and munitions. Britain was never in a comfortable oil position but came through the crisis. It showed that the policy of buying oil on the market in wartime was not viable and it was now realised that secure supplies were needed. The war made Britain more aware of the importance of oil and required the introduction of special administrative arrangements to allocate supplies. The increasing importance of oil meant that it was affecting relations between the Allies.

---

[280] W. H. Long, *Memories* (London,: 1923). pp. 118-30 on rabies, pp. 257-65 on oil; Murphy, 'Walter Long', pp. 314-15; C. A. Petrie, *Walter Long and His Times.* (London: Hutchison & Co., 1936), pp. 212-15.

[281] Jones, 'British', p. 663.

[282] *State*, pp. 195-96.

3 Oil and Inter-Allied Relations, 1917-18

Oil impacted Anglo-American relations because most British oil came from the USA. The US was willing to supply oil to whoever could pay for and transport it, but increasing demand rose led to a shortage of tanker capacity. Both countries were suspicious that the other was putting its post-war interests ahead of the Allied[283] cause when constructing and allocating tankers. Britain dominated the Allied effort in the naval war, meaning that it required far more oil than either France or Italy, and was largely responsible for transporting their oil supplies. All three countries needed increasing quantities of oil as the war progressed. All found themselves in crisis in 1917; an Inter-Allied Petroleum Conference was set up to co-ordinate supplies.

3.1 Oil and Anglo-American Relations

Early in the war it became apparent that Britain could not equip its vastly expanded army solely from its own industries. The USA, the world's leading industrial power, was the obvious place to buy the necessary supplies. In early 1915 J. P. Morgan was appointed sole purchasing agent for the Admiralty and the War Office. A British mission led by Balfour, now Foreign Secretary, was sent to the USA soon after the US entry into the war in April 1917. A British War Mission headed by the newspaper magnate Lord Northcliffe was then established, but this led to conflict between Northcliffe and the British Ambassador to Washington, Sir Cecil Spring-Rice. This was not resolved until both men were recalled in February 1918; Lord Reading was appointed to both positions.[284]

The Americans did not initially realise the severity of various problems facing Britain. On 29 June 1917, Walter Page, the US Ambassador to London, wrote to President Wilson on this subject. He thought that British pride prevented them from accepting the seriousness of their situation until they had no choice but to do so. A financial crisis meant that Britain would not have been able to continue to pay for its imports from the USA without US help. France and Italy would have

---

[283] The USA was officially an Associated Power, but is referred to here as one of the Allies after it entered the war.

[284] K. Burk, *Britain, America and the Sinews of War, 1914-1918* (Boston, MA: Allen & Unwin, 1985), pp. 9-10.

been affected as Britain had been lending to them. Page did not think that this would necessarily have caused the Allies to lose the war without US entry but, coupled with the U-boat crisis, it might have forced an early peace.[285] A few days later the President wrote to Josephus Daniels, the Secretary of the Navy, enclosing a memorandum for Admiral William Sims, the commander of US naval forces in Europe. Wilson said that he could 'not see how the necessary military supplies and supplies of food and fuel oil are to be delivered at British ports in any other way than under convoy.'[286] Significantly Wilson mentioned oil along with food and military supplies. The Admiralty decided in late April to introduce convoys; it took until late July to fully organise Atlantic convoys.[287]

3.1.1 The US Oil Industry

The USA was the world's leading oil producer in 1914. During the next four years, its output increased and its share of world production rose even more, partly but not entirely thanks to falling Russian production. Table 3-1 shows the output of the world's leading producing countries. Appendix 1 gives an expanded version of this table, including all producers.

Table 3-1 Output of the leading global oil producers, tons, 1913-18

Country	1913	1914	1915	1916	1917	1918
United States	35,492,319	37,966,076	42,966,737	47,902,229	50,848,817	53,959,857
Mexico	3,670,899	3,747,915	4,701,501	5,792,245	7,898,967	9,118,332
Russia	8,976,337	9,574,360	9,792,580	10,400,159	8,362,903	3,143,960
Dutch East Indies	1,509,566	1,543,998	1,617,032	1,702,374	1,660,272	1,679,246
Romania	1,854,927	1,755,276	1,646,255	1,224,099	56,567	1,194,705
India	1,110,211	1,037,371	1,148,374	1,188,759	1,131,038	1,146,340
Persia	243,621	381,890	474,553	587,502	937,902	1,131,489
British Empire ex India	431,223	571,496	536,808	557,184	726,628	932,350
Galicia	1,095,506	645,077	666,063	912,535	887,415	667,733
Rest of World	712,919	808,011	993,042	1,043,244	1,076,869	1,093,945
World Total	55,097,528	58,031,470	64,542,945	71,310,330	73,587,378	74,067,957
US as per cent of total	64%	65%	67%	67%	69%	73%

Source: Marian Kent, *Oil and Empire: British Policy and Mesopotamian Oil 1900-1920* (London: MacMillan, 1976), pp. 203-4.

---

[285] A. S. Link et al, eds, *The Papers of Woodrow Wilson.*, 69 vols. (Princeton, N.J.: Princeton University Press, 1966-93). vol xliii, Walter Hines Page to President, 29 June 1917, pp. 48-50.

[286] Ibid. vol. xlii, President to Josephus Daniels, 3 July 1917, with Enclosure for Admiral Sims.

[287] Halpern, *Naval*, pp. 360-63.

Table 3-2 shows that the USA supplied over 75 per cent of oil used by Britain, France and Italy in 1918. Italy had a lower share because it made geographic sense to supply it from British controlled oilfields in Egypt and the East.

Table 3-2 Expected sources of Allied oil supplies, 1918, tons (French converted from metric tonnes in original)

Sources of Supply	Britain	Per Cent	Italy	Per Cent	France	Per Cent	Total	Per cent
Home production	216,000	3.3%	0	0.0%	0	0.0%	216,000	2.4%
USA	5,261,600	79.4%	400,200	47.8%	1,257,600	75.4%	6,919,400	75.8%
Mexico	496,500	7.5%	0	0.0%	0	0.0%	496,500	5.4%
Trinidad	161,000	2.4%	0	0.0%	0	0.0%	161,000	1.8%
Egypt	0	0.0%	400,200	47.8%	0	0.0%	400,200	4.4%
Persia	540,000	8.1%	0	0.0%	48,700	2.9%	588,700	6.4%
Burmah	7,000	0.1%	0	0.0%	0	0.0%	7,000	0.1%
Sumatra	77,000	1.2%	36,000	4.3%	30,400	1.8%	143,400	1.6%
Borneo	144,000	2.2%	0	0.0%	54,800	3.3%	198,800	2.2%
Supplied by UK to France	-277,100	-4.2%		0.0%	277,100	16.6%	-0	0.0%
Total	6,626,000	100.0%	836,400	100.0%	1,668,600	100.0%	9,131,000	100.0%

Source: NA, POWE 33/8: Inter-Allied Petroleum Conference: minutes of meetings, 1918. Fourth Informal Meeting, 27 February 1918, Appendix 4.

Table 3-3 shows the growth in US oil exports between 1914 and 1917. The categories that rose were those where demand from the Allies was increasing; the US Department of Commerce attributed the fall in exports of illuminating oil to the war.[288]

Table 3-3 US oil exports, 1914 and 1917

	1917		1914		Percent change		Change
Exports	Tons	$m	Tons	$m	Volume	Price/ton	Tons
Crude oil	575,000	$7.16	478,000	$6.81	20.3%	-12.6%	97,000
Gas and fuel oil	3,394,000	$32.47	1,550,000	$13.75	119.0%	7.9%	1,844,000
Illuminating oil	2,724,000	$54.66	3,775,000	$74.50	-27.8%	1.7%	-1,051,000
Lubricating oil	884,000	$48.65	642,000	$27.85	37.7%	26.8%	242,000
Gasoline	738,000	$46.94	494,000	$21.70	49.4%	44.8%	244,000
Naptha	651,000	$41.03	133,000	$5.65	389.5%	48.3%	518,000
Residue	2,000	$0.03	370,000	$1.91	-99.5%	227.9%	-368,000
Total Exports	8,968,000	$230.95	7,442,000	$152.17	20.5%	25.9%	1,526,000

Source: NA, FO 115/2297: Foreign Office: Embassies and Consulates, United States of America: General Correspondence. Oil. Nos. 126-191. - Palm Oil. 1917.

The USA did not have unlimited quantities of oil to spare. Administrative arrangements had to be introduced in order to regulate the oil industry. In April

---

[288] NA, FO 115/2297, 'Foreign Office: Embassies and Consulates, United States of America: General Correspondence. Oil. Nos. 126-191. - Palm Oil', 1917.

1916 Congress had, on President Wilson's initiative, set up the Council of National Defense; one of its members, Bernard Baruch, established a number of advisory committees representing different industries. The oil one was headed by A.C. Bedford, the chairman of Standard Oil. Its activities included advising on how to supply the oil needs of the US armed forces and how to balance the needs of the Allies with those of domestic oil industries. In July 1917 Wilson replaced the Council of National Defense with the War Industries Board; Bedford's committee continued in existence. Wilson also requested the US Chamber of Commerce to help in establishing trade bodies that would ensure close co-operation between federal agencies and war industries. Representatives of trade associations were added to the petroleum industry advisory committee, now renamed the National Petroleum War Service Committee. In early 1918 it launched a publicity campaign to persuade the industry of the merits of self-regulation. The industry was keen on co-operation because it offered opportunities for greater efficiency. Wilson was aware that some federal oversight was required and in August 1917 set up the United States Fuel Administration under Harry Garfield. Initially its responsibilities were confined to coal. In January 1918 Garfield persuaded Wilson to add an Oil Division, headed by Mark Requa, a petroleum engineer. He believed in co-operation within the industry and between it and government.[289] The war brought the US oil industry, which had been a target of Anti-Trust action before the war, closer to the government.

The US entry into the war brought many benefits to the Allies, but the expanded US armed forces and war industries required greater quantities of oil. Civilian demand was rising, with the number of cars nearly doubling between 1916 and 1918. An already tight market position was worsened by a cold winter in 1917-18; a coal shortage developed leading to substitution of oil.[290] The average US oil price per barrel rose from $0.81 in 1914 to $1.98 in 1918.[291] Requa persuaded the

---

[289] G. D. Nash, *United States Oil Policy, 1890-1964. Business and Government in Twentieth Century America* (Pittsburgh, PA: University of Pittsburgh Press, 1968), pp. 24-38.

[290] Yergin, *Prize*, pp. 178-79.

[291] "U.S. Crude Oil Wellhead Acquisition Price by First Purchasers", U.S. Energy Information Administration <<http://tonto.eia.doe.gov/dnav/pet/hist/LeafHandler.ashx?n=PET&s=F000000__3&f=A>> (accessed 16 April 2010).

industry to limit prices by the threat of government action if they did not do so voluntarily. An appeal was made to private car users not to drive on Sundays.[292]

3.1.2 Mexico

Table 3-1 shows that Mexican output rose from about 3,750,000 tons in 1914 to over 9,000,000 in 1918. This growth, coupled with declining Russian production, made Mexico the world's second largest producer of oil by 1918, albeit a long way behind the USA. Less than 500,000 tons was supplied by Mexico to Britain in 1918 and none to France or Italy, but Mexico was significant to the Allies. The USA imported around 3,500,000 tons of oil in 1917, an increase of nearly 1,000,000 since 1914; most of this was unrefined crude.[293] US imports from Mexico helped balance US supply and demand and enabled US refined products to be exported.[294] Mexican crude was refined in the USA. The availability of Mexican oil released more US oil for export. All Mexican oil was produced by American or British owned firms.[295] The correspondence of the British Embassy in Washington records concerns over civil unrest and potential German influence in Mexico; British support for the Monroe Doctrine and desire to maintain good relations with the USA meant that Britain took no action independent of the USA in Mexico.[296]

The first and one of the largest oil companies in Mexico was Mexican Eagle, a subsidiary of S. Pearson & Sons, the British group built and controlled by Lord Cowdray.[297] Pearson wanted to exit Mexico because of the unrest in the country; Standard (NJ) was a willing buyer. As well as the strategic aspects, the issue was complicated by Cowdray being President of the Air Board until November 1917, when he resigned after not being appointed to head the newly formed Air Ministry. Pretyman's committee was asked to look into the situation. It reported

---

[292] Yergin, *Prize*, p. 179.

[293] FO 115/2297. 'Exports of minerals oils show big increase', US Department of Commerce, 26 October 1917.

[294] Yergin, *Prize*, p. 178.

[295] FO 115/2272, 'Foreign Office: Embassies and Consulates, United States of America: General Correspondence. Mexico (Land) - (Oil). Nos. 1-75', 1917. Memorandum on Situation of American and British Oil Producing Companies in Mexico, 23 April 1917.

[296] Ibid; FO 115/2273, 'Foreign Office: Embassies and Consulates, United States of America: General Correspondence. Mexico (Oil). Nos. 76-187. - Walker', 1917.

[297] Jones, *State*, pp. 63-77.

in April 1917 that the transaction would give US companies complete control of the US and Mexican oilfields. It would be impossible for Britain to import any oil from these if the USA was hostile in a future war; if it was neutral, even if unfriendly, it might be possible to get oil from British owned Mexican fields. Pearson wanted to reduce its exposure to Mexico as soon as possible. The company had proposed a scheme for the British government to buy its Mexican oil interests for £9,250,000, half their value, with Pearson retaining profits over 5 per cent. After the war the government would have the option to buy Pearson out entirely for a further £9,250,000; if it did not Pearson could re-purchase its interests for the same sum. Pretyman thought that these terms were unattractive to the government. The US entry into the war had made Britain less dependent on Mexican supplies, and the worsening political situation in Mexico made the investment of government funds there less appealing. The committee proposed that if the Standard (NJ) deal went ahead it should be required to purchase the shares via one of its British subsidiaries.[298] The government agreed to neither the sale to Standard (NJ) nor the scheme for it to invest in Pearson's Mexican interests. Cowdray argued that it did not have the right to prevent him selling them, but Standard (NJ) would not buy because of the uncertainty.[299] In 1919 he sold to RDS; three years later the main well was damaged by an influx of salt water.[300]

3.1.3 Tanker Shortages

Finding enough tankers to transport US oil to Europe and getting them there safely were major issues. In September and October 1917 the British Embassy in Washington made a series of requests to the Americans for the allocation of more tankers to the trans-Atlantic route.[301] In March 1918 Long telegrammed Reading with his concerns over fuel oil. The RN might need to carry out extended operations at a time when the safety margin of oil stocks was too low. All safe measures to reduce consumption had been taken. It was essential for all the Allies that RN oil reserves be increased above the danger level. The

---

[298] CAB 24/11, G.T. 576 'Inter Departmental Committee on Petroleum Products', E. G. Pretyman, 26 April 1917.

[299] Jones, *State*, p. 190.

[300] Ibid., p. 217.

[301] FO 115/2297.

Admiralty did not believe that it was possible to achieve the reduced minimum oil stocks by the end of August, even with continued use of the US commercial tankers and of double bottoms. The Admiralty had agreed to end the use of double bottoms in March very reluctantly. The US Government did not seem to appreciate that every three tons of oil delivered in double bottoms reduced cereal imports by four tons because tonnage was wasted in distributing the oil carried in this way. The RN's oil stocks would return to the dangerous situation of the summer of 1917 if it had to do without the oil so carried.[302]

The Inter Allied Petroleum Conference calculated oil demand by Britain, France, Italy and US forces in Europe in the second half of 1918. Lubricating oil, which was to be imported in barrels and so could be carried by any cargo ship, and British domestic production were deducted in order to arrive at total oil imports. This was translated into the number of days that tankers would have to spend at sea to transport this quantity of oil from the USA to Europe. Each tanker was assumed to be unavailable for 55 days per annum because of repairs and docking time, and would spend half the remaining time returning to the USA. The required tanker tonnage was the number of tanker days divided by 155. An adjustment was made for the use of double bottoms; 50,000 tons were expected to be carried by this method in July, August and September, and 10,000 in each of the last three months of the year. Table 3-4 gives the results.

Table 3-4 Tanker requirements, 1 July to 31 December 1918, tons

Country	Domestic Production	Lubricating Oil	Oil Imports,	Tanker Days	Tanker Capacity
Great Britain	108,000	210,000	2,843,100	181,598,350	1,171,602
France		81,000	462,000	36,660,000	236,516
Italy		30,000	407,125	29,808,925	192,316
USA		11,234	435,063	28,536,750	184,108
Total without any use of double bottoms		332,234	4,147,288	276,604,025	1,784,542
Savings from use of double bottoms			180,000		81,290
Estimate of tanker requirements			3,967,288		1,703,252

Source: NA, POWE 33/8: Inter-Allied Petroleum Conference: minutes of meetings, 1918. Fourth Formal Session, 14 September 1918, p. 3.

---

[302] Reading Papers, FO 800/233, Oi/1 'Serious Situation About Oil Fuel', W. Long, 6 March 1918.

No allowance was made for the savings in tanker journey time that were expected to result from the completion of the Clyde-Forth Pipeline. This was first proposed in May 1917 but not approved until May 1918; the first oil flowed on 10 November.[303]

The number of tankers available was then calculated. A loss rate of 1 per cent per month averaged out as six tankers fewer over the whole period. Fuel oil carried in double bottoms had to be transferred to small, coastal tankers that would take it from ports to the fleet. Reduction in the use of double bottoms would release two of these for the Atlantic route, but they would not be able to carry as much oil as had been transported in double bottoms. If all new British and US construction was made available for the Atlantic route there would be a very small surplus of capacity.

Table 3-5 Tanker availability

Source	Tankers	Tanker Capacity, tons
Great Britain	158	1,134,482
USA	55	392,634
France	1	5,059
Italy	6	33,494
Total now available	220	1,565,669
Allowance for sinkings	6	38,366
British construction, average over period	14	101,450
Coastal tankers released by reduction in use of double bottoms	2	12,500
Total for period	230	1,641,253
Required		1,703,252
Shortfall		61,999
US construction, average over period	13	64,988
Surplus if new US tankers all allocated		2,989

Source: NA, POWE 33/8: Inter-Allied Petroleum Conference: minutes of meetings, 1918. Fourth Formal Session, 14 September 1918, p. 4.

A major shortage in general cargo tonnage meant that the Allied Maritime Council wanted to end, or at least reduce, the use of double bottoms. The calculations above assumed that it would be cut to 10,000 tons per month. A decision on this could not be made without knowing whether US tankers currently allocated to the Atlantic route would remain on it and how much of

---

[303] W. M. Brown, 'Avoiding the U-Boats: The Clyde-Forth Oil Pipeline', *Mariners Mirror* 90, no. 4 (2004), pp. 427-37.

new US construction would be allocated to the Atlantic route.[304] The figures for tanker construction given in Table 3-5 give the average availability over the whole six months for vessels completing throughout the period. Table 3-6 gives the full construction programme.

Table 3-6 Tanker construction

Month of Completion	British Tankers	British Tanker Capacity, tons	US Tankers	US Tanker Capacity, tons	Total Tankers	Total Tanker Capacity, tons
Jul-18	2	16,000	2	25,000	4	41,000
Aug-18	3	21,000	4	31,000	7	52,000
Sep-18	8	58,000			8	58,000
Oct-18	10	72,000	4	33,000	14	105,000
Nov-18	6	42,000	2	18,500	8	60,500
Total	29	209,000	12	107,500	41	316,500

Source: NA, POWE 33/8: Inter-Allied Petroleum Conference: minutes of meetings, 1918. Fourth Formal Session, 14 September 1918, p. 4.

This figures show that the situation was still very tight. The Allies had just enough tanker capacity if all new construction was allocated to the Atlantic route and monthly losses were no worse than 1 per cent. During the war the number of tankers available to the Allies increased. Britain's tanker fleet rose slightly although it fell as a proportion of the global total; see Table 3-7.

---

[304] POWE 33/8, 'Inter-Allied Petroleum Conference: Minutes of Meetings', 1918. Fourth Formal Session, 14 Septembet 1918, p. 2

Table 3-7 World oil tankers, 1914-18

Flag	30/06/1914		30/06/1917		30/06/1918	
	Ships	Displacement, 1000 metric tonnes	Ships	Displacement, 1000 metric tonnes	Ships	Displacement, 1000 metric tonnes
British	200	883	198	809	204	930
US	83	259	111	492	144	732
German	46	215	13	54	14	59
Dutch	29	80	35	75	35	75
Norwegian	10	49	20	74	21	79
Belgian	11	29	6	13	5	16
Italian	3	15	6	28	7	42
French	4	16	5	14	5	19
Russian	4	9	40	49	40	49
Mexican	4	13	4	13	4	13
Spanish	1	1				
Romanian	2	8				
Danish	1	1				
Japanese	5	22	4	13	4	13
Greek	1	2				
Other			8	7	10	7
Total	404	1,602	450	1,641	493	2,034

Source: Ferdinand Friedensburg, *Das Erdol in Weltkreig* (Stuttgart: Ferdinand Enke, 1939).

3.1.4 Anglo-American Shipbuilding and the Post-War World.

Britain and the USA were both concerned that the other was biasing its wartime construction and allocation of merchant ships in order to strengthen its post-war position. In April 1917 the British War Trade Intelligence Department stated that it feared that the United States Shipping Board wanted to expand the US merchant marine at the expense of Britain.[305] The Chairman of the US Shipping Board, William Denman, thought that it was Britain that was trying to manipulate the situation to its post-war advantage. He rejected British requests that more US merchant ships be used to supply France and Russia because he suspected that the British wanted to use US ones on the riskier routes. More US and fewer British ships would then be sunk, helping to maintain Britain's dominance of the world trade post-war.[306] In October the War Cabinet discussed the American requisition of merchant ships building in the USA for Britain. Maclay said that '[t]here was evidence...that the United State were out for post

---

[305] CAB 24/9, G.T. 448 'Summary of Blockade Information. March 30 - April 5 1917', W.T.I.D., 6 June 1917.

[306] Burk, *Britain*, p. 112.

bellum development, of which they have always suspected us.'[307] It was decided to point out to the Americans that the loss of these ships caused Britain problems.

In August 1918 Sir Eric Geddes, the First Lord of the Admiralty, told the War Cabinet that the British were taking on most of the naval effort in the war. British warships were responsible for an estimated 1,250,000 out of 1,500,000 miles of escort work per month and 6,000,000 miles of anti-submarine patrolling per month, compared with very little by the others. In the first five months of 1918 the USA had completed 11 warships, excluding small submarine chasers, and the British 203. The British Merchant Marine had declined over the war; the US one had grown. In the last three months 52 per cent of US troops heading for Europe had travelled in British ships. Nearly half of French and Italian imports were carried in British ships. In the first six months of 1918 British yards had constructed 763,000 tons of merchant ships and US ones 838,000 tons. When the USA entered the war it took over 621,000 tons of merchant shipping under construction in the USA for Britain. Britain was building warships and repairing warships and merchant ships, including Allied ones, at the cost of not fully replacing sunk merchant ships. This created a post-war as well as a wartime problem. In the first six months of 1918 6,014 British and 106 Allied warships and auxiliaries were refitted in British yards. Over 13 million tons of merchant ships were repaired, requiring 50 per cent more labour than the warships; 10-12 per cent of these ships were Allied. On 1 April 1918 150,000 tons of merchant ships were under repair in US yards and 1,317,183 in British ones. As more US merchant ships were constructed Britain would have to devote even more effort to repairing US ships instead of building British ones. Britain should receive US merchant tonnage equivalent to the excess labour that it had devoted to warship construction and to the repair of Allied ships. Geddes argued that '[u]nless some arrangement of this character is come to the position of Great Britain as the Carrier of the World is seriously threatened as well as her position as premier Shipbuilding Country.'[308] Table 3-7 shows that the British merchant fleet, along

---

[307] CAB 23/4, 'War Cabinet Papers 227-308', 3 September - 31 December 1917. War Cabinet 253, 19 October 1917, item 15.

[308] CAB 24/60, G.T. 5307 'Naval Effort. Great Britain and United States of America', E. Geddes, 2 August 1918, p. 6.

with most of those in the world, had declined during the war. The US merchant and Japanese ones had increased.

Maclay had written to Geddes a few days earlier. He agreed with Geddes but suggested that he alter some of his numbers, which were inconsistent. Geddes originally claimed that the US had 8,250,000 tons of merchant shipping, but this included vessels confined to the Great Lakes, ships launched but not completed and 850,000 tons of sailing ships; his total for British shipping counted only completed ships and excluded sailing ships. Maclay said that the US merchant fleet totalled 4,750,000 tons on a comparable basis to Geddes's figure of 15,100,000 for Britain.[309] Geddes gave US tonnage as 6,663,000 tons in the final draft of his memorandum, presumably excluding the sailing ships and the incomplete vessels; he left the Lakes ships in as he claimed that these could be and were being used for ocean transport. Maclay claimed a higher growth rate for the US merchant fleet since the start of the war than Geddes, but its size was more significant as a measure of its post-war threat to British interests.

Table 3-8 Overseas tonnage of leading maritime powers, excluding enemy countries, tons

	Aug-14	Gains	Losses	Jun-18	Per cent change
UK and Colonies	18,393,000	5,847,000	-9,140,000	15,100,000	-17.9%
USA including Lakes	3,284,000	4,088,000	-709,000	6,663,000	102.9%
France	2,120,000	460,000	-982,000	1,598,000	-24.6%
Japan	1,023,000	843,000	-293,000	1,573,000	53.8%
Italy	1,589,000	368,000	-883,000	1,074,000	-32.4%
Russia	670,000	163,000	-376,000	457,000	-31.8%
Greece	564,000	44,000	-377,000	231,000	-59.0%
Norway	2,595,000	243,000	-1,448,000	1,390,000	-46.4%
Holland	976,000	537,000	-720,000	793,000	-18.8%
Sweden	899,000	110,000	-247,000	762,000	-15.2%
Spain	806,000	40,000	-193,000	653,000	-19.0%
Denmark	761,000	136,000	-317,000	580,000	-23.8%
Others	1,207,000	674,000	-381,000	1,500,000	24.3%
Total	34,887,000	11,436,000	13,949,000	32,374,000	-7.2%
USA ex Lakes as per Maclay	2,000,000			4,750,000	137.5%

Source: NA, CAB 24/60 GT 5307 'Naval Effort - Great Britain & United States of America', Eric Geddes, 2 August 1918, p. 7, NA, ADM 116/1809, Eric Geddes Papers, A329-2, Maclay to Geddes, 30 July 1918.

---

[309] Geddes Papers, ADM 116/1809, A/439 'Maclay to Geddes', 30 July 1918.

Maclay said that tankers were now around 16 per cent of the US fleet, compared with 20 per cent before the war. The comparable numbers for Britain were approximately 5 per cent and 7 per cent. The American reluctance to supply Britain with as much aid with tankers as it had requested meant that Britain was having to devote a substantial amount of its new build to tankers. Maclay feared that this would result in Britain having too many tankers after the war when there would be less demand for imported oil.[310] He broadly supported Geddes, with his disagreement being over the presentation. Geddes's views were also backed by Albert Stanley, the President of the Board of Trade.[311]

The issue was debated by the War Cabinet on 9 August. Geddes had by then met the US Assistant Secretary of the Navy, Franklin Roosevelt. The USN was willing to build more destroyers and escort vessels, resulting in it taking on a greater share of the naval effort. This left the question of merchant shipping where Britain had suffered heavy losses and was devoting a substantial proportion of its shipbuilding capacity to repairs of US ships. Ships on order for Britain from US yards had been requisitioned. The War Cabinet decided to suggest that it would be appropriate if the British received a share of the new US merchant ships. Sir Chiozza Money of the Ministry of Shipping thought that the US Merchant Marine might overtake the British one by 1920 or 1921. He pointed out that US ships were 50 per cent more expensive than British ones; it might be worth paying this premium to buy US ships now but not after the war.[312]

The issue was referred to a meeting chaired by Balfour and attended by Reading, Maclay and the Third Sea Lord. It decided not to ask the USA to help replace lost British merchant tonnage. Maclay argued that the price would be too high, and it was thought that the US Government would not agree. It was agreed to request the US to alter their ratio of merchant to warship construction to be the same as that of Britain; repairs would be regarded equivalent to construction. The Admiralty requested that five American tankers be transferred to Britain in compensation for the labour used in refitting US destroyers; these would be part

---

[310] Ibid.

[311] CAB 24/60, G.T. 5341 'Naval Effort. Great Britain and United States of America', A. H. Stanley, 6 August 1918.

[312] CAB 23/7, 'War Cabinet Papers 438-79', 1 July - 27 September 1918. War Cabinet 456. 9 August 1918.

of the British order for eight previously taken over by the US government. The Americans were unable to comply because the US was short of tonnage and could transport its troops and their supplies to Europe only with British help. The refitting of US destroyers in British yards continued because it made sense; they returned to active duty in two weeks compared with six or eight if they had to go to the US yards.[313]

Geddes stated that the USN completed very few ships in the first five months of 1918.[314] The US was building a large number of destroyers and other auxiliary craft. Many more would come into service in the rest of 1918 and beyond. It was able to construct more of both these and merchant ships than Britain. In 1932 the USN had 251 destroyers and 81 submarines, most of them part of the wartime programme, compared with 150 and 56 respectively for the RN.[315] Until the USS *Farragut* was laid down in that year no US destroyer had been constructed for over 10 years. Far from not including enough auxiliary ships, the USN's wartime programme had taken it from having too few destroyers relative to its battle fleet to possessing the most destroyers of any navy in the world.[316]

Geddes wrote on 24 August that Edward Hurley, then Chairman of the US Shipping Board, had made a speech in which he made it clear that the USA intended to have the world's biggest merchant marine after the war.[317] A fortnight later Hurley wrote to President Wilson outlining his concerns over British shipping policy. He had always argued that the US merchant fleet was intended to benefit the whole world. It might have sounded better domestically if he had claimed that it would operate principally in American interests, but he did not want to make misleading and potentially harmful statements. He did not believe that the British really thought some of their complaints about the US shipbuilding programme were true. The British would be able to build ships at home after the war at half the cost of the ones commandeered by the US

---

[313] CAB 24/62, G.T. 5508 'Naval Effort of Great Britain and United States of America', E. Geddes, 26 August 1918.

[314] CAB 24/60 G.T. 5307, Geddes.

[315] O'Brien, *British*, p. 135.

[316] Chesneau, *Conway's 1922-1946*, pp. 124-25.

[317] CAB 24/61, G.T. 5494 'Naval Effort of Great Britain and United States of America', E. Geddes, 24 August 1918.

Government and would always have a cost advantage over the US shipping industry. Hurley argued that:

> The British business men are literally dominating the policy of the British government towards us...The figures they furnished us with regard to the ships they could spare were the figures their own shipping interests wanted them to put forward. These figures were quickly revised when the call came for a larger American force in France. The same was true with respect to coal and oil.[318]

This was an early indication that the wartime mistrust over shipbuilding would be followed by peacetime mistrust over oil. Wilson had also received reports from Admiral William Benson, the Chief of Naval Operations, arguing that the British were determined to maintain their naval supremacy. Geddes was sent to the USA in the autumn of 1918. He tried and failed to persuade the Americans to alter their construction programme. His efforts, coupled with his comments on the US naval effort, inadvertently helped to persuade President Wilson of the accuracy of Benson and Hurley's warnings.[319]

The USA did not achieve its ambition of having the world's largest merchant marine. Its fleet was bigger after the war than before, but the British one remained much larger. In 1939, the Britain Empire had 21,000,000 tons of merchant shipping, more than in 1914, albeit a smaller share of the global total. The USA was second with 9,000,000 tons, around 17 per cent of the world aggregate; this excludes the Great Lakes fleet so the comparable figures are 2,000,000 in 1914 and 4,750,000 in 1918.[320]

The two countries co-operated to win the war, but each were suspicious of the other's post-war intentions. This theme of the countries working together but not entirely trusting each other would continue into the post-war era.

---

[318] Link et al, eds, *Wilson*. vol. xlix, Edward Nash Hurley to President, 7 September 1918, pp. 473-74.

[319] O'Brien, *British*, pp. 135-36.

[320] A. S. Milward, *War, Economy and Society, 1939-1945* (London: Allen Lane, 1977), pp. 345-46.

3.2 The Inter Allied Petroleum Conference

In early 1918 Long's committee discussed forming an Inter Allied Petroleum
Conference look at each of the Allies' oil needs and to advise on how best to
achieve the required stocks. It would consider how to make the most economical
use of tanker tonnage and to what extent the specifications of petroleum
products could be standardised for all the Allies. Britain, France, Italy and the
USA would all be represented. At the 18 January 1918 meeting of his committee
Long expressed the fear that Britain could be out voted and suggested that it
should have more delegates than the other countries.[321] At the next meeting it
was proposed that the French and Italian delegates should attend only when
their needs were being discussed. These were very low compared with the
British requirement for oil, and a substantial proportion of them were
transported in British ships and financed by Britain. It was proposed that there
should be five British delegates and two from each of the other three
countries.[322] Differing numbers of delegates actually attended each meeting. The
Conference's main roles were the collation of data and the co-ordination of
efforts; it was an advisory rather than executive body. Five informal meetings
were held in February, mainly concerned with process and method.[323]

3.2.1 France and Oil

Georges Clemenceau, who became Prime Minister of France on 16 November
1917, allegedly said that he would go to his grocer if he needed oil; there does
not appear to be a primary source for this.[324] In English this might appear to
suggest that Clemenceau had so little interest in petroleum that he was
referring to cooking oil, but this is wrong. Eric Melby gives the quote in French,
and the word used for oil is 'pétrole.'[325] The oil industry was not as vertically
integrated in France as in other countries, and petroleum products were often

---

[321] POWE 33/5. 16th Meeting, 18 January 1918, p. 3.

[322] Ibid. 17th Meeting, 30 January 1918, pp. 2-8.

[323] POWE 33/8.

[324] Frank, *Oil*, p. 173, describes the quote as 'apocryphal' and sources Yergin, *Prize*, p. 189, who
sources E. D. K. Melby, *Oil and the International System: The Case of France, 1918-1969* (New
York, NY: Arno Press, 1981), p. 22. He gives no source. Neither do Gruen, 'Oil', p. 116 or
MacMillan, *Peacemakers*, p. 408.

[325] Melby, *France*, p. 22.

sold by grocers.[326] The comment, if Clemenceau ever made it, does not mean that he was dismissing the significance of oil. He was arguing that he would always be able to purchase it for his own use and for France.

France did not experience any great problems with oil supplies until early 1917. Henry Bérenger, a member of the Senate Army Committee and a supporter of increased use of oil by the French Navy, warned in March and again in May that there was an oil crisis. On 14 July he was appointed Chairman of the newly established Comité Général du Pétrole with a wide ranging but advisory remit. Measures were introduced to reduce civilian use, but increased military demand meant that by the end of November stocks were expected to run out within three months. Clemenceau increased Bérenger's powers after becoming Prime Minister. On 11 December Bérenger reported that France was dependent on its Allies for supplies and transport of oil. Three days later Clemenceau attended a meeting of the Comité Général du Pétrole.[327] The immediate need was for tanker tonnage to bring oil to France; the next day Clemenceau issued a plea to President Wilson for extra tanker tonnage. There was a risk that a 'shortage of gasoline would cause the sudden paralysis of our armies and drive us all into an unacceptable peace.'[328] French stocks of gasoline were currently 28,000 tons, compared with a target minimum of 44,000 and consumption of 30,000 tons per month. Wilson must get the US oil companies to allocate an additional 100,000 tons of tankers to France. These could come from the Pacific and from new construction. Clemenceau's final lines to Wilson were:

> There is for the Allies a question of public salvation. If they are
> determined not to lose the war, the fighting French must, by the hour
> of supreme Germanic blow, have large supplies of gasoline which is, in
> the battle of tomorrow, as necessary as blood.[329]

---

[326] G. P. Nowell, *Mercantile States and the World Oil Cartel, 1900-1939* (Ithaca, NY: Cornell University Press, 1994). Note 39, p. 99.

[327] R. W. Ferrier, 'French Oil Policy, 1917-30: The Interaction between State and Private Interests,' in *Enterprise and History Essays in Honour of Charles Wilson*, ed. D. C. Coleman, P. Mathias (Cambridge: Cambridge University Press, 1984), pp. 240-41.

[328] "Foreign Relations of the United States", University of Wisconsin Digital Collections Center http://digital.library.wisc.edu/1711.dl/FRUS. 1917, Supplement 2, The World War, vol. i, File No. 763.72/8161, The Ambassador in France (Sharp) to the Secretary of State, 15 December 1917, p. 646. Also in Link et al, eds, *Wilson.* vol. xlv, pp. 302-3.

[329] "FRUS". 1917, Supplement 2, The World War, vol. i, p. 646.

In January 1918, the US Ambassador to Paris, William Sharp, wrote to the Secretary of State, Robert Lansing, urging the US to act on the French request. Petrol was vital to the war effort; the French had only half the tanker tonnage needed to import the required quantities. Only the US could supply the necessary ships.[330] They were provided, but Bérenger was concerned that the problem had not been permanently solved. On 27 February he told the Inter-Allied Petroleum Conference that 'a drop of petrol is equal to a drop of blood.'[331] France had used only 42,000 tons of oil per month before the war. By the start of 1918 this had more than trebled to 130,000 tons. Oil was required for aircraft, trucks and war industries. Anti-submarine warfare meant greater use of small, oil fired warships. More tractors were being used because farm workers were in the armed forces. Civilians were having to use kerosene instead of electricity and gas for heating and lighting because of the needs of the munitions industry. Oil reserves might have fallen to zero had Wilson not responded to Clemenceau's appeal for extra tankers. France had not been able to construct tankers or to develop its limited home supplies of oil because of the war effort. Bérenger said that it was vital that France was permanently provided with the necessary tankers. This was 'not...a question more or less of agreeable utility or of money. It is a question of life or death, the victory or the defeat of all the Allies.'[332]

3.2.2 Italy and Oil

At the 27 February meeting the Italians said that their requirements were less than those of France and well below British ones, but they were concerned that their stocks 'except for the liquid fuel, which is most required by the navy, who must have a strategical reserve...are very low.'[333] Italy was expected to need 836,400 tons of oil in 1918 before building stocks. The army's demand for meat had reduced the cattle stock, requiring cattle previously used for labour to be replaced by motor tractors.

---

[330] Link et al, eds, *Wilson*. vol. xlv, William Graves Sharp to Robert Lansing, 5 January 1918, p. 492.

[331] POWE 33/8. Fourth Informal Meeting, 27 February 1918, Appendix 2, Note by Henry Berenger.

[332] Ibid. Fourth Formal Session, 14 September 1918, p. 2.

[333] Ibid. Fourth Informal Meeting, 27 February 1918, Appendix 4.

Table 3-9 Italian oil requirements

	Per month	Stocks at 1 February 1918	Month's stocks
Liquid fuel	29,700	94,200	3.2
Kerosene	17,000	2,761	0.2
Aviation spirit	3,000	Not given	
Other spirits	15,500	22,820	1.5
Lubricating oil	4,500	6,000	1.3
Total	69,700		

Source: NA, POWE 33/8: Inter-Allied Petroleum Conference: minutes of meetings, 1918. Fourth Informal Meeting, 27 February 1918, Appendix 4.

3.2.3 Allied Oil Requirements

On 28 February the Conference discussed Allied sources of supply (see Table 3-2) and needs (see Table 3-10). Needs were based on the requirements to increase stocks to a minimum or 'danger line'[334] level. For Britain these were two months for civilian and army stocks and three months plus 225,000 for naval fuel. The level for aviation spirit had not yet been determined. The French needed two months civilian reserves but three months for their army and air service. This was because of the length of the front line and the inferiority of the French railway network to that of the enemy, who controlled the railways of Northern France and Belgium. This required the French to make more use of motor vehicles. All French naval fuel was supplied by the British and was allowed for in the British naval reserves so the French had no need of naval fuel reserves. The Italians too had a long and irregular front line and an inadequate rail network; this necessitated substantial petrol reserves, but they did not quantify these.

The breakdown of oil needs shows that the RN was easily the largest consumer of oil. Britain was the biggest user even excluding navies. The British did not separate out agriculture from other civilian uses, and the French included toluol as a category in its own right. Air forces were not differentiated from the navy and the army; aviation spirit demand has been quoted to show the relative importance of the oil needs of aircraft.

---

[334] Ibid. Fifth Informal Meeting, 28 February 1918.

Table 3-10 Oil needs of different Allied services, 1918, tons (French converted from metric tons in original)

Service	UK	Italy	France	Total
Army	511,600	266,400	455,700	1,233,700
Navy	3,806,500	276,000	268,000	4,350,500
Fabrications de Guerre			161,900	161,900
Agriculture		132,000	71,600	203,600
Other civil uses	1,279,900	162,000	555,200	1,997,100
Local Allied requirements	474,000			474,000
Additions to reserves	554,000		141,100	695,100
Toluol			15,200	15,200
Total	6,626,000	836,400	1,653,500	9,115,900
Aviation Spirit	130,500	36,000	151,700	318,200

Source: NA, POWE 33/8: Inter-Allied Petroleum Conference: minutes of meetings, 1918. Fourth Informal Meeting, 27 February 1918, Appendix 4. The British figures for the RN and other civil uses have been reduced by 94,400 and 182,700 tons respectively to avoid double counting with liquid fuel supplied to France.

On 6 and 7 May the Conference held a formal session at which all the delegates had the full authority of their governments. A further six formal sessions took place, the last on 16 December 1918. The first agreed that it was vital to produce statistics for the oil needs, supply sources and required tonnage of the Allies. Later meetings also covered administrative arrangements, storage and petroleum product specifications. It was an information gathering body rather than an executive one.[335] Yergin points out that it did a good job of distributing the available oil supplies to the Allies but that the dominance of the oil industry by Standard (NJ) and RDS meant that it depended on their networks of to do so.[336]

3.3 Chapter Summary

The Allies depended on the USA to supply much of their large and increasing demand for oil during the war. It had enough oil to do so; sufficient tankers to transport it had to be found and got through the U-boats to Europe. In 1917-18 a number of themes emerged that would become more significant at the peace conferences and later. Britain and the USA co-operated to win the war, but were suspicious of each other's future intentions; this would continue after the war. The British feared that the Americans were planning to usurp their existing position in world trade. The Americans thought that the British were plotting to

---

[335] Ibid.

[336] Yergin, *Prize*, p. 177.

shut them out of post-war commerce. During the war the claims and counter-claims mostly revolved round the size of the two countries' merchant fleets. The British thought that, as an island with a global empire, their wealth and prosperity depended on dominating world trade and having a big enough navy to protect their position. Global trade was not so important to the USA so the British could not see why it required such a large merchant fleet and navy. The Americans did not want to be dependent on the merchant ships and goodwill of another power. Similar disputes would emerge over oil; the British did not see why the USA, by far the biggest producer in the world, needed access to overseas oil. Britain had to have foreign oil because it had little at home. The Americans were concerned that their oil might soon run out; they were the world's biggest consumer as well as its largest producer and needed foreign production to replace the expected domestic decline. Britain's control of the oceans depended in part on its dominance of world coal bunkering. It wanted to maintain its position as the main fuel of the global shipping industry changed from coal to oil; the Americans did not want to become dependent on British goodwill for oil supplies abroad.

France and Italy were slower than Britain and the USA to see the need for oil, partly because they had smaller navies and thus lower demand for oil. Both initially depended on Britain to transport their oil. The French were determined to prevent a repetition of their 1917 oil crisis. They had no major oil company and little oil in their empire. They did have some scope to negotiate with Britain over a share of the potential oil of Mosul, part of which had been allocated to them by Sykes Picot. Pipeline routes from the oilfields to the Mediterranean would cross French territory. French consent would be needed for a Middle Eastern peace settlement; the French intended that it should give them a share of the oil. This would affect Anglo-French post-war relations, and there would be a series of attempts at concluding an Anglo-French oil settlement. The Italians eventually realised that they needed oil; they would try to obtain a share in Middle Eastern oil, but came to the table later than the French and with fewer cards to play. Despite the difficulties in importing oil the Allies did have far more of it than the Central Powers did. The need to secure oil supplies would affect relations between the Allies after the war and in 1918 impacted British war aims.

4 Oil and British War Aims

Britain started with no war aims in the Middle East, but over the course of the conflict it developed a series of goals in which oil played an increasing role. British planners and strategists wanted secure future supplies of oil to avoid dependence on US support. Mosul was the most likely potential source of British controlled oil; obtaining control over it required the consent of France. In December 1918 Clemenceau agreed that Britain should have Mosul. Other disputes delayed the signing of the necessary Anglo-French oil agreement. Attempts to create a British national oil company continued.

4.1 The Oil of Mosul

On 29 July 1918 Slade produced an Admiralty paper on the 'Petroleum Situation in the British Empire'.[337] The same day he met Hankey, who was impressed with his arguments. Slade had gained an important ally since Hankey, as Cabinet Secretary, had a significant influence over British strategy.[338] Hankey then wrote to Sir Eric Geddes suggesting that the Admiralty should look at the question of oil in the context of war aims and of future military operations. It should consider whether its oil justified continuing with operations in Mesopotamia even though the General Staff considered it to be a minor theatre:

> I have been told privately by people with knowledge of oil production that the oil situation of the future is rather uncertain...It was...suggested that the largest potential oilfields at present known are in Persia and Mesopotamia...there are some as far up as Mosul...if this information is correct, the retention of the oil-bearing regions in Mesopotamia and Persia...would appear to be a first class British war aim. I do not remember, however, that it has appeared as such.[339]

On 30 July Hankey met Admiral Sir Rosslyn Wemyss, the First Sea Lord, and persuaded him to circulate Slade's paper to the Imperial War Cabinet along with a covering memorandum that Wemyss dictated in Hankey's presence. Hankey

---

[337] This memorandum appears in several NA files, but none contain all of the subsequent correspondence. ADM 1/8537/240; POWE 33/45, 'Petroleum Situation in British Empire', 1918; CAB 21/119, 'Petroleum Situation in the British Empire and the Mesopotamia and Persian Oilfields', 1918; CAB 24/59 G.T. 5267, Slade.

[338] See S. W. Roskill, *Hankey: Man of Secrets*, 2 vols. (London: Collins, 1970-74).

[339] CAB 21/119.

requested that Wemyss tell Slade to write another paper giving more details on the Mosul oilfields.[340] Wemyss's memorandum stated that the Admiralty wanted:

> to endorse in the strongest manner possible, the general principles and general conclusions set forth [by Slade]...the holding in our hands of the motive power of sea-borne traffic - coal...has proved of inestimable value in that Maintenance of sea power on which the whole edifice of the Empire rests...it is hoped that...the extreme importance of [Mesopotamia] in regard to the Petroleum situation will not be lost sight of.[341]

On 1 August Hankey wrote to Lloyd George suggesting Slade's paper should be considered at the next day's Cabinet meeting along with one by the Allied War Council at Versailles on Palestine and Mesopotamia. Hankey argued that:

> 'there is no <u>military</u> [Hankey's emphasis] advantage in pushing forward in Mesopotamia...there may be reasons other than purely military for pushing on. Would it not be an advantage before the end of the war, to secure the valuable oil wells in Mesopotamia?'[342]

Slade argued that there were two issues regarding oil supply; the strategic position and supply. They were closely linked, but it was possible to obtain sufficient supplies without solving the more vital strategic question. He repeated the argument on bunker fuel that he had put forward in 1916. During the war, Britain had controlled the world's shipping because it controlled the world's supplies of bunker fuel. The future of the British Empire was mostly reliant on this control. Oil was replacing coal as the world's principal bunker fuel, meaning that Britain needed to control as much oil as possible. Loss of control of the world's bunker fuel meant that 'half our sea power is gone and our position becomes a most precarious one.'[343] Oil fired ships had a longer range than coal burners so did not have to refuel as often, further complicating the situation. Oil supplies had to be under entirely British control as foreign concerns would use 'every means at their disposal, honestly or dishonestly, openly or secretly, to

---

[340] CC, Hankey Papers, HNKY 1/5, 'Diary: Vol. 3, 20 July 1918 - 3 Dec. 1922'. 1 August 1918. The meeting was on 30 July but Hankey says in his diary that he forgot to record it until two days later.

[341] CAB 24/59 G.T. 5267, Slade.

[342] CAB 21/119. Hankey to Prime Minister, 1 August 1918.

[343] CAB 24/59 G.T. 5267, Slade, p. 1.

hamper the development of British interests.'[344] He alleged that foreign oil companies were making £20-25 million per annum from the British market.

Table 4-1 shows that the USA supplied over 60 per cent of UK imports in 1913. Romanian and Russian supplies had been cut off since 1914, increasing the importance of US oil to Britain. US reserves were expected to last only 20-25 years at the current rate of consumption, which was rising. Expected increases in Mexican output would be taken by the USA. Britain would not be able to obtain significantly more oil from its other pre-war suppliers, including Russia, Romania, Burma or the Dutch East Indies. Slade commented that what mattered was not a country's oil output but its exportable surplus, shown in Table 4-2. The figures shown are for Britain only. Canada took 9 per cent of the USA's exportable surplus and the rest of the British Empire 5 per cent, giving a total of 30 per cent for the Empire. Slight discrepancies between the two tables are because of rounding errors.

Table 4-1 UK oil imports, 1913

USA	62.3%
Romania	11.6%
Russia	7.7%
Dutch East Indies	7.7%
Mexico	4.1%
Other	6.5%

Source: 'CAB 24/59, G.T. 5267', Slade, p. 1.

Table 4-2 Exportable surplus of leading oil producers, 1913

1913	Total output, tons	Exportable surplus, tons	Exportable surplus, per cent of total output	UK imports, tons	UK imports, per cent of exportable surplus
USA	33,150,000	7,120,000	21%	1100000	16%
Romania	1,880,000	940,000	50%	230000	19%
Russia	8,370,000	670,000	8%	130000	19%
Mexico	3,480,000	1,740,000	50%	70000	4%
Dutch East Indies	1,500,000			125000	8%

Source: 'CAB 24/59, G.T. 5267', Slade, p. 2.

British demand would not return to pre-war levels after the war. Naval use would fall, but demand from the Mercantile Marine would rise. Civilian use of

---

[344] Ibid.

motor vehicles would increase because fewer horses would be available, and a large number of military surplus vehicles would be sold cheaply after the war. Slade expected demand to stay at the current 6,000,000 tons per annum, at least while naval stocks were being built up; see Tables 4-3 and 4-4. These figures differ slightly from those in Table 3-10 because they were prepared at different times. Demand from other countries would also rise; the USA and Germany both planned to have large merchant fleets. The Germans had suffered from British control of coal for shipping and did not intend to allow the same to happen with oil.

Table 4-3 UK imports as of 7/18, tons

Fuel oil	4,300,000
Motor spirit	750,000
Kerosene	600,000
Lubricating oil	350,000
Total	6,000,000

Source: 'CAB 24/59, G.T. 5267', Slade, p. 4.

Table 4-4 Expected UK post war oil demand, tons

RN and Mercantile Marine	3,500,000
Build up of Naval stocks	1,000,000
Other uses	1,500,000
Total	6,000,000

Source: 'CAB 24/59, G.T. 5267', Slade, p. 4.

The most important potential oilfields in the world were those of Persia and Mesopotamia. There were other undeveloped oilfields in the world but exports from those in the Americas were likely to go to the USA and others, including those of Papua, Nigeria, the Gold Coast, New Brunswick, Argentina, Portuguese West Africa, Timor, Madagascar and Algeria, were relatively small. Control of the oilfields of Persia and Mesopotamia was vital:

> In Persia and Mesopotamian lie the largest undeveloped resources at present known in the world...

> It is not too much to estimate that the oil lands of Persia and Mesopotamia which will extend over an area of 360,000 square miles, or more than twice the size of the oil land of Russia, should not in the future provide a supply equal to that now given by the United States.

> If this estimate is anywhere near the truth, then it is evident that the Power that controls the oil lands of Persia and Mesopotamia will control the source of supply of the majority of the liquid fuel of the

future. It this control is combined with that of coal, then that Power will hold the control of bunker fuel and will be in a position to dictate its own terms to all shipping in case of war.[345]

Britain had to be wary of German penetration of the oil market. If Germany could not control the world oil market by winning the war, it would try to do so by peaceful means afterwards. Slade, Vice Chairman of APOC, launched an attack on RDS, which he claimed was 'inimical to British control [and]...in intimate relations with and trading with Germany so far as it can without danger of being black-listed.'[346] Slade concluded by calling on the Admiralty to 'urge'[347] the government to:

1. Defend the Persian oilfields that were vital to victory.

2. Expedite development of the Persian and Mesopotamian oilfields by entirely British interests.

3. Ensure explorations for and development of oil in the British Empire by entirely British interests.

4. Encourage and help British companies to take control of as many foreign oilfields as feasible. The output should be distributed by British companies.

5. Exclude foreign interests from the British oil industry.

Slade's second paper was based on reports made by German geologists before the war and by APOC geologists on behalf of the British military. It gave details of the areas of oil seepage and argued that there were substantial indications of oil over an area of around 50,000 square miles. A German paper, presumably captured or decoded although Slade gave no provenance for it, said that the oil provinces of Mesopotamia and Persia had the 'greatest importance after that of the Suez Canal'[348] as German objectives. The Cabinet did not immediately act

---

[345] Ibid., p. 6.

[346] Ibid., p. 7.

[347] Ibid., p. 8.

[348] CAB 24/60, G.T. 5313 'Memorandum on the Reported Oil Fields of Mesopotamia and Part of Persia', E. J. W. Slade, 2 August 1918.

upon Slade's papers but passed them onto the Cadman's Petroleum Executive on the proposal of Long. On 3 August Slade visited Hankey to complain about this because he 'doubted the discretion of Cadman'[349] and feared that he was too close to RDS.

Hankey continued to press the case for British control over the oilfields of Mesopotamia and Persia. On 3 August his attempt to enlist Balfour's support had elicited the reply that this 'was a frankly imperialistic war aim.'[350] Hankey could not understand 'allowing such humbug to stand in the way of our vital national needs!'[351] Later in the month Hankey tried a slightly different tack, writing to Balfour arguing that nobody, including President Wilson, would want to return Lower Mesopotamia to Turkish rule. He contended that the only alternative was for them to be under some form of British rule. The water supply of Lower Mesopotamia was dependent on territory allocated to France under Sykes-Picot but it guaranteed the water supply of the British territory. Hankey argued that Britain would be justified in advancing until it controlled enough territory to secure the water supply. He then added that '[i]ncidentally this would give us most of the oil-bearing regions.'[352] Slade received support from General Sir Frederick Sykes, the Chief of the Air Staff, who wished 'to endorse with all possible emphasis the views set forth [and]...also the recommendations made by...Slade.'[353] Sykes thought that the survival of the Empire depended on air power. The vital importance of oil for both the RAF and the RN meant that measures had to be taken to secure oil supplies and a large buffer zone was needed between the oilfields and hostile powers. Others were critical of Slade.

Long had a number of objections to Slade's paper, several of which he recorded in the margin of his copy. Warwick Brown accurately describes them as being 'caustic.'[354] Long wondered who the foreign interests that Slade believed were acting against British interests were and whether they were really making £20-25 million per annum in Britain. He questioned Slade's assumptions about rising oil

---

[349] HNKY 1/5. 3 August 1918.

[350] Ibid. 3 August 1918.

[351] Ibid. 3 August 1918.

[352] CAB 21/119. Hankey to Balfour, 12 August 1918.

[353] CAB 24/60, G.T. 5376 'Petroleum Situation in the British Empire', F. Sykes, 9 August 1918.

[354] Brown, 'Royal Navy', p. 164. Note 40.

consumption post war and argued that his conclusions were a matter for the Petroleum Executive, not the Admiralty.[355] Cadman reported to Long that Slade's paper had not been seen by either Tothill, who as Fourth Sea Lord was responsible for naval supply, transport and logistics and was 'very upset'[356] by the affair, or Pretyman, the Civil Lord. Cadman had met Slade who commented that he had previously put a paper to the War Cabinet in order to block a proposal by the Board of Trade. Cadman regarded Slade's paper as putting forward the views of APOC and found it 'extraordinary'[357] that a company should be able to approach the War Cabinet in this manner. Slade and Greenway thought the company's relationship with the government meant that it should consult them more often. Cadman told them that the government wanted the help of all, but Standard (NJ) and RDS were Britain's main oil suppliers. The government did not want to give the erroneous idea that it favoured APOC. Slade alleged that Shell had obtained confidential APOC documents but does not appear to have repeated his claim that Cadman was the source.[358] A correspondence between Slade and Long then ensued. Slade claimed that Shell was trading with Germany. He did not directly accuse the Petroleum Executive of being responsible for the alleged leaks to Shell but did comment that they went back to the time that it was set up.[359] Long wanted evidence of Slade's allegations against the Petroleum Executive. He would investigate the claim that Shell was trading with the enemy but this was a separate issue from the alleged leaks.[360] Slade and Long eventually agreed that further correspondence on the issue would serve no purpose.[361]

The controversy over Slade's paper led to some back-tracking by the Admiralty. Pretyman said that:

> The paper appears to be an exparte statement by the Anglo Persian
> Oil Company who are in bitter rivalry with the Royal Dutch Shell. Many
> of the statements made are to my knowledge inaccurate or
> exaggerated, and the whole of the questions raised are now under

---

[355] POWE 33/45. G.T. 5267.

[356] Ibid. Cadman to Long, 7 September 1918.

[357] Ibid.

[358] Ibid.

[359] Ibid. Slade to Long, 10 and 24 September 1918.

[360] Ibid. Long to Slade, 16 and 25 September 1918.

[361] Ibid. Slade to Long, 27 September 1918.

consideration by the Committee appointed by Mr Walter Long of which Lord Harcourt is Chairman and on which I represent the Admiralty.[362]

He and Tothill took their objections to Wemyss, who explained in a memo to Geddes that in future papers on oil would be forwarded to them. Wemyss claimed that he was aware of his 'ignorance of oil politics and [his] principal concern in the subject is strategical.'[363] Geddes submitted a memo to the War Cabinet explaining that:

> On reperusal of the Memorandum I find that there are passages in it which deal with contentious questions of oil company politics...The endorsement, however, of the Memorandum by the First Sea Lord and myself refers only to the contention that the oil bearing districts of Mesopotamia and Persia are of very great national importance to us.[364]

Matters of oil company politics would be left to the Petroleum Imperial Policy Committee chaired by Lord Harcourt.

A War Cabinet meeting on 13 August 1918, with the Dominion Prime Ministers present, discussed war aims. Balfour said that at the start of the war he had thought that it was unfortunate that Britain had to go to Mesopotamia since the territory occupied would be at risk from attack by the Russian or Turkish Empires. The situation had now changed. Britain had promised to hand it over to an Arab state but 'must be the guiding spirit there.'[365] A further issue that had recently emerged was oil. Mesopotamia contained what were claimed to be very large oilfields. Balfour said that:

> With every desire not to acquire more territory than we can help out of this war - in that I believe I differ from some of my colleagues ; I am anxious to keep down the extension of the British Empire as much as possible—I am very reluctant to see anything done which would endanger our obtaining oil from this region. I do not care under what system we keep the oil, whether it is by a perpetual lease or whatever

---

[362] ADM 1/8537/240. Pretyman to First Lord, 12 September 1918.

[363] Ibid. Wemyss to First Lord, 25 September 1918.

[364] CAB 24/64, G.T. 5710 'A Note in Reference to the Admiralty Memorandum on the "Petroleum Situation in the British Empire" (Paper G.T. 5267)', E. Geddes, 17 September 1918.

[365] CAB 23/43, 'War Cabinet Minutes', 1917-18. Meeting of War Cabinet 457, 13 August 1918, p. 10.

it may be, but I am quite clear that it is all-important for us that this oil should be available.[366]

Curzon stated that if Britain lost Baku then these were the only other significant ones available. Balfour replied that he understood that the Mesopotamian ones were superior to those of Baku. A map of the Mesopotamian oilfields was consulted and Lloyd George said that he was 'in favour of going up as far as Mosul before the war is over.'[367] Long missed this meeting because of illness but submitted a memorandum that discussed only the future of German colonies. Britain must not return any that could be used by Germany as submarine bases, wireless stations or coal and oil depots to support attacks on British commerce in a future war.[368] Long made no reference to Mosul or Slade's paper; the correspondence indicates that his objections to that document were to the process by which it was circulated and to the oil company politics involved. Slade's paper had, via its influence on Hankey, put Mosul onto the agenda for the discussion of British War Aims. Lloyd George, Curzon and Balfour had all agreed Mosul's oil was vital for Britain. Curzon could be relied upon to back the expansion of the British Empire. Later in 1918, Edwin Montagu, the Secretary of State for India, complained to Balfour that:

> And then there is the rounded Lord Curzon, who for historical reasons of which he alone is master, geographical considerations which he has peculiarly studied, finds, reluctantly, much against his will, with very grave doubts, that it would be dangerous if any country in the world was left to itself, if any country in the world was left to the control of any other country but ourselves, and we must go there, as I have heard him say, "for diplomatic, economic, strategic, and telegraphic reasons."[369]

Curzon may have seen oil as simply another reason to advocate expansion, but the arguments over oil had influenced Lloyd George and Balfour. The Prime Minister had not previously commented on this issue, but now favoured the acquisition of Mosul. In 1916, Balfour had argued that the oil problem was one of

---

[366] Ibid., p. 10.

[367] Ibid.

[368] Ibid. G.T. 5515 Memorandum for the War Cabinet, W. H. Long, 24 August 1918.

[369] BL, Balfour Papers, MSS. 49748: vol. lvi 'Papers Relating to Foreign Affairs', 1914-1918. Montagu to Balfour, f. 304. Part of this quote was incorporated into the title of an essay; Neilson, 'Diplomatic.'

transport as it could be bought on the world market.[370] After a further two years of war and an oil crisis, he accepted the vital need for British access to Mosul's oil. His concern was to obtain it in a manner that did not expand the British Empire unnecessarily.

4.1.1 The Seizure of Mosul.

By the time that Mosul became a British war aim the forces in Mesopotamia had been reduced in size. In April 1918 two Indian Divisions were transferred to Palestine in order to partially replace British troops who were being sent to France because of the German offensive there.[371] General Sir Edmund Allenby's offensive in Palestine was delayed by these changes. By early October Damascus had fallen and the Ottoman Army was in full retreat. General Marshall was ordered on 7 October to deliver the final blow to the enemy.[372] He wrote in his memoirs that these orders created significant transport problems. His force had been required to keep open the lines of communication to Persia across poor roads, leading to a high rate of unserviceability amongst its motor vehicles.[373] The transport difficulties were overcome, and the bulk of the Ottoman Sixth Army had been destroyed by 30 October.[374] Sir Arnold Wilson, the Acting Civil Commissioner of the British occupied part of Mesopotamia and the Political Resident in the Persian Gulf, wrote in his memoirs that he had for some time been communicating with the British Government over the need to occupy Mosul vilayet. He argued that, whether Mosul was to be British or French, it must be occupied by the time that hostilities ended. The vilayets of Basra, Baghdad and Mosul should be under the same government.[375]

Ottoman forces remained in occupation of the city of Mosul and Marshall ordered a column under General Fanshawe to capture it. Marshall was informed of the armistice with the Ottoman Empire on 1 November but did not pass this

---

[370] CAB 37/154/3.

[371] D. L. Bullock, *Allenby's War: The Palestine-Arabian Campaigns, 1916-1918* (London: Blandford, 1988), p. 112.

[372] Barker, *Neglected*, p. 455.

[373] W. Marshall, *Memories of Four Fronts* (London: Ernest Benn Limited, 1929), p. 318.

[374] A. T. Wilson, *Mesopotamia, 1917-1920: A Clash of Loyalties. A Personal and Historical Record.* (London: Oxford University Press, 1931), p. 16.

[375] Ibid., pp. 17-18.

information onto Fanshawe. The next day the Ottomans informed Fanshawe of the armistice and asked him to withdraw his force to the point that it had reached when the armistice was signed. Marshall ordered him to press on and take the city of Mosul. The Ottoman commander, Ali Ihsan, protested but eventually signed terms of surrender with Marshall. The latter thought that the problem was that archaic military terms had been used in the armistice with the Ottoman Empire. Marshall admitted in his memoirs that he was not certain that he was in the right.[376] According to Wilson the problem was that the armistice said that all garrisons in Mesopotamia should surrender but did not define either Mesopotamia, a term not used in the Ottoman Empire, or garrison.[377] Britain was now in possession of all of the Mosul vilayet and its potential oil. Later there would be disputes with Turkey over whether or not this territory should be part of the new state of Iraq. The Turks would have had a greater chance of winning this argument if they had retained control of all of Mosul in 1918.

4.1.2 Persia

Persia remained neutral throughout the war, but neither side respected its neutrality. Britain's main objective in Persia was to protect its existing positions, which were concentrated in the south. The Russians in the north adopted a more aggressive approach than the British, defeating the enemy but causing great resentment amongst the local population.[378] The main British interests in Persia were oil, the Gulf and the protection of India. In June 1917 the Viceroy of India sent a telegram warning of the risk that Persia would either descend into anarchy or else an anti-British government would come to power. In either case the South Persia Rifles, a locally recruited but British officered and controlled force, would fall apart taking Britain's military position in South Persia with them. Shiraz would have to be evacuated and action taken to protect the Gulf ports. The route to Herat would be open to the Ottomans who could then take the war to Afghanistan and the Indian border. The oilfields and Arabistan would be threatened along with the communications of the British forces in Mesopotamia. The Viceroy argued that the best solution was to placate the

---

[376] Marshall, *Memories*, pp. 323-25.

[377] Wilson, *1917-1920*, pp. 17-18.

[378] Fatemi, *Oil*, pp. 62-72.

democratic politicians, if necessary by payment.[379] The British concentrated on holding the south, ruling through local leaders described as 'puppets'[380] by an Iranian historian.

In June 1918 Curzon explained to the Imperial War Cabinet that Persia was weak and was a major problem for Britain, which wanted to maintain Persia's autonomy and integrity. The collapse of Russia had opened the north to the enemy, but the British, in co-operation with the remaining Russian forces, had so far kept them out. There was a lot of trouble in the south. The South Persian Rifles was unpopular with the Persian government and the British government was trying to come up with a better solution. A cordon of Persian and Indian troops protected Afghanistan. Having Persia as a friend would be a positive, but having it as an ally would create difficult obligations.

> [The] main object is to deny Persia to the enemy, to have a friendly
> Government there, and to prevent her from becoming a focus of
> German intrigue in her own territories, or a danger to Afghanistan.[381]

In the same meeting Curzon argued that Germany had won so much in the east that it could afford to make great concessions in the west. The Germans wanted to destroy the British Empire and could do so in the east. Britain must retain Palestine and Mesopotamia to protect Egypt and the Persian Gulf respectively. There was no disagreement with Curzon's views.[382]

4.2 The Petroleum Imperial Policy Committee

On 29 May 1918 Long set up the PIPCO '[t]o enquire into and advise His Majesty's Government as to the policy to be followed in order to ensure adequate supplies of oil for the Naval, Military and Industrial purposes of the British Empire.'[383] It was chaired by Harcourt who had left office when Asquith was replaced as Prime

---

[379] CAB 24/17, G.T. 1193 'Persia. Telegram from Viceroy', Viceroy, 25 June 1917.

[380] Fatemi, *Oil*, p. 69.

[381] CAB 23/43, p. 9.

[382] Ibid., pp. 9-10.

[383] POWE 33/13, 'Negotiations Regarding Petroleum Policy of His Majesty's Government: Vol 1 Reports and Proceedings of Petroleum Imperial Policy Committee', 1918-19, p. 4.

Minister at the end of 1916 and been created a Viscount in 1917. Its members were:

Viscount Harcourt (Chairman);
Viscount Inchcape (Treasury);
E. G. Pretyman (Civil Lord of the Admiralty);
Sir Frederick Black (Director of Contracts, Admiralty);
Professor Sir John Cadman (Director, Petroleum Executive);
Alwyn Parker (Foreign Office);
Lancelot Smith (Board of Trade);
B. A. Kemball Cook (Ministry of Shipping);
Sir Harry MacGowan;
Sir John Ferguson;
Colonel Sir Robert Horne;
Colonel R. S. Williamson;
J. C. Clarke (Deputy Director, Petroleum Executive);
Secretary: Captain A. S. Jelf, Malay States Civil Service.

Kemball Cook joined the committee on 30 September 1918 and Black on 31 October 1918. Parker was succeeded as Foreign Office representative by the Hon. C. H. Tufton on 24 October 1918. He was replaced by E. Weakley on 21 December 1918. Inchcape was a government director of APOC, and Black was appointed one on 4 February; he ceased to be a government representative on 30 June but remained on the board until 27 March 1923.[384] Unlike most previous oil committees no serving naval officers were members. Horne had worked under Eric Geddes on organisation of the railways of the Western Front and then followed him to the Admiralty, but his presence was probably due to his legal expertise; he was an advocate specialising in commercial and shipping law. Cadman had argued that the committee should include a corporate lawyer and businessmen.[385] Inchcape was a shipping tycoon, MacGowan an industrialist, and Ferguson a banker.

The PIPCO's report was published in February 1919. Long, who set it up, had objected to much of Slade's July 1918 paper. Harcourt, its Chairman, and Cadman, a member, had both been previously criticised by Slade, who was only a witness and not a member. Its introduction repeated Slade's arguments, less the oil company politics. Oil, which Britain lacked, was replacing coal, which it

---

[384] Ferrier, *History*. Appendix 8.4, p. 651.

[385] POWE 33/12, 'Imperial Policy Oil Committee: Formation', 1918. Cadman to Batterbee, 4 March 1918.

had in abundance. The control of bunker fuel was vital to the future of the British Empire. Britain was dependent on the USA for oil supplies; rising demand and potentially declining output in the USA meant that the Americans might not be able to meet British needs even if they remained friendly. This shows that these views had been widely accepted.[386] The committee decided that the way to ensure Britain's oil supplies was to have a large oil company under British control. It reopened the 1916 debate on how to moving RDS from Dutch to British control. Most of its time was taken up with discussions and negotiations on how to achieve this. The witnesses who appeared before the PIPCO were all men whose could advise on this course of action; directors of APOC, Burmah, Mexican Eagle and RDS and corporate lawyers. [387] No debate on why this was the solution was recorded. It seemed to be decided from the start that it was; the question was how to achieve it.

Harcourt and Deterding came to an agreement. The British registered subsidiaries of RDS would remain British in perpetuity. A majority of their directors must be British born British subjects. A British Government nominee would have to agree to changes in Shell's board of directors and Articles of Association and to asset disposals. The shareholding split of 60 per cent Royal Dutch and 40 per cent Shell would remain. RDS's British companies and its operations in Romania, Mexico, Venezuela and part of Russia would be British controlled. Its operations in the Dutch Empire would have remained Dutch controlled as this was required by Dutch law. RDS, via Anglo-Saxon or another of its British subsidiaries, would obtain a stake in the TPC equal to that of APOC. Anglo-Saxon and APOC would each have 34 per cent and the British Government 2 per cent. If other parties, presumably meaning the French, did not take up all of the remaining 30 per cent, then any balance would be divided evenly between Anglo-Saxon and APOC. The shares of these two companies and the British Government would be put into a voting trust, with a majority of the three members deciding how the full block was voted. The Deutsche Bank's stake in TPC had been seized by the British Treasury because it was an enemy owned shareholding in a British registered company. This offered an opportunity to re-allocate the capital of TPC. Sir Frederick Black dissented from a number of

---

[386] POWE 33/13, pp. 5-6.

[387] Ibid., pp. 8-9.

points in the Agreement. He was concerned that Britain had given up too much in Mesopotamia in return for British control over Shell. He worried that the Mesopotamian oil production would be controlled by RDS and the French. APOC should have been consulted over the marketing arrangements for the Mesopotamian Oil. Insufficient attention had been paid to the Romanian oilfields.[388] Deterding was motivated by a desire to obtain a share of the TPC and a need for British Government support in Romania and Russia.[389] The deal was approved by the Cabinet on 5 May 1919. It lacked the political will to push it through, and the companies found that they had enough other opportunities. It was not completed.[390]

The report included as appendices a number of reports on British oil policy. Themes that came out of them were the need to develop the oil resources of the British Empire and to keep these under British control, and the significance of distribution and transport networks. The first of them was the 1916 Board of Trade Memorandum that was considered earlier.[391] The next gave figures for the oil production and consumption of the British Empire; these showed that the British Empire needed very substantial oil imports and that even India, which contributed most of the Imperial production from the Burmese oilfields, was a net importer. The figures are summarised in Table 4-5:

Table 4-5 British Empire oil output and demand, tons

	1913	1914	1915	1916	1917
Indian output	1,110,211	1,037,371	1,148,374	1,188,759	1,131,038
Rest of Empire output	243,621	381,890	474,553	587,502	937,902
Empire output	431,223	571,496	536,808	557,184	726,628
Indian demand	1,398,679	1,359,691	1,419,759	1,440,601	1,297,792
Rest of Empire demand	3,321,506	4,114,285	3,770,707	4,694,357	6,195,288
Empire demand	4,720,185	5,473,976	5,190,466	6,134,958	7,493,080
Empire imports	4,288,962	4,902,480	4,653,658	5,577,774	6,766,452
Persian output	243,621	381,890	474,553	587,502	937,902

Sources: POWE 33/13, Negotiations regarding petroleum policy of His Majesty's Government, Vol. 1 reports and proceedings of Petroleum Imperial Policy Committee, pp. 108-11 for demand. Some of its output figures were only estimates, so these have been

---

[388] Ibid., pp. 15-26.

[389] Jones, *State*, p. 212.

[390] Ferrier, *History*, p. 260.

[391] POWE 33/13. Appendix A, pp. 103-8.

taken from Marian Kent, *Oil and Empire: British Policy and Mesopotamian Oil 1900-1920* (London: MacMillan, 1976), Appendix VIII, pp. 203-4.

Appendix C comprised a memorandum on 'The Petroleum Position of the British Empire'[392], written by Harcourt for the Imperial War Conference, and the subsequent discussion on the subject by the Conference that took place on 22 July 1918.[393] Long chaired the meeting, which was attended by Cabinet ministers from Australia, Canada, Newfoundland, New Zealand and South Africa, including the Prime Ministers of all but South Africa. The Indian delegation included Montagu, but the only other British Cabinet Minister present was the Home Secretary, Sir George Cave. Various civil servants, military officers and advisers, including Cadman, attended. The main purpose of the meeting was for Harcourt to acquaint the representatives of the Dominions with the oil situation, especially the need to end Britain's reliance on imports from the USA. He stated in his memorandum that:

> every effort must be made now, and in the future, not only to develop existing oilfields in British territories or spheres of influence, but to acquire new fields that will be from the outset in British commercial hands and under British control. It seems clearly to be of first rate importance that no foreign influence under any guise, shall be permitted in British territories.[394]

An open ban on foreigners could lead to retaliation against British oil prospectors outside the Empire. A possible solution was to refuse to award licences for oil exploration, development and transport on Crown Land to foreigners. A pipeline to the coast would almost always have to pass over some Crown Land. A resolution was passed unanimously that:

> The Conference takes note of the Memorandum on the question of petroleum, and, having regard to the great and growing importance of petroleum and its products for naval, military, and industrial purposes, desires to commend the suggestions contained in the Memorandum to the serious consideration of the Governments concerned.[395]

---

[392] Ibid. Appendix C, 'The Petroleum Position of the British Empire', Viscount Harcourt, pp. 112-13.

[393] Ibid. Imperial War Conference, 14th Day, 22 July 1918.

[394] Ibid., p. 113.

[395] Ibid., p. 127.

A shortened version of Slade's July memorandum was included. The comments directly critical of RDS were removed, but he still claimed that foreigners were making £20,000,000 to £25,000,000 profit from supplying oil to Britain.[396] In reply to questions, he said that he was concerned that pre-war negotiations between Royal Dutch and Germany would be renewed after the war. Britain did not need to control all of RDS; its transport and distribution business would be enough. If feasible, he would have British control over it all, but it depended on the price; RDS would be more likely to participate in a purely transport and distribution company than to give up control of its oilfields.[397]

The opinions of Burmah, Mexican Eagle and APOC, the main British oil companies other than Shell, were given in Appendices E, F and G. Greenway of APOC argued that Standard (NJ) and RDS dominated the world oil market. This meant strategic risks and higher prices for Britain. He repeated Slade's claim, which Slade had insisted was not made on behalf of APOC, that these groups were taking annual profits of £20,000,000 to £25,000,000 out of the British Empire. Greenway once again put forward the idea of an all British distribution company comprised of APOC, Burmah and Mexican Eagle, completely excluding Shell. He claimed that such a group would have a good enough network to distribute what he claimed would be a combined output of 4,000,000 tons of oil per annum, potentially rising to 9,000,000 tons. The Empire would need 5,000,000 to 6,000,000 tons in peacetime. He claimed that this scheme was proposed in the national interest, whilst proposals from RDS was motivated by profit.[398]

J. T. Cargill, the Chairman of Burmah, thought that the first thing that had to be done was to ensure that all potential oilfields in the British Empire were thoroughly explored; Burmah had in the past been hampered by local regulations. British companies had been harmed by unfair price competition from foreign rivals; this should be banned. He emphasised the importance of refining and distribution facilities, and of an Imperial bunkering network.[399] On 8

---

[396] Ibid. Appendix D, Memorandum By Admiral Sir Edmond Slade on the Petroleum Situation in the British Empire, 9 October 1918, p. 127.

[397] Ibid., p. 44.

[398] Ibid. Appendix G, Memorandum by Mr C. Greenway on the National Oil Policy, 19 September 1918, pp. 141-44.

[399] Ibid. Appendix E, Memorandum by Mr J. T. Cargill, Chairman, Burmah Oil Company, 8 October 1918, pp. 134-38.

October 1918 he told the PIPCO that RDS and Standard (NJ)'s main advantages were their distribution and transport facilities, which would be very expensive to replicate. Pretyman was concerned that Greenway's scheme would result in a monopoly, which would be unpopular with the public. Cargill agreed but thought that this risk was less than that of not developing fully the oil resources of the Empire.[400] Lord Cowdray's submission concentrated mainly on the need to find new sources of oil in the Empire. It was more important that he helped to do so than that he held onto his share of Mexican Eagle. He believed that there was oil in Britain and intended to find it.[401] His efforts produced only a small field found at Hardstoft near Mansfield in Derbyshire in 1919. The ending of government support in 1922 curtailed drilling in Britain until the late 1930s.[402]

The final appendix was a memorandum written by Long in February 1919, arguing that there was a vital need for a permanent petroleum department. The importance of oil meant that it should not be attached to another department; Long argued that the Petroleum Executive could not have carried out its tasks as efficiently if this had been the case. He stated that:

> Such a Department must be in charge of a Minister of the Crown, who would be responsible to His Majesty's Government for petroleum policy.
>
> The need for a clearly defined and settled oil policy in daily becoming more apparent.[403]

The independent Petroleum Executive would be retained for a few years, but in 1922 it would be taken over by the Board of Trade as a cost cutting measure.[404]

---

[400] Ibid., pp. 46-47.

[401] Ibid. Appendix F, Memorandum by Lord Cowdray on the Importance of this Country and the Dominions Having Their Own Sources of Petroleum, 5 December 1918, pp. 138-40.

[402] Payton-Smith, *Oil*, p. 17.

[403] POWE 33/13. Appendix H, The Need for a Permanent Petroleum Department, W. H. Long, 27 February 1919, pp. 144-45.

[404] Payton-Smith, *Oil*, p. 40.

4.3 The Versailles Peace Conference

It did not take long after the signing of the Versailles Treaty for it to be heavily criticised; John Maynard Keynes, a member of the British delegation, published his famous attack soon after it was signed.[405] A modern view from Alan Sharp is that a 'fairer assessment would be that the settlement was not perfect, it contained the potential seeds of future conflict, but also the potential for a more hopeful future.'[406] The introduction to the book of papers presented at an international scholarly conference in 1994 argued that most academic specialists would agree; this view has not percolated down to the popular view. The Treaty did undergo revision in the 1920s; this process might have continued had the Great Depression not occurred. [407] Zara Steiner argues that popular histories and statesmen still criticise the Peace Treaty, but academic specialists agree that it was the best compromise that could have been achieved. It might have succeeded if the USA had joined the League of Nations, Britain and France had worked together, or the Germans had accepted it.[408] One popular history that tries to put forward a more positive view of Versailles is Margaret MacMillan's *Peacemakers*.[409] It rates four stars on Amazon.com; it is noticeable that most of the negative reviewers focus their criticism on its revisionism.[410]

4.4 The Paris Peace Conference: Aims and Structure

The most important countries at Versailles were Britain, France and the USA; the actions of each were driven by its leader; Lloyd George, Clemenceau and Wilson respectively. The focus on this trio became even stronger once the Council of

---

[405] J. M. Keynes, *The Economic Consequences of the Peace* (London,: 1919). vol. xi, p. 130.

[406] Sharp, *Versailles*, p. 213.

[407] Boemeke et al, *The Treaty of Versailles : A Reassessment after 75 Years*, pp. 3-4.

[408] Z. S. Steiner, *The Lights That Failed : European International History, 1919-1933* (Oxford: Oxford University Press, 2005), pp. 15-70; 'The Treaty of Versailles Revisited,' in *The Paris Peace Conference 1919 : Peace without Victory?*, ed. M. L. Dockrill, J. Fisher (Basingstoke: Palgrave, 2001), pp. 13-33.

[409] MacMillan, *Peacemakers*.

[410] "Reviews of Paris 1919: Six Months That Changed the World by Margaret Macmillan", Amazon <<http://www.amazon.com/Paris-1919-Months-Changed-World/dp/0375760520/ref=sr_1_3?s=books&ie=UTF8&qid=1281368112&sr=1-3>> (accessed 9 August 2010). These reviews are of the US edition. Other references to this book are to the UK edition.

Four was established in March 1919. The fourth member was Vittorio Orlando, the Italian Prime Minister, who absented himself for a period after Italian claims to Fiume were rejected in early April. The Council of Four replaced the Council of Ten, which had added the foreign ministers of these four countries and two Japanese representatives; it was too unwieldy.

The three had different objectives. Clemenceau wanted security for France against future aggression from Germany, which had a much larger population. Ideally he would have liked to restore France's 1814 frontier or more realistically to have established an independent Rhineland Republic. He settled for Allied occupation of the left bank for 15 years and a demilitarised zone on the right bank. Germany handed over its fleet and evacuated Belgium as part of the armistice and had lost its colonies during the war. This meant that Germany appeared to be less of a threat to Britain than it was to France; Lloyd George regarded it as a potential trading partner. The 1918 General Election did produce demands for large reparation payments; it left Lloyd George as the Liberal Prime Minister of a Conservative dominated Coalition Government. Wilson was motivated primarily by his desire to establish the League of Nations and by the principle of self-determination; this was not uniformly applied, with many non-European peoples being deemed to need some form of guidance. This took the form of mandates, which were allocated to Western countries over former German colonies and those parts of the Ottoman Empire populated by non-Turkish peoples. Different types of mandate reflected the assumption that Arabs were closer to being capable of self government than were Africans or Pacific Islanders, requiring less supervision and guidance.

4.5 Aims in the Middle East

Versailles and the subsequent treaties with the former Ottoman Empire created the current shape of the Middle East and are frequently blamed for the instability of the region. There was a general feeling that the Ottoman Empire should be stripped of its non-Turkish territories, restricting the Turks to Turkey. Anatolia was clearly Turkish, but there were disputes about whether or not Turkey should include Constantinople, the Straits, Smyrna (now Izmir), Kurdistan and Armenia. The dissolution of the Ottoman Empire was motivated by a desire to punish it for entering the war, a belief that it had ruled its non-Turkish peoples badly and the principle of self-determination. It would provide an example of the uneven application of self-determination; Arabs, unlike Europeans, were not deemed to be ready for full independence and would be guided and supervised by Western mandatory powers.

4.5.1 British Aims in the Middle East

In November 1918 the Foreign Office's Political Intelligence Department argued for a Turkish state, with safeguards for minorities in Anatolia and European Turkey; there was some doubt over the inclusion of Constantinople, but the Black Sea Straits should be under international control. The Dodecanese Islands should go to Greece via a friendly agreement with Italy. Armenia should be independent, but under the guidance of a power friendly to Britain. Existing trucial relations between Britain and Arab rulers should be maintained; it was hoped that a similar one would be signed with the Hedjaz. The development of Mesopotamia needed the aid of a major power for an unknown period; this should be Britain. Because Kurdistan controlled Mesopotamia's water supplies it had also to be under a British mandate. Syria would not need as much guidance as Mesopotamia but would need help from a Western power for a short time. Britain had fewer interests than in the rest of the Arab world so was happy for this to be somebody else provided that it was friendly to Britain. The main British interests in Syria were its relations with Mesopotamia and the Hedjaz, access to Damascus and Alexandretta and the route of a Mesopotamia to Haifa railway. Britain had a number of interests in Palestine; strategic ones were its proximity to the Sinai Peninsula, the Suez Canal and Aqaba and the route of the Mesopotamia to Haifa railway. If a single power were to oversee Palestine it should be Britain or possibly the USA. An international administration had some advantages over even a friendly foreign one, but it would not achieve Britain's political aims. These were to reconcile the different religious communities, prevent disorder and encourage Jewish immigration without antagonising the Arabs. [411]

---

[411] M. L. Dockrill et al, *British Documents on Foreign Affairs—Reports and Papers from the Foreign Office Confidential Print. Part II, from the First to the Second World War. Series I, the Paris Peace Conference of 1919* (Frederick, Md.: University Publications of America, 1988). vol. xi,

On 4 February 1919 Sir Hubert Llewellyn Smith, the Permanent Secretary at the Board of Trade and Head of the Economic Section of the British Delegation, sent Lloyd George a paper on British economic aims in the Alexandretta area. He argued that the issue of the pipeline across French territory would not create difficulties with the French, because the French would benefit from their minority stake in Mesopotamian oil. Negotiations with RDS must be completed before any proposals were made to the French. The issue of British participation in Algerian oilfields had also to be resolved.[412] Britain had always had far more trade than France in the Alexandretta area. British trade interests in Mesopotamia meant that Britain had to have free access to Alexandretta; it was the best port between Smyrna and Port Said and could become the main port for the Baghdad Railway and its connections. The oil pipeline from Mesopotamia to the Mediterranean was expected to terminate there.[413] The Admiralty disagreed on the destination of the pipeline; it must terminate at a British controlled port. Ideally no great power should control any of the Syrian or Anatolian ports. If France or Italy were granted concessions on the coast Britain should ask for Tripoli in modern Lebanon. It was not as good a port as Alexandretta, but suitable harbour facilities could be constructed. The cost would be justified by the oil pipeline and the need to counter any development of Beirut and Alexandretta into French naval bases.[414]

The Admiralty expanded on and slightly modified its views on a meeting on the Baghdad Railway held by the British Delegation in Paris on 15 February. Its principal interest was oil pipeline, which must be safe in wartime, completed quickly and terminate at a British controlled port. If Beirut and Alexandretta were French controlled the outlet should be Tripoli or Haifa; the latter was now preferred. The RAF agreed with these points; the pipeline was important to it as Egyptian oil was unsuitable for aircraft. The General Staff wanted a railway route from Baghdad to the Mediterranean that was as far from the frontier as possible. The Armed Forces argued that the border of British controlled territory

---

The Turkish Settlement and the Middle East; the Far East, Doc. 18: Memorandum Respecting the Settlement of Turkey and the Arabian Peninsula, pp. 51-72.

[412] NAS, Lothian Papers, GD40/1/37, 'Middle East - 11 Nov. 1917 - 30 April 1919', 1919. Llewellyn Smith to Prime Minister, 4 February 1919, pp. 31-32.

[413] Ibid. 'British Economic Desiderata in Alexandretta and its Hinterland', pp. 33-36.

[414] Ibid. Note by Admiralty, Tripoli (Syria), pp. 37-38.

must be significantly to the north of that proposed in the Sykes-Picot Agreement in order to allow a safe route for the pipeline and railway.[415]

Three days later the British Delegation produced a memorandum on the Middle East. It broadly agreed with the November memorandum, but argued that the new Turkish state needed foreign advisers. There were some caveats to the principle of self-determination. There was no clear majority in some areas, such as Thrace, Armenia and Constantinople. The historic treatment of the Armenians and the future potential for Jewish emigration meant that these groups deserved a greater say than was justified by their numbers. There were instances, such as the opening of the Straits and access to the Holy Places in Palestine, where global interests outweighed those of the local population. The Arabs should eventually decide if they wanted to join together in a single federations; poor communications plus economic, social and historic differences between the different Arab countries ruled this out for now. The independent Kingdom of the Hedjaz was now regarded as an independent state, since it had been recognised as an Allied belligerent by the Britain, France and Italy. Mesopotamia, including Mosul, and Syria were both clear and viable sub-divisions of the Arab lands. A single Kurdish state could not be established without violating the integrity of Persia; southern Kurdistan should become part of Mesopotamia because it controlled its water and needed its markets. Mesopotamia and Syria would both need the guidance and assistance of a mandatory power. The people of Lebanon, defined as far as possible as the Christian inhabited area, could choose whether to join Syria or to be independent. In the latter case they would need a mandatory power. In Palestine international interest in the Holy Places and the desires of potential Jewish immigrants out-weighed self-determination of the current inhabitants. A mandatory power should be appointed in order to ensure that the Arabs and Jews were treated equally and learnt to work together, and that people of all religions could access their holy places. No comment was made on who each mandate should be allocated to.[416]

---

[415] Dockrill et al, *BDFA*. vol. xi, Doc. 32: Minutes of Meeting respecting the Future of the Baghdad Railway, 15 February 1919, p. 130.

[416] Ibid. Doc. 34: Memorandum by the British Delegation, Paris, on British Policy in the Middle East, pp. 136-53..

In February 1919 the Intelligence Department of the Naval Staff produced a report on Middle Eastern oil, arguing that control of Mosul and its oil should be a British objective. The Naval Section of the British Delegation forwarded it to the Political, Economic and Military Sections of the Delegation, Sir Louis Mallet of the Foreign Office and Sir Arthur Hirtzel of the India Office on 20 March. [417] The report repeated Slade's view that it was vital that Britain to controlled its own oil supplies; Persia and Mesopotamia were the best available options. A detailed description of the prospects of finding oil in this region was given. Most of it had yet to be surveyed, but there were good reasons to think that it was a single oilfield, split by the Turkish-Persian frontier. There was thought to be oil close to Baghdad as well as around Mosul. As the Persian and Mesopotamian oilfield was a single structure it should be developed as such. In Persia British rights were well established; the situation in Iraq was less clear-cut. Political stability in Mesopotamia was required with a government that was friendly, or at least neutral, towards Britain. [418]

4.5.2 Britain, France and Mosul

The oil of Mosul was significant in determining the borders of Iraq and Syria, and the allocation of mandates. Historic British interests meant that it would have the Mesopotamian mandate. Britain wanted the oilfields to be part of its mandate territory. Protection of the oil pipeline and control of the Mediterranean port that it terminated at required Britain to have the mandate for Palestine. There were other reasons, including its proximity to Egypt, naval control of the eastern Mediterranean and promises previously made to Zionists in the Balfour Declaration. Britain's desire for Mosul's oil meant that Britain had to be the mandatory for both Mesopotamia and Palestine.

Clemenceau had little interest in colonies, although others in France were determined to obtain Syria. In December 1918 he came to London. During his visit he had a private conversation with Lloyd George; no official record was kept, but Lloyd George described the conversation to Hankey, who wrote the following in his diary:

---

[417] FO 608/97/15, 'Mines and Minerals: Oilfields of Persia and Mesopotamia', 1919.
[418] Ibid.

> All went well and they all had a magnificent reception. Afterwards I saw LLG at 10 Downing St. He said Clemenceau had been really affected by his welcome. LLG had seized the opportunity to demand first Mosul and then Jerusalem [Hankey originally wrote Palestine and Mesopotamia but scored it out] in the peace terms. Clemenceau, in his malleable state, had agreed, but had said "But Pichon will make difficulties about Mosul.[419]

Lloyd George's version, given in his memoirs, was similar, except that he said that he made his requests in reply to a specific question from Clemenceau. Britain wanted at least two changes to Sykes-Picot:

> Deprived of the grain and oil supplies of [Mosul], Irak would have been seriously crippled financially and economically. The second was the partition of Palestine into three separate areas under different administrations.

> When Clemenceau came to London after the War I drove with him to the French Embassy through cheering crowds who acclaimed him with enthusiasm. After we reached the Embassy he asked me what it was I specially wanted from the French. I instantly replied that I wanted Mosul attached to Irak, and Palestine from Dan to Beersheba under British control. Without any hesitation he agreed. Although that agreement was not reduced into writing, he adhered to it honourably in subsequent negotiations.[420]

The British claimed that these offers came without conditions. Clemenceau said that France needed something in compensation for its concessions. He stated at the Council of Four meeting on 21 May 1919 that Britain had broken various promises. In Autumn 1918 he had seen how Britain was acting in Syria and asked Lloyd George what Britain wanted. He was told Mosul and Palestine. Relations had not improved. The British had not acted on a promise to help Clemenceau with Faisal, the leader of the Arab delegation to Paris, who was arguing in favour of independent Arab Emirates. Clemenceau had given up more Syrian territory for a British railway. Britain would not discuss the withdrawal of their troops from Syria until its borders had been set. The day before a French mandate over Anatolia had been proposed, but now Lloyd George wanted to give it to the USA. Clemenceau blamed Curzon for this. Clemenceau had to consider French public opinion. France had the largest financial involvement of any country in Turkey,

---

[419] HNKY 1/5. 4 December 1918. Stephen Pichon was the French Foreign Minister.

[420] D. Lloyd George, *The Truth About the Peace Treaties.*, 2 vols. (London: Victor Gollancz, 1938). vol. ii, p. 1038.

and should not be excluded because of the Muslim or Italian issues. Lloyd George said that he had agreed to give Syria to France in return for Mosul; Clemenceau replied that an agreement to give Syria to France had already been signed. Lloyd George responded that it had been accepted in London that France should have Syria, but Mosul should be part of Mesopotamia; it was part of the same watershed. The railway was needed to transport Mesopotamian oil, in which France had a half share, so its construction was in French interests. Lloyd George claimed that there had been no mention of French interest in Asia Minor until the day before.[421]

In mid May 1919 it had been provisionally decided that the USA would receive the mandates for Constantinople, Greece that for Smyrna, France south Anatolia and Italy north Anatolia. Lloyd George then changed his mind and decided that, apart from Smyrna going to Greece, the Turkish lands should not be divided up. He was influenced by warnings from Montagu about the impact on Muslim sentiment in India if the Caliphate lost Constantinople and Balfour's opinion that the Turks were entitled to have a single state.[422] This change of heart was one of the British actions that provoked Clemenceau's anger at the 21 May meeting of the Council of Four.

Christopher Andrews and A. S. Kanya-Forstner say that evidence in French archives on this point is limited; what there is tends to support the French position that Mosul and Palestine were given up in return for British acceptance of the French claim to the remainder of Syria. André Tardieu, one of Clemenceau's chief aides, claimed that the British had promised to support the French position on the Rhineland.[423] Edward Fitzgerald notes that Clemenceau did not give up all of Mosul's oil; Sykes-Picot gave France only about half the areas of oil seepage, and it was likely to be developed by a British firm. Etienne Clémentel, the French trade and industry minister, was arguing in favour of continuing Allied control of raw materials in peace time. US opposition prevented this happening, but Clemenceau supported him at the time. Bérenger, the French oil expert, thought that the solution to France's oil problems was co-

---

[421] "FRUS". vol. v, pp. 760-64.

[422] Dockrill, Goold, *Peace*, pp. 197-99.

[423] C. M. Andrews, A. S. Kanya-Forstner, 'The French Colonial Party and French Colonial War Aims, 1914-1918', *Historical Journal* 17, no. 1 (1974), p. 104.

operation with Britain, whose oil companies possessed expertise that France's small ones did not.[424] Alan Sharp argues that Clemenceau must have wanted something in return, suggesting that this was British support over the Rhineland.[425] Paul Helmreich quotes Victor Berard as telling the French Senate in June 1920 that this was part of the reason. Helmreich comments that Clemenceau later claimed that Mosul was given up in return of guarantees that other French aims in the Middle East would be achieved.[426] Michael Dockrill and Douglas Goold suggest that the British promised France the rest of the territory granted to it by Sykes-Picot, half of Mosul's oil and support in the event of an unprovoked German attack on France.[427] Britain did offer France a guarantee against German attack. At the last minute Lloyd George made it conditional on Congress approving a similar US offer, which it did not.[428]

4.6 Chapter Summary.

The war showed the need for oil; it was not certain that Britain would be in as good a situation in a later conflict unless it took action to strengthen its position. The Allies depended on US supplies and Britain could not guarantee that these would be available in the future. Even if the USA remained friendly it might be unable to provide enough oil since its own demand was rising, and it was feared that its supply would shortly peak. Action had to be taken to secure oil reserves for Britain.

One possible method of guaranteeing Britain's oil supplies was to establish a large British controlled oil company. Many mistrusted RDS because it was 60 per cent foreign owned. Some wanted to re-organise it in order to provide a British majority, whilst others, such as Slade, wanted to exclude it. RDS's critics never explained why a global oil company would want to act against the interests of Britain, whose navy controlled the oceans and was the world's largest consumer of oil. Shell, the British part of the group supported the Allies because it was a

---

[424] Fitzgerald, 'France's', pp. 723-25.

[425] Sharp, *Versailles*, pp. 189-90.

[426] P. C. Helmreich, *From Paris to Sèvres : The Partition of the Ottoman Empire at the Peace Conference of 1919-1920* (Columbus, OH: Ohio State University Press, 1974), p. 17.

[427] Dockrill, Goold, *Peace*, p. 145.

[428] Sharp, *Versailles*, pp. 119-20.

British company. Royal Dutch, its Dutch partner, agreed because it was in its interests to do so. The wartime attempts to form a British national oil company failed, but the idea would be resurrected in the early 1920s. The war had shown the importance of oil; it was starting to influence international relations. Policy makers had to decide whether it was to better to secure future supplies by control of companies or of oil bearing territories. The most obvious available oil territory was Mosul.

Britain, France and Italy all wanted their own sources of supply. The USA, worried that its oil might run out, did not want to be cut out of overseas oilfields. This affected British relations with France, Italy and the USA and strategy towards the Middle East. Britain wanted Mosul and its oil. France agreed to this request but in return expected British support elsewhere, notably in its efforts to prevent a future threat from Germany and in its aims in Syria. The Allies had united to defeat the Central Powers but now had different objectives, which led to disputes at Versailles. France did not receive the support that it expected from Britain, which now regarded Germany more as a trading partner than as a potential enemy. It was not yet realised that the control of oil bearing territory was more important than the nationality of the companies that exploited it. This damaged Anglo-American relations since it made the US oil companies fear that they were being excluded from the Middle East.

5 Oil and the Middle East in Allied Diplomacy, 1919-22

The Treaty of Versailles with Germany was signed on 28 June 1919, but separate treaties had to be negotiated with the other Central Powers. The Paris Peace Conference continued until January 1920 and was followed by other conferences. The San Remo Conference of April 1920 determined the terms of the Treaty of Sèvres that was signed with the Ottoman Empire on 20 August 1920. This did not produce a lasting settlement and had to be re-negotiated at Lausanne in 1923 following Turkey's victory in the Greco-Turkish War. Throughout the negotiations it was clear that Britain would end up with a mandate over Iraq. The question was whether Mosul, and its oil, would be included. In December 1918 Clemenceau had agreed with Lloyd George that Britain could have Mosul. Disagreement over what France expected in return delayed the signing of an Anglo-French oil agreement. Two were signed and cancelled before a third was ratified. The similarities between them show that they were victims of other disputes rather than being cancelled because of disputes over oil. The Treaty of Sèvres appeared to have given Britain its objectives, but it could not be enforced. The San Remo Agreement angered the Americans because it seemed to exclude them from Middle Eastern oil. Turkey revived under General Mustafa Kemal and British relations with France and Italy worsened. A revolt in Iraq might have led to Britain leaving but for the oil.

5.1 The Long-Bérenger Agreement

On 8 April 1919 Walter Long and Henry Bérenger, the politicians responsible for oil in Britain and France respectively, signed an Anglo-French oil agreement. In Britain it created controversy between the Foreign Office and the Petroleum Executive and Lloyd George cancelled it. Curzon was informed by telephone on 13 June that Lloyd George had only recently found out about the agreement, which Clemenceau had also not known about, and now wanted to know the extent of the talks. [429] Curzon said that they started with a letter of 6 January

---

[429] E. L. Woodward et al, eds, *Documents on British Foreign Policy, 1919-1939. First Series*, 27 vols. (London: H.M.S.O., 1946-86). No. 684, Letter from Sir G. Clerk to Mr Kerr (Paris), 17 June 1919, p. 1092.

from the French Ambassador to the Foreign Office proposing an Anglo-French oil agreement. Curzon thought that oil should not be discussed until the peace conferences had resolved all the territorial issues. A meeting took place at the Admiralty on 15 January. Ernest Weakley, representing the Foreign Office, argued Curzon's view. The meeting decided that Britain should indicate its willingness to co-operate with France before France obtained US help with oil and the Peace Conference forced Britain into adopting such a policy.

On 1 February another French note indicated that talks between Bérenger and Cadman had been positive. A British Inter-Departmental Conference in Paris discussed the issue. Two days later Cadman asked Balfour's permission to inform Bérenger that Britain was willing to offer France 20 to 30 per cent of the TPC in return for their facilitation of the construction of a pipeline to the Mediterranean and British access to Algerian oil development. Balfour initialled a minute written by Sir Louis Mallet of the Foreign Office Paris delegation making this request. On 6 February Curzon asked Balfour to discover the nature of Cadman's discussions with Bérenger and argued against any talks on an Anglo-French oil agreement. A fortnight later Curzon sent Balfour a statement setting out the differences between the views of the Foreign Office and the Petroleum Executive. On 20 February Cadman told Weakley that he had not given the French any details during their talks. The next day Curzon reiterated to Balfour his objections to the oil agreement.

The Foreign Office heard no more until 15 March when it received a copy of a provisional agreement between Long and Bérenger. Two days later a despatch from Balfour said that it was inadvisable to continue negotiations until the territorial settlement was clearer. This was subject to consultation with Cadman, and Bérenger being informed that Britain would allow France a stake in the TPC. On 1 and 11 April Sir George Clerk, Curzon's private secretary, received private letters from Charles Tufton of the Foreign Office Paris delegation. The first implied that Mallet thought that the Cabinet and the relevant departments in London were being consulted over discussions. The second included a revised draft agreement. Curzon was unclear about the authorisation of this and called a meeting of the Inter-Departmental Committee on Eastern Affairs. Long said that Balfour had given approval in Paris. The Long- Bérenger Agreement was part of the more significant negotiations between the British Government and RDS. The meeting concluded that the Government should approve the Long-Bérenger Agreement subject to it being accepted by the Foreign Office and the RDS agreement by the War Cabinet.[430]

Long gave his version in November in a memorandum urging that the decision to cancel the oil agreement should be reconsidered. His timetable of events was similar, except that there had been a meeting between Bérenger, Cadman and other oil experts on 17 December 1918, before the French Ambassador wrote to the Foreign Office; his interpretation was different. He stated that the Foreign Office had been kept fully informed of events, had been represented at meetings to discuss the issue and had been invited to comment on drafts. Mallet, Tufton and Malkin of the Foreign Office had attended a meeting in Paris on 1 February 1919. It had agreed that the French should have a 25 per cent stake in Mesopotamian oil. Hirtzel of the Indian Office had suggested that the Arabs should receive a share. Mallet had met Cadman before writing his memorandum of 3 February that set out the case for co-operation with France and was initialled by Balfour. Cadman suggested that the Foreign Office should carry out the negotiations. Mallet replied that Cadman should do so because of their technical nature; Cadman was authorised to offer the French up to 30 per cent. The draft agreement was shown to the Foreign Office, India Office, Colonial Office, Board of Trade and Admiralty. The first two suggested changes that were accepted by France. Long argued that this showed that any lack of communication was not the fault of the Petroleum Executive. He was kept fully informed and attended most meeting with French Ministers; there was no doubt that they were authorised by their Prime Minister and government to act for France. Long had been given full authority over all oil issues by the Cabinet. He insisted that other departments be kept fully informed and that their consent be obtained prior to the drawing up of any agreements.[431]

The problem was a lack of communication between the Foreign Office delegates in Paris and the Foreign Office in London. Cadman consulted closely with the former, and they were influenced by him. The British in Paris thought that the oil issue should be resolved before the mandates were allocated. The Foreign

---

[430] Ibid. Enclosure in No. 684, The Long-Berenger Oil Agreement, pp. 1093-95.

[431] CAB 24/92, C.P. 59 'Oil Supplies', W. Long, 4 November 1919.

Office in London wanted to leave the oil problem until after the mandates had been dealt. The situation was compounded by slow communications; correspondence took too long to get first from Paris to London and then to reach the senior men at the Foreign Office. Weakley received documents from Cadman on 6 February and forwarded them immediately to Curzon, who did not receive them until 17 February.[432]

The agreement that was signed by Long and Bérenger on 8 April said that:

> France and Great Britain...have...agreed on the basis of a common policy to be followed in the near East and in the countries adjacent to the Mediterranean for the exploitation of various oilfields.

> The principles of this policy are those of cordial co-operation and reciprocity in all those countries where the oil interests of the two nations can usefully unite.[433]

It stated that, if Britain received the Mesopotamian mandate, it would endeavour to obtain for the TPC the rights that it had received from the Ottoman government in 1914. The TPC would be British controlled; its capital would be divided 70 per cent British, 20 per cent French and 10 per cent the Mesopotamian government. Should the latter not want to take part its stake would be divided evenly between Britain and France. The French government would do everything in its power to enable the construction of two oil pipelines from Mesopotamia and Persia to a port or ports on the Mediterranean and of the necessary facilities at the ports. The two countries would together choose the routes of the pipelines and the ports to be used. They would act together in Romania. Nationals of both were given access to oil concessions in the other's colonies, subject to compliance with local laws. Provision was made for the agreement to be extended to apply in Galicia and Russia.[434] The agreement between the British government and RDS allocated the British share as RDS 34 per cent, APOC 34 per cent and the government 2 per cent; it provided for others to receive 30 per cent.

---

[432] Kent, *Oil*, pp. 141-42.

[433] Woodward et al, eds, *DBFP*. vol. iv, p. 1089.

[434] Ibid., pp. 1090-92.

The agreement was cancelled by Lloyd George on 21 May in a letter to Clemenceau. It confirmed a statement made by the Prime Minister at the meeting of the Council of Four held earlier that day that:

> as you regard the British proposal for railway and pipe-line for the Mosul area to Tripoli as a departure from the Agreement which we entered into in London in December last, I do not propose to proceed further with the proposed arrangement which I hereby withdraw.[435]

At the meeting Lloyd George admitted that half the oil of Mesopotamia belonged to France, but he tore up an agreement splitting it 70 per cent to Britain, 30 per cent to France. This suggests that it was not the oil agreement itself that he objected to and that he cancelled it for other reasons.

Lloyd George was concerned that the oil agreement was signed while he was negotiating with France over the borders of Syria. The former affected the latter, so he should have been informed of the oil agreement, which he found out about only by chance. He thought that the oil should not be discussed until the boundaries had been set; Britain access to the Mediterranean had to be settled before it could negotiate about oil. He also believed that policy considerations should not be confused by negotiations that involved private oil companies.[436]

As well as arguments with France over Syria, the oil agreement had the potential to affect Anglo-American relations. On 13 May Leland Summers of the American Commission to Negotiate Peace had written to Llewellyn Smith asking for information about a rumoured Anglo-French oil agreement; he was particularly interested in Romania.[437] He was informed that the plans for co-operation had ended, or at least been suspended. They were not intended in any way to keep the USA out of Romania.[438]

The Cabinet were not told of the agreement or its cancellation until 20 August. It decided that Curzon should discuss the future of Turkey and of Syria with

---

[435] Ibid. Note 2, p. 1092.

[436] Ibid. No. 689, Mr Davies to Earl Curzon, 11 July 1919, p. 1100.

[437] Ibid. Note 1, p. 1095.

[438] Ibid. No. 686, Sir H. Llewellyn Smith to Mr Summers, 25 June 1919, pp. 1098-99.

Balfour and that the War Office should look at and report on the significance of the oasis of Tadmor (Palmyra) to the Mosul to Mediterranean railway and pipeline.[439] Curzon wrote to Balfour on the same day. There had been three Cabinet meetings over the previous 30 hours. He noted that the ministers keenest on British expansion were the radicals such as Lloyd George, Montagu and Barnes, whilst Conservatives like Milner, Chamberlain and himself wanted to limit British involvement;[440] Montagu had complained to Balfour in 1918 that Curzon could always find reasons to expand the British Empire.[441] Curzon told Balfour that:

> I am so convinced that Palestine will be a rankling thorn in the flesh of whoever is charged with its Mandate that I would withdraw from this responsibility while we yet can...The Prime Minister clings to Palestine for its sentimental and traditional value...Others (of whom you would probably be one) think that, irksome as will be the burden, we cannot now refuse it without incensing the Zionist world...

> As a "sine qua non" of course Mesopotamia, including Mosul, must be entrusted to us. A boundary must be found between Syria and Mesopotamia; and at this point the Prime Minister attached and importance, which I should be inclined to think excessive, to the necessity of having a railway and a pipeline exclusively from Mesopotamia to a Mediterranean port.[442]

The cancellation of the Long-Bérenger Agreement did not end plans for an Anglo-French oil agreement. Britain and France both needed Mosul's oil. France needed oil industry expertise that its companies did not possess. Britain required a railway and a pipeline from the oilfields, including the Persian ones, to a port on the Mediterranean. The French had to agree to either the use of French territory or to British mandates including a suitable route and pipeline. France needed British support in Europe and may have tried to use the oil to gain this, but it was in a weak bargaining position. Sykes-Picot gave it only half the potential oilfields. It had no large oil company to exploit them. France required British or American help over oil, and it was Britain that cancelled the oil agreement. Signing such a deal before the treaties were signed and mandates allocated

---

[439] CAB 23/12, 'War Cabinet Papers 616-35', 15 August - 27 October 1919. 20 August 1919, War Cabinet 619.

[440] BL, Balfour Papers, MSS. 49734: vol. lii 'Lord Curzon, 1915-23'. Curzon to Balfour, 20 August 1919, ff. 154-58.

[441] Balfour Papers Mss. 49709. Montagu to Balfour, f. 304.

[442] Balfour Papers Mss. 49734. f. 158.

would have antagonised the Americans. Lloyd George objected to signing an oil agreement before territorial questions were settled, not to the idea of having one.

5.2 Greenwood-Bérenger Agreement

Long wanted an Anglo-French oil agreement. He concluded his November memorandum by stating that:

> I would earnestly beg the Cabinet to re-consider the matter in the light of the facts disclosed in this Memorandum, which show how greatly we are committed to the French Government, and also in face of the great overwhelming fact that oil is becoming every day more vital to our national life; and that if we lose the opportunities which have grown out of the war, we shall probably never be able to regain our position, and shall undoubtedly suffer once again from a shortness of supplies which will greatly hamper our national action.[443]

5.2.1 Anglo-French Middle Eastern Disputes

The arguments at the 21 May meeting of the Council of Four meant Britain continued to occupy Syria. A commission that was to be sent to the Middle East to report upon the wishes of the locals became a solely US one, the King-Crane Commission. In July it reported that a French mandate over Syria would result in a war between France and the Arabs. The Arabs wanted the USA with Britain as second choice. They opposed separating Syria and Palestine and Zionist plans and Jewish immigration.[444] The Americans were favoured by the Mesopotamians; there was no second choice, but the Commission thought that Britain might be acceptable despite complaints about its military occupation. Britain was the best qualified candidate. The risk that the mandatory power might exploit Mesopotamia's agriculture, oil and other resources had to be guarded against, as did the possibility of Indian immigration; the locals feared this as threat to their culture.[445] On 15 September Lloyd George handed the leaders of the American, French, Italian and Japanese delegations an aide-memoire setting out British

---

[443] CAB 24/92 C.P. 59, Long, p. 2.

[444] "FRUS". vol. xii, Mr C. R. Crane and Mr H. C. King to the Commission to Negotiate Peace, 10 July 1918. pp. 749-50.

[445] Ibid. pp. 799-802.

plans to withdraw from Syria by 1 November. British troops would then occupy Mesopotamia, including Mosul, and Palestine, defined by its ancient borders. In accordance with the principles of Sykes-Picot, France should permit the Arab State to give Britain the right to build a railway and an oil pipeline from Mesopotamia to Haifa. The British were prepared to submit any dispute over the route to an arbitrator appointed by Wilson. Clemenceau said that France would replace the British troops, but would not comment on the remainder of the aide-memoire. The Syrian question had to be considered along with the fate of the rest of Turkey.[446]

Earlier in September Balfour had pointed out some inconsistencies in the British position. Britain talked as if oil in its sphere belonged to it, but all nations were supposed to be treated equally in mandated territories. France had agreed to give Britain Mosul. Britain was now asking that France must give it territory to construct a British railway and pipeline in order to exploit Mesopotamia's oil and wheat. The French would argue that there should be no problem in sending its products along a partly French railway to an international port in French territory or even by sea via the Suez Canal. Britain should not have given France Mosul in Sykes-Picot. It did because Kitchener did not want Britain's sphere to border Russian territory. These factors had to be considered when negotiating with the French.[447]

5.2.2 Syria and France

French objectives in Syria conflicted with the goals of the Arab nationalists. In September 1915 Admiral Wemyss visited Cairo. Senior British officials told him that possession of Homs, Hama, Damascus and Aleppo, the four largest cities in modern Syria, was vital to the Arabs, whose support Britain needed. Agreeing to

---

[446] Ibid. vol. viii, Meeting of Council of Heads of Delegations, 15 September 1919, pp. 205-8, 216-17.

[447] Woodward et al, eds, *DBFP*. No. 165, Memorandum by Mr Balfour (Paris), 9 September 1919, pp. 373-74.

this would require substantial concessions by the French, who would have to be compensated elsewhere.[448]

By the end of the war, a British army under General Allenby had conquered Palestine and Syria. Allenby's forces included an Arab army, commanded by Faisal, the eldest son of Sharif Hussein of Mecca, who was helped by British advisers, most famously Colonel T. E. Lawrence. In November 1918 Lawrence wrote a series of anonymous articles in *The Times*, exaggerating the contribution of the Arab army to the campaign. He claimed that the Arabs had been the first Allied troops to enter Damascus. It had been planned that they would be the only ones to enter the city, but the Australian Light Horse moved through it in an attempt to cut off the retreating Ottomans; they were welcomed by the locals, who had already raised the Arab flag.[449] Syria was supposed to become French territory but was occupied by the British who allowed Faisal to administer it. He had to delegate the work to others since he spent much of 1919 at the Paris Peace Conference. He agreed with Clemenceau that he would become King of Syria with France exercising a loose trusteeship. This was unacceptable to the Arab nationalists who wanted full independence. Faisal followed rather than led his supporters. In March 1920 the Syrian National Congress proclaimed him as King of Syria. A month later France was allocated the mandate over Syria at San Remo. Alexandre Millerand had replaced Clemenceau as French Prime Minister in January. His government wanted to govern Syria in its own way, which had no place for the Arab nationalists. A short war followed, resulting in defeat for the Arabs. On 28 July 1920 Faisal went into exile. Britain managed to offend both the French, by initially supporting Faisal and the Arab nationalists, and Faisal and the Arab nationalists, by withdrawing its support.[450]

5.2.3 Anglo-French Rapprochement

In December 1919 the British and French met in an effort to settle their differences in the Middle East. Wilson had been incapacitated by a stroke since

---

[448] CC, Wemyss Papers, WMYS 3/1, 'Gallipoli Campaign'. Report dated Sat. 30 October 1915, P. and O. Karmala. Month unclear on original, but Wemyss was not serving in the Mediterranean in January, the only other month of 1915 in which the 30th was a Saturday.

[449] Fromkin, *Peace*, pp. 332-42.

[450] Ibid., pp. 435-46.

October. In November the US Senate had voted against ratifying the Treaty of Versailles. On 12 December Berthelot sent a note to Curzon, who had replaced Balfour as Foreign Secretary in October. Uncertainty over the future involvement of the USA in resolving European and Eastern issues had led Lloyd George and Clemenceau to decide that Britain and France should settle their differences. A meeting the day before had shown that this could be achieved with some compromises on both sides.[451] The French were prepared to allow passage of the British railway across their territory from Haifa to Damascus and Mosul. In return for Mosul they wanted half of the oil of Mesopotamia and Kurdistan.[452] E. G. Forbes Adam and Robert Vansittart of the Foreign Office, commenting on Berthelot's memorandum, noted that this was a significant increase from the 20 or 25 per cent given to France by the Long-Bérenger Agreement. The French now appeared to want a share of the oil rather than a stake in the operating company. Adam and Vansittart were inclined to be generous to France for political reasons; the success of the League of Nations and British policy depended on Anglo-French friendship. They did not feel able to comment on the oil requirements of the two countries but suggested that adjustments of Middle Eastern frontiers in favour of France might be made if British needs made it impossible to give France half the oil. This would make it impossible to have the railway and pipeline entirely in British territory or to maintain Britain's monopoly of political influence in the Arabian Peninsula.[453]

The French position on oil was given in a note prepared by Bérenger for Clemenceau in early December.[454] According to a British summary of it written by Weakley, it began by detailing the major efforts undertaken by Britain to obtain control of oil and to rid itself of reliance on American oil. Bérenger thought that British policy in the Caucasus, India, Persia and Mesopotamia was mainly based on oil rather than territorial considerations. France had a great

---

[451] Dockrill et al, *BDFA*. Doc. 41: French Note and Memoranda by the British Peace Delegation regarding Turkish Settlement. December 1919, p. 212.

[452] Ibid. p. 217.

[453] Ibid. Doc. 43: Second part of M. Berthelot's note of 12 December regarding Arab countries, with comments of the Political Section of the British Peace Delegation, E. G. Forbes Adam, Robert Vansittart, 18 December 1919, pp. 233-34.

[454] According to the editors of DBFP, no copy of this document can be found in the Foreign Office archives. They assume that it is the note communicated by Berthelot to Curzon on 11 December 1919.Woodward et al, eds, *DBFP*. vol. iv, note 1, p. 1111. The following comments are based on a British summary of it prepared by Weakley.

need for oil and should insist on obtaining a fair share of the oil of south Russia, Mesopotamia, especially at Mosul and Kirkuk, Romania and Persia. Bérenger appeared to Weakley to be arguing for a restoration of the Long-Bérenger Agreement. Weakley wrote that there could be no question of allowing France a share of Persian oil. Sir Hamar Greenwood, who had recently succeeded Long as Minister in Charge of Petroleum Affairs, suggested reviving Long-Bérenger. He thought that the French share might be 18 per cent rather than 20 per cent. Weakley thought that the French would ask for up to half. He regarded Long-Bérenger as being a fair deal.[455] On 21 December Greenwood and Bérenger signed an agreement very similar to the Long-Bérenger. It included two railways instead of one; there were still two pipelines.[456] A series of Anglo-French meetings in late December and January decided to abandon the concept of mandates in Anatolia; it would remain officially Turkish with Italian and French spheres of influence. The Greeks would receive territory in Thrace and would control Smyrna for five years after when its sovereignty would be determined by a plebiscite; the Greeks had been authorised by the Council of Four to land troops at Smyrna in May. The Straits would be under international administration.[457]

5.3 The San Remo Agreement

The Greenwood-Bérenger Agreement quickly ran into problems. On 23 January 1920 a Conference of Ministers decided that the profits from Mesopotamian should go to the State rather than to private companies. The only ministers present were Lloyd George, Bonar Law, Churchill and Montagu; Greenwood, the Minister in Charge of Petroleum, and Long, his predecessor, were absent. Nobody from the Petroleum Executive gave evidence.[458] The decision was contrary to the agreement signed with RDS that gave it 50 per cent of the TPC. The French then demanded 50 per cent of the oil as they had accepted 25 per

---

[455] Ibid. No. 703, Memorandum by Mr Weakley on M. Berenger's note to M. Clemenceau relative to petroleum, 13 December 1919, pp. 1111-13.

[456] Ibid. No. 705, Memorandum of Agreement between Sir Hamar Greenwood, His Majesty's Minister in Charge of Petroleum Affairs, and Senator Henry Berenger, Commissioner-General of Petroleum Products in France, pp. 1114-17.

[457] Dockrill, Goold, *Peace*, pp. 204-7; Sharp, *Versailles*, pp. 181-82.

[458] CAB 23/37, Conclusions of a Conference of Ministers: Oil Situation in Mesopotamia, 23 January 1920.

cent only because of the RDS stake.[459] On 18 March Long urged that the agreements made with RDS and the French Government should be ratified. He was very worried about future oil supplies, believing that it was vital to obtain British control over Shell. This would diversify British supplies, reducing the dependence on the USA. RDS might now come to an agreement with the big US oil companies or the French.[460] Robert Horne, the President of the Board of Trade, backed Long's views in a memorandum of 16 April.[461] Further support came six days later from Frederick Kellaway, who had recently succeeded Greenwood as Minister in Charge of Petroleum. The Petroleum Executive thought that it would be a mistake to exclude private companies from the venture; development of the oilfields was a risky and expensive enterprise that required expertise not possessed by the government. France was being offered 25 per cent of the oil on the grounds that it was inheriting Deutsche Bank's stake in TPC. Excluding RDS would suggest that the pre-war TPC concession was invalid; France would then expect 50 per cent and other oil companies would be reluctant to deal with the British Government.[462]

Four days before Kellaway produced his memorandum, Lloyd George told Millerand that he was happy to deal with the French government but not with the oil companies. They were unpopular; giving them Mesopotamian oil would create problems with Parliament. Britain was willing to give France 25 per cent of the oil on the same terms as Britain received its oil. meaning after charging the costs of administration of Mosul. He invited Millerand to submit the French oil proposals in writing.[463] Marian Kent describes this 'giving the Frenchman a face-saving way out'[464] The San Remo Agreement, sometimes called the Cadman-Berthelot Agreement, was being negotiated and was signed by the Prime Ministers on 18 April. This was very similar to the previous agreements; the French would now receive 25 per cent of the oil if the British Government developed it, or a 25 per cent stake in a private company formed to carry out

---

[459] Kent, *Oil*.

[460] CAB 24/101, C.P. 903 'Oil Supplies', W. H. Long, 18 March 1920.

[461] CAB 24/101, C.P. 1085 'Mesopotamian Oilfields', R. S. Horne, 16 April 1920.

[462] CAB 24/101, C.P. 1118 'Mesopotamian Oilfields', F. Kellaway, 22 April 1920.

[463] Woodward et al, eds, *DBFP*. No. 2, Notes of a Conversation between the Prime Minister and M. Millerand, 18 April 1920, pp. 9-10.

[464] Kent, *Oil*, p. 154.

the work. Native interests would be allowed up to 20 per cent; half of the first 10 per cent would come from the French share and the balance from all pro-rata to their stakes. The British Government would support any agreement France made to buy up to 25 per cent of any of APOC's Persian oil sent through French mandated territory by pipeline.[465] The agreement was published on 24 July 1920. It was attacked by the Americans who were angry at being excluded from the Mosul oilfields.[466]

5.4 Treaty of Sèvres

The April 18 meeting between Lloyd George and Millerand was part of the San Remo Conference between the Allies, lasting from 18 to 26 April. It followed on from the First London Conference, which ran from 12 February to 10 April. The USA did not attend London and participated only as an observer at San Remo. These determined the terms that would be offered to the Ottoman Empire, with the decisions being taken by Britain and France.[467] They were largely those that the two countries had discussed at their meeting in December and January. Britain would have the mandates for Mesopotamia and Palestine, and France those for Syria and Lebanon. The League of Nations, which was supposed to allocate mandates, would be left to agree to what had already been decided.[468] The Greeks would receive territory in Thrace and would control Smyrna for five years; a plebiscite on its future would then be held. Anatolia and Constantinople remained Turkish, but the Straits would be controlled by an international commission. Another commission would ensure close supervision of Turkey's finances by Britain, France and Italy. Partition of Anatolia would have angered the Americans and broken the Covenant of the League of Nations, so the three agreed that they would prioritise French interests in Cilicia and Italian ones in Adalia. The Armenians received independence but no help to maintain it. The Allies occupied Constantinople in March in order to force Turkish acceptance of the Treaty. Turkey signed it on 10 August. It was destined not to last. The Allies

---

[465] PP, *Miscellaneous. No. 11 (1920). Memorandum of Agreement between M. Philippe Berthelot, Directeur Des Affaires Politiques Et Commerciales Au Ministère Des Affaires Étrangères, and Professor Sir John Cadman, K.C.M.G., Director in Charge of His Majesty's Petroleum Department*, HMSO 1920 [Cmd. 675].

[466] Kent, *Oil*, p. 155.

[467] Sharp, *Versailles*, pp. 194-95.

[468] Dockrill, Goold, *Peace*, pp. 174-75.

lacked the will and resources to enforce an old style treaty that ignored Arab and Turkish nationalism.[469]

5.5 Iraq

In August 1919 Field Marshal Sir Henry Wilson, the CIGS, told Churchill, then the War Secretary, that Britain's strategic position had changed since 1914. There would be no threat of a European war or an invasion of Britain for years. The potential risks faced in Egypt, Iraq and India were far higher than any threats to the Empire before 1914. He feared that a crisis in one of these, or Ireland, might spread to the others. He wanted an expeditionary force to be available to be sent to the Empire.[470] In November Churchill circulated four papers on Iraq to the Cabinet. The General Staff argued that costs could be saved by reducing the Iraqi garrison if Britain withdrew from either Mosul or Northern Persia. It opposed the first option because the potential oil would justify the cost, both human and financial, of obtaining control of Iraq, which was important for imperial communications. The threat was now from local disturbances in remote areas, rather than from Turkey. A railway from Basra to Baghdad to Kirkuk, and eventually to Mosul, was necessary. Further extensions were not in British interests, which were better served by a Haifa to Baghdad line.[471] In February 1920 General Radcliffe, the DMO, wrote to Wilson saying that a proposal by Churchill to reduce the garrison of Iraq to 4,000 British and 16,000 Indian troops would meant that it would be impossible to hold more than Basra and the Persian oilfields. He argued that;

> In Mesopotamia, or especially in the Mosul Vilayet, is the one
> potential asset which has come to us from the war. It is surely worth
> some sacrifice in the present to reap its unbounded possibilities in the
> future.[472]

---

[469] Ibid. pp. 207-14.

[470] K. Jeffery, ed. *The Military Correspondence of Field Marshall Sir Henry Wilson 1918-1922* (London: Bodley Head, 1985). Wilson to Churchill, 7 August 1919, pp. 120-22.

[471] CAB 24/93, C.P.120 'The Situation in Mesopotamia with Notes as to Expenditure', W. S. Churchill, 12 November 1919.

[472] NA, WO 32/5227, 'Reduction of Garrisons in Mesopotamia', 1919-21. DMO to CIGS, 9 February 1920.

G. H. Bennett points out that Lloyd George agreed and said so publicly.[473] During a debate on Foreign Affairs in the House of Commons H. H. Asquith, the Leader of the Opposition, argued that Britain was maintaining an expensive garrison in Iraq, which had no natural frontiers; Britain should withdraw to Basra.[474] Lloyd George responded by saying that he could see why somebody might advocate a complete evacuation of Iraq but not why Asquith wanted to stay in Basra whilst:

> withdrawing from the more important and the more promising part of Mesopotamia. Mosul is a country with great possibilities. It has rich oil deposits.[475]

He added that Britain had an obligation to the people of Iraq. When the peace treaty with Turkey was signed Britain would claim the mandate for Iraq, including Mosul; this would mean helping and advising an Arab government.[476]

Churchill was concerned by the costs of staying; the budget and the responsibility for policy had to be made clear. On 1 May he argued that Iraq was garrisoned by 60,000 British and Indian troops at an annual cost of £18,000,000 to the War Office; it had no responsibility for policy, which was driven by the Foreign Office. The Colonial Office possessed the expertise to run a country like Iraq; it should decide policy subject to financial constraints determined by the Treasury. Churchill suggested annual expenditure of a maximum of £7,000,000, £5,000,000 of which would be on the military. The military must be entitled to decide what they could do within the budget available. He argued that Iraq could be defended more cheaply if the responsibility for doing so was transferred from the War Office to the Air Ministry; he was Secretary State for the Air as well as for War. He concluded by saying that:

> In considering the future profit which may be drawn from the Mesopotamian oilfields, it is necessary always to bear in mind the capital charges which are accruing. Every year we go on at the present rate of expenditure adds £1,000,000 a year at 5 per cent, to what Mesopotamia will ultimately have to produce in order to yield a

---

[473] G. H. Bennett, *British Foreign Policy During the Curzon Period, 1919-24* (New York, NY: Macmillan, 1995), pp. 105-6.

[474] *Parliamentary Debates, Fifth Series, House of Commons*, vol. cxxvii. 25 March 1920, cols. 644-45.

[475] Ibid. 25 March 1920, col. 662.

[476] Ibid. 25 March 1920, cols. 662-64.

profit. Even if the oilfields bear out our most sanguine hopes, we are burdening them to an intolerable extent with capital charges, and what would be a thoroughly good business for the British Empire, if developed gradually and thriftily is being daily deteriorated by the sterile charges which are mounting up.[477]

In January 1920 a meeting of ministers had argued that the oil could pay for the entire administration of Iraq.[478] Churchill pointed out that this would not be the case if the costs of staying were too high. British policy in Iraq over the next few years was driven by a desire to stay there because of promises made to the Arabs, the oil and protection of the route to India versus a need to do so cheaply.

5.5.1 Revolt

In the summer 1920 a revolt against British rule broke out in Iraq. It was largely suppressed by the end of the year but raised questions over the cost of the British presence and how Iraq could best be governed.[479] The cost of occupation might have been justified by oil but, as Peter Sluglett points out, this was an argument that might have satisfied the British press but would have outraged foreign powers.[480] During the revolt, Arnold Wilson, the British Civil Commissioner, reported to the Secretary of State for India that Standard (NJ)'s local representative, W. H. Gallagher, was in contact with the rebels. Gallagher appeared to have had talks with them, but Wilson produced no evidence that Standard (NJ) was actively aiding them.[481]

For a while it appeared that Britain might have to evacuate Mosul. In June 1920 Churchill told Lloyd George that the costs of garrisoning Iraq could not be cut

---

[477] CAB 24/106, C.P. 1320 'Mesopotamia', W. S. Churchill, 1 May 1920.

[478] CAB 23/37, 'Conclusions of a Conference of Ministers: Oil Situation in Mesopotamia', 23 January 1920.

[479] M. Gilbert, *The World in Torment: Winston S. Churchill, 1916-1922* (London: Heinemann, 1975), pp. 490-97; C. Tripp, *A History of Iraq*, 3rd ed. (Cambridge: Cambridge University Press, 2007), pp. 39-44.

[480] Sluglett, *Britain*, p. 34.

[481] BL, Arnold Wilson Papers, MSS. 52455: vol. i c 'Correspondence with India Office', 1917-1920. Telegrams from Civil Commissioner, Baghdad to Secretary of State for India, no. 7321, 17 June 1920, f. 129, no. 7779; 26 June 1920, f. 134; no. 10967 9 September 1920, f. 190.

unless Britain's responsibilities there were reduced.[482] In December Churchill informed General Sir Aylmer Haldane, the GOC Iraq, that Sir Percy Cox, recently appointed High Commissioner in Baghdad, had said that garrisoning Iraq would cost £20,000,000 to £25,000,000 in each of the next two to three years. As this was too much to justify Britain remaining, Haldane was to prepare a plan for withdrawal. He should also give his view of the General Staff's view that the Basra vilayet could be held by a single division. This would give Britain a foothold and would protect the Persian oilfields.[483] There were two separate oil issues affecting Britain's presence in Iraq; Basra covered the existing Persian oilfields and the Abadan refinery, but the potential oilfields were in Mosul.

The Cabinet considered the issues of Iraq, the Middle East and Palestine on 31 December 1920. Churchill said that the revolt in Iraq had been put down, and the military position was now secure. The troops from Persia were to be withdrawn once the passes opened in the spring. The Mosul vilayet could not be evacuated before then; withdrawing from it in the summer would probably to lead to attacks from the Arabs, Turks and possibly Bolsheviks. Any decision to withdraw to the Basra vilayet could not be implemented until March 1922, meaning military expenditure in Iraq of £20-22,000,000; it would be hard to persuade Parliament to grant this sum on the Army Vote. The alternatives were to withdraw rapidly to Basra, leaving anarchy and chaos behind, or to establish a department to be responsible for the policy in Iraq and the budget to implement it. In the subsequent discussion it was argued that withdrawing to Basra would be a major political error. Britain could not take Iraq's only port and ignore the rest of the country. Military commitments could be cut in two years' time after a new Arab government had been established and a lasting peace negotiated with Turkey. Cox had suggested that Faisal would be acceptable as King to the Iraq Arabs; the trouble in Iraq was mostly external. If Faisal became King, supported by the Arabs, then the garrison could be reduced to one division in Baghdad and Mosul and a brigade in Basra. Curzon pointed out that France had said that it would consider British support for Faisal in Iraq as an unfriendly act. The Cabinet decided to further consider the idea of making Faisal King of Iraq. The discussion

---

[482] Churchill, Gilbert, eds, *Companions.* vol. iv, part 2, Winston S. Churchill to David Lloyd George, 13 June 1920, pp. 1119-20. Original reference Churchill Papers 16/47.

[483] Ibid. Winston S. Churchill to General Haldane, 17 December 1920. Original reference Cabinet Papers CAB 23/23.

then turned to Churchill's proposal for a Department for Middle Eastern Affairs. The question was whether it should be part of the Colonial or the Foreign Office; Parliamentary objections ruled out a new department with its own minister. The Foreign Office was already responsible for affairs much of the region, but the Cabinet decided that the new department should be part of the Colonial Office; it already did similar work elsewhere and the Foreign Office had no experience of administration.[484]

5.5.2 The Cairo Conference

At the start of 1921 Lloyd George invited Churchill to became Colonial Secretary in place of Lord Milner, who wanted to leave the government. Churchill agreed, provided that the Middle East Department would be set up immediately, the Colonial Office would be responsible for the Palestinian and Iraqi mandates, and he would have full powers to cut British expenditure in the Middle East. He decided that British expenditure in Iraq could be limited if it were run by an Arab government. Security would be provided by British police, Indian troops and the RAF. Making Faisal king was one option; another was to give the throne to his brother Abdullah. Some form of election would be required, but local customs meant that this need not be conducted under Western methods.[485]

Churchill formally took office as Colonial Secretary on 15 February, although he had been preparing for the job since the start of the year. The method of governing Britain's middle eastern territories would be decided by a conference at Cairo in March. He was keen to ensure that the Arabs did not do anything that would damage Anglo-French relations; he ordered T.E. Lawrence to tell Faisal that Britain could support him only if his supporters ceased their anti-French agitation. Churchill favoured reconciling Turkey, but Lloyd George's pro-Greek policy meant that he had to allow for the risk of conflict with Turkey.[486] Before departing for Cairo Churchill told Sir George Ritchie, the President of the Liberal Association in Dundee, his constituency, that Britain could not continue to spend large amounts of money in Iraq. Britain's African colonies offered far greater

---

[484] CAB 23/23, 'Cabinet Minutes and Papers 59(20) - 82(20)', 3 November - 31 December 1920. Cabinet 82(20), 31 December 1920.

[485] Gilbert, *World*, pp. 507-12.

[486] Ibid., pp. 531-32.

opportunities for development. He made no mention of oil. Britain would have to leave Iraq unless a cheaper way of staying could be devised. This would damage Britain's reputation, since Britain had invaded Mesopotamia, evicted the Ottoman government, accepted the mandate and promised to introduce a better form of government than had previously existed. He hoped that the problem could be solved by installing an Arab government and ruler, needing the backing of only a small British military force.[487]

On 14 March, the third day of the conference, Churchill informed Lloyd George that he expected unanimous agreement that Faisal was the best option. Talks had been taking place between Britain and Turkey and he wanted to know whether he could assume that there would be no trouble with Turkey in Mosul; it would be easier to reduce the garrison if this was the case. He intended to withdraw troops as quickly as possible.[488] Two days later Churchill informed the Prime Minister that unanimous agreement had been reached. Faisal would rule Iraq, with Kurdistan being ruled separately under a High Commissioner until the Kurds decided to join Iraq. The scheme would save £5,500,000 in 1921-22 and reduce the cost of the garrison to £5-6,000,000 in each of the next three years. The whole country, including Mosul and Kirkuk, could be held until local levies were ready.[489] The same day Churchill received a reply from Lloyd George to his initial telegram; appointing Faisal would cause problems with France unless the first move came from the Iraqis. Britain could not assume that fighting between Greece and Turkey would not lead to Turkish action in Mosul. It had warned the Turks that Britain would supply munitions to Greece if they did move against Iraq. He was happy with the intention to rapidly cut costs in Iraq.[490] Churchill reported back that he had spoken to Bekir Samir, the Turkish Foreign Minister, who had said that they had no interest in Iraq as they wanted to leave the Arabs alone.[491] It would emerge that, while the Turks had no interest in Arab territory,

---

[487] Churchill, Gilbert, eds, *Companions*. vol. iv, part 2, Winston Churchill to Sir George Ritchie, 23 February 1921, pp. 1371-72. Original reference Churchill Papers 5/24.

[488] Ibid. Winston S. Churchill to David Lloyd George, 14 March 1921, pp. 1389-90. Original reference Churchill Papers 17/18.

[489] Ibid. Winston S. Churchill to David Lloyd George, 16 March 1921, pp. 1392-95. Original reference Churchill Papers 17/15.

[490] Ibid. David Lloyd George to Winston S. Churchill, 16 March 1921, pp. 1395-96. Original reference Churchill Papers 17/18.

[491] Ibid. Winston Churchill to David Lloyd George, 16 March 1921, pp. 1396-97. Orginal reference Lloyd George Papers.

they regarded Mosul as being Turkish. The remainder of the Cairo Conference dealt with other issues in the Middle East, including Palestine and Transjordan. On 22 March the Cabinet decided to offer the throne of Iraq to Faisal. To avoid problems with the French Faisal should be told informally that the throne of Iraq was vacant; Britain would be happy if the Iraqi people offered it to him, provided that he accepted the conditions of the mandate and agreed not to take any action against the French. If he accepted it should be suggested to him that he should return to Mecca; from there he should put himself forward as a candidate at the appropriate moment. Churchill's recommendations on Kurdistan and on cuts in the garrison of Iraq were accepted.[492]

5.5.3 From the Cairo Conference to the End of the Coalition

In December 1920 Faisal met Philip Kerr, Lloyd George's private secretary. Faisal said that in order to establish an Arab government in Iraq, reducing British commitments and expenditure in the country, Britain had to regain the confidence of the people, which it had lost. A strong Arab government was needed, but it would have to have British help and support. Without it, the country might descend into anarchy, or be re-conquered by Turkey. Kerr was left with little doubt that Faisal would like to head such a government.[493]

The British appointed Iraqi Council of State unanimously elected Faisal as king on 11 July 1921.The majority of Iraqi Arabs were Shias, but Faisal and most of the Council were Sunnis; he was not an Iraqi. There had been some co-operation between Sunnis and Shias before and during the Iraqi Revolt; this did not last. His leadership of the Arab Revolt against the Ottoman Empire during the war did give him support from Arab nationalists, especially Iraqis who had joined his army. The British organised a referendum in which 96 per cent of the votes were cast in favour of Faisal becoming king. There was little opposition and no other candidate; the British had deported Sayyid Talib, the most likely local contender. The Kurds and supporters of Turkey, who opposed Arab rule, and

---

[492] CAB 23/24, 'Cabinet Minutes and Papers 1(21) - 16(21)', 4 January to 24 March 1921. Cabinet 13 (21), 22 March 1921.

[493] NAS, Lothian Papers, GD40/17/1350, 'Memorandum on Interview with Emir Faisal, 20 December 1920, About Mesopotamia and British Policy There; 31 December 1920', 1920.

southern Shias, who wanted a theocracy, did not vote. Faisal was crowned on 23 August.[494]

Churchill was concerned that costs were not being reduced enough in Iraq. The Cairo Conference had decided that it could be garrisoned by 12 battalions, 2 of them British. The War Office now wanted 7 of the battalions to be British, increasing the cost from £4,500,000 to £10,000,000. British troops needed greater staff and administrative support than local or Indian troops. This was too much for Iraq to support. The alternatives were to give up the mandate or to adopt a proposal by Air Chief Marshal Sir Hugh Trenchard, the Chief of the Air Staff, to control the country from the air by RAF bombers. Britain's intention had been to rule through a government and monarch accepted by the people rather than to hold the country by force. Faisal could govern supported by the RAF, four Imperial battalions and native levies. Eventually, Iraq should be independent, friendly to Britain and beneficial to British commercial interests with hardly any call on the British Exchequer. This would not happen if an expensive British garrison had to be financed.[495] The proposal for air control was accepted; the military commander in Iraq would come from the RAF, and would be responsible to the Colonial Office.[496]

The resurgence of Turkey meant that it posed a threat to Iraq; the War Office feared that air control would mean that the garrison was too small to hold more than the Basra vilayet. In November 1921 Laming Worthington-Evans, the War Secretary, told the Cabinet that if Kemal wanted to attack Britain he would do so in Mosul and that there was nothing that Britain could do militarily to stop him.[497] The next month Churchill warned the Cabinet that pro-Turkish and anti-Faisal propaganda had taken place; a small Turkish incursion had led to the capture of Rowanduz, a Kurdish town to the south of the Iraqi frontier. Capturing Mosul would increase Turkish prestige, allow them to hold southern

---

[494] Tripp, *A History*, pp. 44-48; J. S. Yaphe, 'The View from Basra: Southern Iraq's Reaction to War and Occupation, 1915-1925,' in *The Creation of Iraq, 1914-1921*, ed. R. S. Simon, E. H. Tejirian (New York NY: Columbia University Press, 2004), pp. 32-33.

[495] CAB 24/126, C.P. 3197 'Policy and Finance in Mesopotamia 1922-23', W. S. Churchill, 4 August 1921.

[496] Sluglett, *Britain*, pp. 40-41.

[497] CAB 24/129, C.P. 3494 'Possibility of a Turkish Offensive in Northern Iraq', L. Worthington-Evans, 21 November 1921.

Kurdistan and give them a base to later attack Baghdad, and give them the oilfields. They could obtain much needed revenue by offering the concessions to France and the USA. French problems in Syria might be eased if Iraq were Turkish as the French would appear relatively liberal and pro-Arab in comparison. There were fears that Standard (NJ) was encouraging a Turkish attack on Iraq in the hope of winning the oil concession, It was not known if the US Government was aware of this, but its attitude to mandates, the north Persia oil concessions and Persian railways suggested that it would not be unhappy to see the Turks retake Iraq if it meant US companies getting a stake in the oil.[498]

Turkish agitation continued throughout 1922. In early February Worthington-Evans was concerned that Churchill's plan to rely on air power to control Iraq meant that Britain could not hold Baghdad and should withdraw to Basra in order to defend the port, the Persian oilfield and the Persian Gulf.[499] By early October he was arguing that the Iraqi levies could not be relied upon; Imperial troops should not be stationed in Mosul unless reinforced, which was impossible. The General Staff had agreed to keep them there only subject to the conditions agreed at the Cairo Conference, which had not been implemented. Troops were to remain in Mosul for now, but in the event of a major uprising in Kurdistan, there would be no alternative but to withdraw them.[500] The air control policy worked; Cox reported later in the month that the Turks were withdrawing thanks to the actions of the RAF.[501]

Faisal did not prove to be as compliant as the British had hoped.[502] He wanted to replace the mandate with a treaty setting out Britain's rights and obligations towards Iraq. This was not agreed until October 1922 and not ratified by the Iraqi Chamber of Deputies until June 1924.[503] Faisal confronted Britain during the negotiations; Helmut Mejcher, Peter Sluglett and Charles Tripp agree that this could have lost him his throne had he not been removed from the scene by

---

[498] CAB 24/131, C.P. 3566 'Foreign Incitement of the Turks to Attack Iraq', W. S. Churchill, 13 December 1921.

[499] CAB 24/133, C.P. 3708 'Iraq', L. Worthington-Evans, 8 February 1922.

[500] CAB 24/138, C.P. 4192 'The Situation in Northern Iraq', 5 October 1922.

[501] CAB 24/139, C.P. 4295 'Turkish Designs in Iraq', Devonshire, 22 October 1922.

[502] Sluglett, *Britain*, p. 37.

[503] Ibid., pp. 49-61.

appendicitis in the summer of 1922. This gave Cox the chance to close opposition newspapers and political parties and to order the bombing of insurgents. This show of British intent persuaded Faisal to come to an agreement when he recovered.[504] Air control of Iraq worked for Britain.

The difficulties in coming to an agreement with Faisal made Churchill wonder if it was worthwhile for Britain to stay in Iraq. He told Lloyd-George in September 1922 that the threat from Turkey meant that extra troops had had to be kept at Mosul, meaning that expenditure was greater than planned. Problems with the USA had prevented development of the oil. He suggested that Britain should give Faisal an ultimatum that it would leave unless he agreed to Britain's terms. Whether Britain left entirely or held onto Basra was less important.[505] Lloyd George wanted to stay, putting Mosul's oil forward as a reason to do so. He claimed not to have been closely involved in the decision to invade Mesopotamia in 1914, which he thought was a mistake. Having done so, Britain could not go back on its obligations to the Arabs. He concluded by saying that:

> I was anxious that the Anglo-Persian should bore to ascertain the value of the oil deposits. We have, however, done practically nothing in that respect. If we leave, we may find a year or two after we have departed that we have handed over to the French and the Americans some of the richest oilfields in the world...On general principles, I am against a policy of scuttle, in Iraq as elsewhere, and should like you to put all the alternatives, as you see them, before the Cabinet on Thursday.[506]

The Lloyd George Coalition lost office before the issue could be considered.

5.6 Anglo-Italian Relations and Oil

In September 1920 the Italian government wrote to the British government suggesting that Britain and France might alter the San Remo Agreement in order to accommodate Italian interests. Curzon told the Italian Ambassador that San Remo was based on co-operation in regions where Britain and France already had

---

[504] Mejcher, *Imperial*, p. 294; Sluglett, *Britain*, p. 48; Tripp, *A History*, p. 52.

[505] Churchill, Gilbert, eds, *Companions*. vol. iv, part 3, Winston S. Churchill to David Lloyd George, 1 September 1922, pp. 1973-74. Original reference Churchill Papers 17/27.

[506] Ibid. David Lloyd George to Winston S. Churchill, 5 September 1922, pp. 1977-78. Original reference Churchill Papers 17/27.

major interests, including Mosul. The pipeline across the French mandate in Syria would bring oil to Europe, benefitting Italy and other countries.[507] The Italians tried again during the 1922 Genoa Conference. On 19 April Carlo Schanzer, the Italian Foreign Minister, wrote to Lloyd George asking that Britain and France state that the San Remo Agreement did not discriminate in any way against Italian oil interests. Italians should have the same rights as Frenchmen to be awarded concessions in the British Empire. Italy should receive a share of any oil concessions obtained by Britain and France in former enemy countries.[508] The Foreign Office argued that there was no need to go beyond a Note of 22 July 1921, stating that the San Remo Agreement did not stop Italians from co-operating with British or French oil interests.[509] It was not prepared to give any preference to Italians, but was happy to stay that there was no discrimination against them. They had the same rights as any other nationality in British colonies.[510] This did not satisfy Schanzer, who was facing criticism on this issue in the Italian parliament.[511] His problem was that Italy, unlike France, had nothing to offer Britain in exchange for a share of the oil.

5.7 Mustafa Kemal Rejects Sèvres

In January 1920, the newly elected Turkish Chamber of Deputies voted in favour of the National Pact, which had been issued by Kemal in Angora, now Ankara. It called for the establishment of an independent Turkey comprising the parts of the Ottoman Empire inhabited by ethnic Turks. A British led Allied force occupied Constantinople in March and dissolved the Chamber of Deputies. Many of its members fled to Angora, where a Turkish National Assembly was set up, with Kemal as its president. It declared that the Sultan was a prisoner without freedom of action; his decisions should be ignored.[512] This left the Allies with the

---

[507] Woodward et al, eds, *DBFP*. vol. xiii, No. 318, Note from Earl Curzon to the Italian Ambassador, 17 September 1920, pp. 346-47.

[508] PA, Lloyd George Papers, LG/F/86/7/2, 'Schanzer to the Prime Minister', 19 April 1922.

[509] PA, Lloyd George Papers, LG/F/86/7/5, 'Foreign Office to Sir P. Lloyd Greame', 28 April 1922; Lloyd George Papers, LG/F/86/7/4, 'G.L.H. Lloyd to Sir Edward Grigg', 27 April 1922. G. L. H. Lloyd to Sir Edward Grigg

[510] PA, Lloyd George Papers, LG/F/86/7/6, 'Lancelot Oliphant to J.D. Gregory', 11 May 1922.

[511] PA, Lloyd George Papers, LG/F/86/7/7, 'P. Lloyd-Greame to Sir Edward Grigg', 14 May 1922.

[512] Fromkin, *Peace*, pp. 427-29.

problem of how to enforce the Treaty of Sèvres. One possibility was that Greece could launch an offensive from Smyrna.

5.7.1 Britain and Greece

Britain had traditionally backed the Ottoman Empire to protect its interests in the Middle East, most crucially the route to India. Russia was the main threat so the need for a British proxy in the region diminished after the 1907 Anglo-Russian Agreement. The Ottomans moved closer to Germany and entered the war against the Allies. Greece was divided during the First World War: King Constantine, Kaiser Wilhelm's brother-in-law, was personally pro-German but thought that neutrality was the best policy for Greece. The pro-Allied Prime Minister, Eleftherios Venizelos, was forced to resign. In June 1917 an Allied ultimatum led to the abdication of Constantine in favour of his son Alexander; Venizelos returned to power and took Greece into the war on the Allied side. Greek policy was based on the *Megali* Idea, that all Greeks should be part of the Greek State.[513] Lloyd George, who was close to Venizelos, believed that Greece could replace the Ottoman Empire as Britain's proxy in the Middle East. He had some, but not universal, support within the British government for this view. The Foreign Office's PID backed him. Curzon, while happy to see the Turks removed from Europe, did not want to see the Greeks installed in Asia Minor. The War Office, especially Henry Wilson, favoured a return to supporting Turkey, albeit a reduced Turkish state.[514] The India Office were concerned over the reaction of India's large Muslim population if the Ottoman Empire was treated harshly at the peace conference.[515]

Venizelos appeared to have achieved Greece's aims at Sèvres; an offensive to defeat the Kemalists was required in order to hold them. Venizelos hoped for British financial and military support; this was not forthcoming. The War Office was concerned that Kemal would be forced into an alliance with the Russian Bolsheviks. The India Office also had reservations about the pro-Greek policy. In October 1920 King Alexander died. Venizelos lost an election the next month.

---

[513] E. Daleziou, 'Britain and the Greek-Turkish War and Settlement of 1919-1923: The Pursuit of Security by "Proxy" in Western Asia Minor.' (University of Glasgow, 2002), pp. 23-25.

[514] Ibid., pp. 71-74.

[515] Ibid., p. 34.

The new government organised a plebiscite that returned Constantine to the throne. Most British Conservatives had accepted Lloyd George's policy of supporting Greece whilst Venizelos, a strong supporter of the Allies, was in power; now that he was gone many backbenchers favoured a return to the old policy of using Turkey as Britain's Middle Eastern proxy. [516] The French had accepted with the Greek policy only because of Venizelos. [517] In January 1921 Aristide Briand became Prime Minister of France. He wanted to withdraw the French garrison from Cilicia, which was both expensive and in a strategically dangerous position between the Kemalists and Syria. He sent Henri Franklin-Bouillon on two diplomatic missions to Angora. In the autumn France and Turkey signed a peace agreement, meaning that France recognised Kemal's government as being that of Turkey. France gave Kemal significant quantities of military equipment. [518] Italy, which regarded Greece as a rival, had already come to terms with Kemal. [519]

In March 1921 the Greeks launched an offensive in Turkey. It was unsuccessful; the Greek government, believing that it was politically impossible to stop now, renewed the attack in July. It was initially successful, but in late August and early September the Greek forces were routed by Kemal. Greece appealed to its erstwhile allies for help but received no aid and only sympathy from Lloyd George. By September 1922 the Greek Army had been evacuated from Asia Minor, many Greek civilians had fled to Greece and Smyrna was in flames. Kemal now turned his attention to Constantinople and Eastern Thrace. It appeared that Britain and Turkey might go to war. Churchill had argued for reconciliation with Kemal, but now agreed with Lloyd George that Britain must fight for the Gallipoli Peninsula. British and Turkish forces faced each other at Chanak. British public opinion was against the war; Canada and Australia refused to send troops. The French and Italian ones on the spot stayed in their camps. The crisis was averted by negotiations between Kemal and the local British commander, General Sir Charles Harrington, who did not carry out his orders to deliver an

---

[516] Ibid., pp. 148-62.

[517] Fromkin, *Peace*, p. 432.

[518] Ibid., pp. 536-37.

[519] Ibid., pp. 531-33.

ultimatum that might have meant war. Kemal had achieved the National Pact but agreed to delay his occupation of European Turkey.[520]

5.7.2 The End of the Lloyd George Coalition

The Greek-Turkish War brought down the Lloyd George Coalition. In March 1921 Andrew Bonar Law had resigned from the government and the leadership of the Conservative Party on the grounds of ill health. He now returned to politics. On 7 October 1922 *The Times* published a letter in which he argued that Britain could not act alone. It had been right to stand up to the Turks at Constantinople but needed help from other countries in such circumstances. Account had to be taken of Muslim feelings. The main issue was that Lloyd George had ignored the wishes of the Conservatives who made up the majority of his Coalition. On 19 October 1922 a meeting of Conservative MPs decided to withdraw their support from the Coalition. Bonar Law became Prime Minister the same day and called an election for 15 November, which his party won.[521] Many of the Conservative members of Lloyd George's Cabinet refused to join the new administration, but Curzon remained Foreign Secretary and Stanley Baldwin became Chancellor of the Exchequer. His former post of President of the Board of Trade went to Sir Philip Lloyd-Greame, who had been responsible for oil as Secretary for Overseas Trade. The change of government meant that all policies, including those on oil and Iraq, would be reconsidered. The new government would have to renegotiate the peace treaty with Turkey.

5.8 Chapter Summary

Britain wanted the Mesopotamian mandate, which would give it control of Mosul's oil. It had other interests there, but only the oil required Mosul to be part of Mesopotamia. Protection of the pipeline to the Mediterranean and control over the port at which it terminated required Britain to have the Palestinian mandate. There were other reasons, such as protection of Egypt and the Suez Canal and fulfilment of promises to the Zionists, but the oil strategy needed a friendly mandatory. The USA was considered, but Britain preferred to

---

[520] Ibid., pp. 540-52.

[521] Daleziou, 'Britain', pp. 273-75.

take on the task itself even before the USA decided not to take on a mandate. The San Remo Agreement and the Treaty of Sèvres appeared to give Britain all that it wanted but did not last. San Remo angered the Americans because it shut them out of Mosul's oil, with consequences for Anglo-American relations. The similarity between it and the previous attempts at an Anglo-French oil agreement shows that the earlier ones were not ratified because of other disputes rather than oil. Clemenceau had agreed to allow Britain Mosul but expected a share of the oil and British support elsewhere. The French soon decided that Sèvres had been rather better for Britain than it was for themselves. The decision by the Council of Four to allow the Greeks to land at Smyrna had severe consequences. Turkish resistance under Mustafa Kemal was galvanised; the dictated Treaty of Sèvres had to be re-negotiated at Lausanne in 1923.

The revolt in Iraq led to a re-examination of Britain's position there. The garrison was too expensive, but many policy makers were reluctant to leave; the oil was a factor in their deliberations. A cheap solution, which was to govern via Faisal with most of the military support coming from the RAF, allowed Britain to stay. Italy's attempts to obtain a share of Mosul's oil were rebuffed; it could offer nothing in return. The Chanak Crisis that followed Turkey's victory over Greece brought down the Lloyd George Coalition. Britain's oil strategy was now to obtain secure supplies from Iraq. This affected its Middle Eastern policy and its relations with other countries, including France, the USA, Italy and Turkey. The new Conservative Government under Andrew Bonar Law would have to consider this strategy and whether to stay in Iraq. This would affect the new peace treaty that had to be negotiated with Turkey. This came at a time when the RN's plans required greater oil reserves.

6 Post War Oil Planning for the Royal Navy

Civilian oil use was increasing, but the largest user remained the RN. Oil was soon to completely replace coal as a naval fuel in an era where the balance of naval power had changed. The defeat of Germany and the inability of France and Russia to finance large navies after years of conflict meant that the RN had no rivals in Europe. It had two globally; the USN and the IJN. The strength of the RN had been informally based on a two power standard for many years, although it was not adopted officially until 1889, when the powers were France and Russia. Germany became the main rival in the early twentieth century. In 1908 the Asquith Government defined the two power standard as being the strength of the second and third largest powers plus 10 per cent. This was replaced in 1912 by a new measure of a 60 per cent margin over the second largest navy. The abandonment of the two power standard is often regarded as a sign of the decline of the RN, but Phillips O'Brien points that it meant different things at different times and to different governments.[522] Eric Grove notes that the size of other navies meant that the RN in practice still had a two power standard.[523] In 1919 the Cabinet proposed to return to a 60 per cent margin over the biggest fleet other than the USN. The RN successfully argued for a one power standard including the USN; this was the only standard that might allow the construction of battleships.[524]

6.1 The One and Two Power Standards

After the First World War Britain's only naval rivals were the USA and Japan. They were not likely to combine. Britain had been allied to Japan since 1902. This did not prevent the Admiralty for planning for a war with it. It was doubtful if the alliance would be renewed because its existence increased Anglo-American tension.[525] The USN was sometimes included in calculations of the two power standard and sometimes omitted.[526] Beatty's papers include a draft

---

[522] O'Brien, *British*, p. 4.

[523] Grove, *Royal Navy*, p. 102.

[524] Ibid., pp. pp. 144-45.

[525] O'Brien, *British*, pp. 162-65.

[526] Ibid., pp. 37-40.

memorandum by the Admiralty Board stating that the USN had been excluded from two power standard calculations because these were based on possible combinations against Britain; it would be very difficult for the USN to co-operate effectively with a European navy against Britain. The Monroe Doctrine and the US reluctance to become involved in European affairs were also factors. The paper admitted that these views were disputed by some. Since the USA was now involved in Europe and had realised that it needed a navy at least as big as the RN these arguments were no longer valid. The paper is undated, but is in a file containing correspondence between Beatty and Long from February 1919 to June 1922.[527] It ignored the plans drawn up in 1907-8 to fight a possible alliance between the USA and Germany.[528] Some of the comments in it suggest that it may have been a draft of a Cabinet memorandum written by Long on 12 August 1919; he had been First Lord since January. This did not include any mention of the history of the two power standard, or the USN's inclusion in or exclusion from it.[529]

Long wrote that the only navy that needed to be considered was the USN; the RN would be only slightly bigger than it by 1923-24 if the US 1916 programme was completed; some of the US battleships would superior to any British ones. He did not think that the USA would 'become an aggressive power'[530], but Britain's policy had always been that no power should be superior to it at sea. The USA would gain supremacy unless Britain persuaded to reduce its construction programme or embarked upon one of its own. Long wanted to know for how long it should be assumed that there would not be a war with a major power or a combination of smaller powers jointly possessing the strength of a great power. Five years was easier for planning, as the planned strengths of the IJN and USN in five years time were known. A 10 year period would enable greater cuts in naval expenditure.[531] On 15 August 1919 a Cabinet meeting decided that the armed forces should plan on the basis that the British Empire would not be involved in a

---

[527] NMM, Beatty Papers, BTY/13/28/14, 'British Naval Officers and Officials: Long, W H, 1st Viscount (1858-1924), Letters and Papers 25 Feb 1919-21 Jun 1922'.

[528] O'Brien, *British*, pp. 37-38.

[529] CAB 24/86, G.T. 7975 'Post-War Naval Policy', W. H. Long, 12 August 1919.

[530] Ibid., p. 1. 'Oil Fuel Reserves', O. de B. Brock, 24 May 1921.

[531] Ibid.

major war for 10 years. The pre-war standard on the size of the RN should not be altered without Cabinet authority.[532]

On 13 February 1920 Long wrote a memorandum arguing that Britain had two options for its naval policy; persuade the US Government to limit the USN to equality with the RN; or carry out a construction programme that would make the RN equal to the currently planned size of the USN. His preference was for the former since '[a]n Alliance or an Entente with the United States based on equality in Naval Material is, in fact, required to reach the ideals we each aim at.'[533] If agreement could not be reached the RN had to be built up to a one power standard. In November he pointed out that it had been agreed that the RN would maintain a one power standard. The USN's construction programme meant that it would be larger than the RN by the end of 1923. Like many people he thought that war between Britain and the USA was impossible. This did not mean that Britain could afford to have a smaller navy than the USA. Britain's prestige and power were based on its naval supremacy. It was only because war with the USA was thought to be highly unlikely that the Admiralty was prepared to accept equality with the USN. Without new construction the RN would fall behind the IJN in quality of ships; comparing the strengths of navies involved more than just counting the number of ships.[534]

The August 1919 Cabinet meeting was the first occasion on which what came to be known as the 10 year rule was mentioned. Stephen Roskill argued that it dominated British naval policy until it was abandoned in 1932.[535] John Ferris has shown that it was not until 1925 that the Treasury and the 10 year rule became the key shapers of British defence policy. In August 1919 the 10 year rule was just a component of defence planning.[536] It gave a timescale for defence planning, including the period over which naval oil reserves could be established. War between the UK and the USA might seem unlikely but could not be ignored by naval planners whilst tensions, including a naval building race,

---

[532] CAB 23/15, 'War Cabinet Papers "A" Minutes 531a - 634a', 12 February - 24 October 1919. War Cabinet Meeting, 15 August 1919.

[533] CAB 24/98, C.P. 645 'Naval Estimates and Naval Policy', W. H. Long, 13 February 1920, p. 3.

[534] CAB 24/115, C.P. 2176 'Naval Policy and Construction', 22 November 1920.

[535] Roskill, *Naval*, pp. 214-15.

[536] J. R. Ferris, *The Evolution of British Strategic Policy, 1919-26* (Basingstoke: Macmillan, 1989), p. xii.

remained between the two countries. Plans for war with the USA were drawn up, but the RN was less confident about fighting the USA than Japan. Plans produced in January 1921 said that a war with the USA would be very unpopular and should be ended as soon as it was shown that the British Empire could resist; a long conflict would favour the Americans.[537] The one power standard had implications of its own for the RN's oil policy. Oil reserves had to be built up round the world in order to give the reduced fleet the mobility to protect British interests around the world. Oil had to be stored at home, in the Mediterranean, in the Far East and on the routes to the Far East.

6.2 Oil and Naval Plans in 1918-19.

On 18 September 1918 Geddes, then First Lord, requested the views of the Admiralty on oil. On 1 December these were brought together in a number of memoranda.[538] Tothill, the Fourth Sea Lord, analysed the availability of oil. He concluded that global oil supplies should remain adequate to meet world demand; many potential fields had not been fully exploited; better oilfield practices should reduce the high level of waste of oil; coal could be converted into oil; and the introduction of internal combustion engines should cut oil demand. His view of the future of oil supplies was right, although for the first two reasons rather than the last two. He did wonder if it was correct for Britain, with its large coal deposits, to lead the way in using oil. He wanted Britain to develop oil production in the UK or easily accessible places and coal conversion plants.[539] Pretyman, the Civil Lord, stressed the need to avoid dependence on US oil; these supplies would be cut off if the USA was hostile and even if it remained friendly its exports were likely to decline because of rising domestic demand.[540] Creating a single British oil company would mean having a monopoly in the Empire, leading to criticism in Parliament. US oil was of better quality than Mexican and in a more suitable location than RDS's fields in Dutch East Indies. His view was that:

---

[537] NMM, Beatty Papers, BTY/8/1/8, 'War with Japan', 4 January 1921; NMM, Beatty Papers, BTY/8/1/7, 'War with the USA', 4 January 1921.

[538] ADM 167/57, 'Memoranda, Mar. - Jan. 1919', 1919. 'Various Aspects of the Oil Situation', 1 December 1918.

[539] Ibid. 'II. Adequacy of Supply, Memorandum by Fourth Sea Lord', pp. 3-4.

[540] Ibid. 'I. Sources of Supply, Memorandum by Civil Lord', p. 1.

> The Admiralty has therefore, I think, less to expect from the
> formation of an All British Oil Combine than from the development of
> supplies in Egypt, Mesopotamia, Persia and any other British
> possession within 4,000 miles of the UK and we should press the
> Foreign Office to bear this in mind when peace conditions are
> considered.[541]

Tothill thought that exploitation of oilfields in British territory required either the formation of a state controlled oil company or else ensuring that there were big, British controlled companies. He wanted APOC to operate only in Persia and Mesopotamia and RDS to be brought under British control.[542] Wemyss, the First Sea Lord, dealt with the strategic aspects of oil. His paper was largely a summary of the views out forward by Slade in his memorandum of 29 July 1918, with Slade's controversial views on RDS omitted. Britain had to continue to control the world's supply of bunker fuel, whether this was oil or coal. Future control of oil depended on control of the Persian and Mesopotamian oilfields. These had to be entirely British; any foreign interests, however small, would be working against Britain. Wemyss argued that 'absolute security is required.'[543]

The first sentence of Wemyss's memorandum was that [i]t is no exaggeration to say that our life as an Empire is largely dependent upon our ability to maintain the control of bunker fuel.'[544] This sentence was copied from Slade's July paper.[545] In October 1918 the Board of the Admiralty considered a memorandum on the likely oil bunkering needs of the RN and the Mercantile Marine after the war.[546] The authors were the Directors of Operations Division (F), Trade Division and Stores.[547] It was impossible at this stage to estimate accurately post war requirements, but where coal was now required increasing amounts of oil would be needed in the future. The governments of Canada, South Africa, Australia and New Zealand would control oil stocks in their countries and should keep them up

---

[541] Ibid. 'III. Control of Supplies (a) Memorandum by Civil Lord', p. 6.

[542] Ibid. 'III. Control of Supplies (b) Memorandum by Fourth Sea Lord', p. 7.

[543] Ibid. 'IV: Strategical Aspect of Oil Fuel Supply (a) Memorandum by First Sea Lord'. Underlined in original.

[544] Ibid., p. 7.

[545] CAB 24/59 G.T. 5267, Slade, p. 1.

[546] ADM 167/53, 'Board Minutes, Aug. 1917 - Dec. 1918', 1917-18. 16 October 1918, No. 427, 'Post-War Oil Storage and Bunkering Abroad', p. 207.

[547] N. Tracy, ed. *The Collective Naval Defence of the Empire, 1900 to 1940* (Aldershot: Scolar, 1997), p. 236.

to an agreed level. Commercial supplies might be counted if it could be certain that the required level of naval oil would always be available. In Crown Colonies the government should set up storage at naval bases and in locations where commercial facilities would be uneconomic. British companies should be encouraged to provide storage at foreign ports and might be subsidised for doing so where it was otherwise uneconomic. Where possible, such as in South America, facilities should be established in several different countries in case political problems prevented British warships from using some ports.[548]

In calculating the oil needs of each station the size of force that might be sent there in an emergency was estimated. Sufficient oil should be provided to supply this force for three months at a monthly war expenditure of 5,000 tons for battleships and battle cruisers, 2,000 tons for light cruisers and 1,000 tons for destroyers. The potential force to be provided for in the south Atlantic, Cape, East Indies or Pacific was two battle cruisers and six light cruisers; requirements for this were rounded to 70,000 tons. British firms owned storage for 76,000 tons in south east America, but these could not be relied upon as all were in foreign countries. Facilities at Ascension, St Helena, the Falklands and Sierra Leone would have to be developed; only the last had any chance of being commercially viable, so the others would have to be financed by the government. New storage facilities would have to be developed in East Africa and the Cape. More than enough was available from commercial sources in the East Indies. The shortfall in the Pacific would be made up in Canada and by signing contracts with suppliers in French (Tahiti), Peruvian (Callao) and Chilean (Valparaiso) territory. It was possible that battleships might have to be sent to China so 120,000 tons should be provided for a force of four battleships, six light cruisers and eight destroyers. Commercial supplies on British territory totalled 117,000 tons; the balance would be provided at Hong Kong if necessary. Larger supplies were needed for the Mediterranean Fleet and for Canada, where battleships might have to be sent. A list of Australian and New Zealand ports where supply might be provided was given; the quantities to be available at each should be discussed with the local governments.[549] The Board accepted these conclusions and recommendations. It passed part of it to Harcourt's PIPCO as an expression

---

[548] ADM 167/53. Appendix, p. 209.

[549] Ibid. Appendix, pp. 209-11.

of the Admiralty's views on oil bunkering. The Admiralty did not want to take any action that would speed up the change from coal to oil, but all measures should be taken to ensure that Britain continued to control world fuel bunkering when this did occur.[550]

On 28 December Tothill told the Admiralty Board that RN oil reserves in home waters should equal 12 months' war expenditure. This meant 4,500,000 tons, requiring an additional 2,750,000 tons of storage to be provided at a cost of about £1 per ton. It was agreed to explain to the War Cabinet that these reserves were needed to reduce dependence on the USA. The only other potential sources were Persia, Mesopotamia and carbonisation of coal; none of them would be realised for many years and might never fully provide for the navy.[551] Long, still Colonial Secretary and with responsibility for oil, agreed.[552] On 17 January 1919 the Cabinet accepted that home oil reserves should be built up to 4,500,000 tons. Curzon suggested that Baku might be an alternative source of supply. Wemyss was tasked with writing a report on this option.[553] He concluded that, even on optimistic assumptions, Russia and Romania might together supply 350,000 tons of fuel oil per annum; these would have to come through the Dardanelles. At most 200,000 tons of this would come from Russia; it had not supplied the RN before the war. The majority of Russia's oil was used domestically; exports were mostly lubricating and lighting oil. Romania was expected to be able to export 700,000 tons per annum once all its wells were repaired; a quarter would be fuel oil.[554]

In October 1919 G. H. Ashdown, the Director of Stores, wrote that:

> The provision of additional tankage is likely to be a difficult matter owing to the present financial situation. It is, however, a question which should be dealt with at the earliest possible moment in view of the growing requirements for supply of oil, not only to H.M. Ships, but

---

[550] Ibid. 31 October 1918, No. 439, 'Post-War Oil Storage and Bunkering Abroad', p. 220.

[551] Ibid. 28 December 1918, No. 554, 'Oil Fuel Reserve for Navy in Home Waters.'; CAB 24/72, G.T. 6594 'Oil Fuel Reserve for Navy in Home Waters', R. E. Wemyss, 3 January 1919.

[552] CAB 24/73, G.T. 6634 'Oil Fuel Reserve for Navy in Home Waters', W. H. Long, 8 January 1919.

[553] CAB 23/9, 'War Cabinet Papers 514-52', 8 January - 31 March 1919. War Cabinet 517, 17 January 1919, '3. Oil Fuel Reserves', pp. 2-3.

[554] CAB 24/74, G.T. 6703 'Oil Fuel Reserve. Petroleum Production in Russia', R. E. Wemyss, 25 January 1919.

to increasing numbers of oil burning merchant ships. For the time being, the demand for oil has out grown the means of supply.[555]

Captain Barry Domvile, the Director of Plans, wrote to the Deputy Chief of the Naval Staff and the Fourth Sea Lord arguing that Ashdown had raised two questions that had to be considered. How much reliance could be placed on commercial stocks? How should oil reserves be divided between onshore storage and mobile supplies in tankers? In answering these a number of points had to be born in mind. Oil, unlike coal, did not deteriorate in storage. War in the Pacific would require oil to be provided for the fleet both on transit to the east and at its bases once it arrived. It must be decided whether money was better spent on tankers or on permanent storage. The safety of oilfields and refineries and the threat from submarines had to be considered. The Petroleum Executive had taken action to try to get control over as much oil as possible. Domvile repeated the argument already made by Slade and Wemyss that Britain had to control the world's oil bunkering. He wrote that 'it will be as necessary for us to control the oil bunkering facilities in the next war, as it was for us to control the coal bunkering facilities on the late war.'[556] He recommended that the issue be reviewed by the Naval Staff; this was accepted.

6.3 Oil Reserves for Merchant Shipping

In December 1919 Long, now First Lord, requested that the Admiralty and the Petroleum Executive prepare a memorandum for the Cabinet on the need to have an oil reserve for British merchant ships. The final draft was submitted in February. It argued that most British merchant shipping companies were converting some of their vessels to oil and using oil for new ships. Even if the maximum effort was devoted to producing creosote from coal, it would take 40,000,000 tons of coal to produce 2,000,000 tons of oil. This would cover only a third of British merchant shipping and naval demand. The lack of storage and tankers meant that Britain had to take action if it wanted to control oil bunkering in the same way as it controlled coal supplies; the vital need to do so was reiterated. The Admiralty had to provide oil stocks for commercial use;

---

[555] ADM 1/8577/351, 'Oil Fuel Supplies for H.M. Ships in Event of War', 1919. 'Provision for Supplies of Oil Fuel for H.M. Ships on Certain Stations', Memorandum by D. of S., 6 October 1919.

[556] Ibid. 'Supply of Oil Fuel in War Time', D. of P., 20 October 1919.

private owners of oil storage facilities were unlikely to be willing to maintain sufficiently large reserves. Allowing merchant ships to use naval stocks should be avoided as it would restrict naval movements. The Admiralty should build up a war reserve of 12 months consumption for commercial use as well as naval stocks. On the basis of demand during the war, and assuming that 75% of large merchant ships were oil-burners in 10 years time, 1,500,000 tons of oil were needed to give a reserve of 12 months' commercial use. The memorandum, signed by Long and Greenwood, concluded that:

> (a) That a twelve months' war reserve shall be laid down at home and at each important bunkering station abroad as a national necessity in war for commercial purposes. This reserve to be in addition to the approved reserve for Naval purposes;

> (b) That the commercial war reserve stock be provided and maintained by the State.[557]

Commercial shipping did not adopt oil as quickly as the authors of this paper expected; in 1930, over 60 per cent of the world's merchant shipping burnt coal.[558]

6.4 Oil and War Plans in 1920-21

The Cabinet had approved an oil reserve of 12 month's war consumption for the RN, to be built up over 10 years. In February 1920 Domvile argued that the need for economy and the strategic aspects of oil reserves had not been properly considered in late 1918, when it was decided to establish stocks of 4,500,000 tons at home and 336,000 overseas. Expenditure on storage in location that could not be defended or had little value in wartime was a waste.

In a conflict with the USA all oil supplies from the Americas and the Caribbean would be cut off. The main operational theatre would be the North Atlantic, meaning that substantial oil stocks would be need in the UK, at least until Middle Eastern supplies significantly increased. Until then one year's reserves might be too little. Stocks would also be needed in Canada or Newfoundland and in

---

[557] CAB 24/98, C.P. 601 'Oil Fuel Reserve for British Oil-Burning Merchant Ships', A. a. P. Executive, 5 February 1920.

[558] Brown, 'Royal Navy', p. 197.

Bermuda. Home reserves could not be used in a war with Japan; it would require more tankers than had been available in the recent war to transport the difference between demand and the production of Persia, Burma and British North Borneo from home to the western Pacific and Indian Ocean. Reserves should at least cover this balance for 12 months. Singapore would be the main base; the risk of raids meant that not all the oil reserve should be put there. The 1,500,000 tons needed should be split Singapore 685,000 tons, Hong Kong 15,000, Australia 400,000 and Burma 400,000. France and Italy were then the only possible European opponents. Neither was likely to be able to equal the threat to British sea communications, including oil imports, that Germany had posed in the last war. Unrestricted submarine warfare was unlikely and had reached its zenith in 1918. Six months' supply would be enough, divided UK 2,250,000 tons, Malta 200,000 and Gibraltar 100,000. Malta could be supplied from the east and Gibraltar from the UK and the USA. The location for storage of oil reserves should be based entirely on war needs. Supplies had to be mobile so a number of tankers should be kept overseas in wartime. Reserves built up by commercial companies to supply merchant ships should not be included when calculating naval reserves. Oil reserves were needed in all the possible main theatres of war; the North Atlantic, Mediterranean and western Pacific. Half the necessary storage should be built up in five years. Oil for a fleet transiting to the East had to be stored on the Suez and Cape routes. There should be oil reserves for escort vessels at key trade ports. [559]

On 26 May 1921 the Board of the Admiralty noted that the Cabinet had not replied to its arguments that oil reserves for commercial use were needed. Naval reserves of 4,500,000 tons at home had been approved, but another 3,500,000 tons were needed overseas. [560] Vice Admiral Sir Osmond de Brock, the Deputy Chief of the Naval Staff, put forward the reasoning behind this request. The RN could not keep a fleet big enough to deal with a Japanese threat in the Far East and maintain a force at home capable of facing a hostile USA or a combination of European powers. The mobility of the fleet was key; fuel had to be stationed in the main potential theatres of operation and on the routes to them. Home

---

[559] ADM 1/8607/102, 'Naval Oil Fuel Reserve', 1921. Memorandum by Director of Plans, 5 February 1920.

[560] Ibid. Extract from Board Minutes, 1352: 'Oil Fuel Reserves', 26 May 1921.

storage was being built up, but more was required on the route to and in the Far East. Japan ought to be deterred from acting against British interests if the RN was able to move quickly to the Far East. If the USA and Japan were to go to war with each other with Britain neutral a strong British fleet would be needed in the Far East in order to protect British interests. Britain had not needed substantial fuel reserves overseas before 1914 because most warships burnt coal; the most likely theatre of operations was in home waters where coal was readily available. An oil fired fleet that might have to operate outside of European waters needed oil reserves overseas and tankers to transport oil from the storage facilities to the fleet. De Brock gave the size of fleets required against each of the USA and Japan in 1930 and their annual oil consumption. The main bases would be Bermuda in a war with the USA and Singapore if the opponent was Japan. Storage would be located at a number of bases; the total reserves required exceeded the annual consumption because of the need to transport oil from the storage base to the operating one. The oil needs of a war in Europe would be met mostly by home reserves and Persian output with 300,000 tons of storage being required in the Mediterranean. Table 6-1 on the next page gives his figures for wars with the USA or Japan, assuming that:

1. The figures for Persia, Trinidad and Burma, which were all British controlled oilfields, were based on oil production rather than storage.
2. Allowance was made for quantities consumed by the fleet en passage to the Far East and requirements for secondary operations.
3. Australian stock was assumed to be positioned so as to be approximately equivalent to Singapore in respect of distance from any advanced Naval anchorage.
4. An additional 460,000 tons oil fuel at Singapore and another 48 oilers would be required to maintain supply at a base 2,500 miles beyond Singapore. No immediate provision was made for this, which would be considered along with the issue of separate commercial reserves abroad; these could only be properly considered when merchant shipping requirements could be more clearly defined. An output of about 480,000 tons from Dutch Borneo might possibly be available.
5. All commercial requirements in the Far East were to be met from Naval reserves provided in that area.
6. The Mediterranean figure was calculated after allowing for requirements for secondary operations.[561]

---

[561] Ibid.

Table 6-1 Oil requirements and proposed supply arrangements

WAR IN THE EAST			(Base Singapore)			
Class of Ship	No.	Estimated annual consumption oil fuel Tons	Source or Base	Quantity Tons	Equivalent at Singapore Tons	Requiring Oilers
Battleships	12		Singapore	1,200,000	1,200,000	
Battle Cruisers	8	480,000	Rangoon	400,000		
					468,000	3
Light Cruisers	26	624,000	Burmah	100,000		
Flotilla Leaders, T.B.D.s	80	960,000	Persia	1,530,000	1,224,000	30
Submarines	30	36,000	Aden	100,000		
					123,000	2
Various	10	240,000	Colombo	225,000		
Attendant Oilers	58	370,000	Hong Kong	15,000	15,000	
			Australia	400,000	400,000	
			Add for repairs			7
TOTAL	224	3,430,000		3,970,000	3,430,000	42
WAR IN THE WEST			(Base Bermuda)			
Class of Ship	No.	Estimated annual consumption oil fuel Tons	Source or Base	Quantity Tons	Equivalent at Bermuda Tons	Requiring Oilers
Battleships	22	1,320,000	U.K.	4,500,000	3,779,000	66
Battle Cruisers	7	420,000	Trinidad	72,000	72,000	
Light Cruisers	28	672,000	Persia	720,000	525,000	21
Flotilla Leaders, T.B.D.s	126	1,512,000				
Submarines	30	36,000	Halifax	100,000	100,000	
			Bermuda	500,000	500,000	
Various	18	648,000	Mediterranean	170,000	170,000	3
Attendant Oilers	59	504,000				
			Add for repairs			18
TOTAL	290	5,112,000		6,062,000		108

Source: ADM 1/8607/102, 'Oil Fuel Reserves', O. de B. Brock, 24 May 1921. Enclosure 2 to Board Minutes, 26 May 1921.

From the aggregate requirements for wars with the USA and Japan de Brock subtracted the home reserve and the annual output of the Persian, Burmese and Trinidadian oilfields. He added the extra reserves needed in the Mediterranean for a European war, the requirements for storage in New Zealand, Africa, the Falklands and the Pacific coast of Canada and working stock. This gave a total of 3,500,000 tons of reserves needed in the Empire outside of the UK. Substantial investment in oil storage facilities was required if this was to be achieved storage by 1930. He hoped that the Dominions could be encouraged to help.[562] His breakdown is given in Table 6-2:

Table 6-2 Proposed naval oil storage overseas

Station	Proposed fuel reserve, tons	Base	Quantity, tons	Existing 21/3/21, tons	Expected total 21/3/22, tons
Mediterranean	300,000	Gibraltar	80,000	11,200	11,200
		Malta	180,000	22,400	47,400
		Port Said	20,000		16,000
		Suez	20,000		
East Indies	730,000	Aden	100,000		
		Colombo	225,000		
		Kilindini	5,000		
		Rangoon	400,000		
Africa	48,000	Cape	24,000		
		Sierra Leone	24,000		
North America & West Indies	660,000	Bermuda	500,000	16,000	16,000
		Halifax	100,000		
		Jamaica	10,000		16,000
		Canada (Pacific)	50,000		
South America	24,000	Falkland Is.	24,000		
China	1,215,000	Singapore	1,200,000		
		Hong Kong	15,000		32,000
Australia	400,000	To be decided later	400,000		
New Zealand	26,000	Wellington	10,000		
		Fiji	16,000		
Working Stock	97,000	Bases abroad	97,000		
TOTAL	3,500,000			49,600	138,600

Source: ADM 1/8607/102, 'Oil Fuel Reserves', O. de B. Brock, 24 May 1921. Enclosure 1 to Board Minutes, 26 May 1921.

---

[562] Ibid.

De Brock's list of oil depots did not include any of three Pacific Island that in 1919 had been surveyed as potential fleet oiling bases. These were Fanning, one of the Line Islands, and two of the Cook Islands, Penrhyn and Suvarov. A report recommended building oil storage and airfields on them and considered how to defend them. The Admiralty decided that it was impracticable to develop them.[563]

The 26 May Board meeting led to the preparation of a memorandum, which the Board discussed on 17 June. It sent it to the CID, recommending that the oil reserves be increased by at least 500,000 tons of oil each year with more being added when allowed by economic circumstances.[564] It was very similar to de Brock's paper of the month before. Oil was so superior to coal as a fuel for ships that the switch to oil was necessary. This meant that the British Empire had lost control of global fuel supplies. Britain had to build up both oil reserves and tankers to transport them. Oil had to be drawn from either oilfields or storage facilities near fleet bases. Until these could be developed in other parts of the world the RN could not operate effectively outside home waters and the Mediterranean. There had to be a year's reserve of oil at for the fleet at its main bases and supplies on its route to the Far East. Oil stocks needed to be provided for detached squadrons in areas where these might be expected to operate. The recommendations for the distribution of reserves were similar to de Brock's a month previously. The Dominions and India should provide 1,000,000 tons of the 3,500,000 tons of storage required overseas; their defence depended on the mobility of the fleet. The need for a separate 12 month reserve for merchant ships was needed was repeated; the RN would not have spare tankers or oil in wartime, and commercial companies would not maintain reserves of more than three months. The Admiralty suggested 1,000,000 tons, admitting that it was hard to estimate the amount needed.[565] The final draft was sent to the CID under the name of Lord Lee, First Lord since February. Nothing should be done that might encourage British merchant ship owners to speed up the change from coal to oil. The commercial reserve would be additional to naval stocks, held at naval bases but to be allocated to merchant ships in wartime. The total reserves

---

[563] Roskill, *Naval.* p. 270 and note 3.

[564] ADM 1/8607/102. Extract from Board Minutes, 1364: 'Oil Fuel Reserves', 17 June 1921

[565] Ibid. 'Reserves of Oil Fuel', Admiralty, 4 June 1921.

remained 4,500,000 tons at home, 3,500,000 overseas and 1,000,000 for merchant ships. By March 1922 2,000,000 would have been completed.[566]

The CID asked for some changes to be made in view of the economic climate.[567] The Naval Staff's response requested total reserves of 2,713,000 tons in the Far East and on the route to Singapore. Table 6-3 shows that there were a few reductions compared with de Brock's figures, but most of the difference between this number and the previous 3,500,000 tons was because this paper did not consider stocks other than in the Far East and on the route there. Commercial reserves were excluded. The time taken to establish these reserves would depend on tanker availability and the production of Eastern oilfields. The Admiralty expected that a 12 month supply would be available in seven or eight years time.[568] The CID noted that this was the minimum acceptable to the Admiralty. The cost would be £2,000,000 in the first year, with later expenditure still to be determined. The CID agreed generally with the Admiralty's view, wanting the project to go ahead. The Chancellor of the Exchequer missed the meeting, and his views had to be heard. He had stated previously that £1,500,000 could probably be found in the first year.[569]

---

[566] Tracy, ed. *Collective*. [175] 'Reserves of Oil Fuel', memorandum by Lord Lee of Fareham, First Lord of the Admiralty, 21 June 1921, pp. 290-95. Original reference CID 145C, CAB 4/5.

[567] CAB 24/128, C.P. 3367 'Reserves of Oil Fuel for the Royal Navy', M. P. A. Hankey, 5 October 1921.

[568] CC, Roskill Papers, ROSK 7/188, 'Oil and Naval Fuel Reserves'. 'Naval Oil Fuel Reserves', Note by the Naval Staff, 26 July 1921, original reference CID 147-C.

[569] CAB 24/128 C.P. 3367, Hankey.

Table 6-3 Planned naval oil fuel reserves, 1921

Base	Naval Staff, July	De Brock, May
Australia	400,000	400,000
New Zealand - Wellington	10,000	10,000
New Zealand - Fiji	16,000	16,000
South Africa - Simonstown	24,000	24,000
Gibraltar	69,000	80,000
Malta	124,000	180,000
Port Said	4,000	20,000
Suez	20,000	20,000
Aden	100,000	100,000
Ceylon	225,000	225,000
Hong Kong		15,000
Kilindini		5,000
Rangoon	400,000	400,000
Sierra Leone	24,000	24,000
Singapore	1,200,000	1,200,000
Unallocated	97,000	97,000
Americas and West Indies		684,000
Total	2,713,000	3,500,000

Source: ROSK 7/188, 'Naval Oil Fuel Reserves', Note by the Naval Staff, 26 July 1921, original reference CID 147-C, ADM 1/8607/102, 'Oil Fuel Reserves', O. de B. Brock, 24 May 1921.

6.5 Post War Domestic Oil Policy

The RN was by far Britain's largest user of oil, but there was also growing civilian demand. The Petroleum Executive was established in wartime because of a crisis over Britain's oil supplies; in peacetime, the government had to decided whether or not to retain a separate body to co-ordinate oil policy. The idea of oil company mergers aimed at bringing RDS under British control returned in the early 1920s.

6.5.1 Domestic Demand

Before the war the oil industry had tried to replace coal with oil as the principal fuel of Britain's ships, railways and factories. This effort mostly failed except for the RN. The Admiralty put the technical advantages of oil first. Commercial

companies emphasised the cheapness and ready availability of British coal.[570]
Table 6-4 shows that British imports of oil rose significantly from 1900 to 1914.
The growth was mostly in petrol for internal combustion engines and fuel oil for
the RN.

Table 6-4 British imports of petroleum products, tons

Year	Total	Kerosene	Fuel Oil	Petrol	Lubricating Oil	Gas oil	Crude & other spirits
1885	288,000						
1890	410,000						
1895	691,000						
1900	995,000	840,000			155,000		
1905	1,171,000	614,000	48,000	73,000	185,000	249,000	2,000
1910	1,348,000	541,000	134,000	215,000	229,000	224,000	5,000
1913	1,904,000	613,000	371,000	394,000	265,000	257,000	4,000

Source: G. Jones, The State and the Emergence of the British Oil Industry (London: Macmillan, 1981), p. 32. Converted from imperial gallons in original. Not split before 1900.

After the war British railways, merchant shipping and industry continued to
favour coal, which was still providing 90 per cent of the country's primary fuel
needs in 1950. Industry did not switch to oil until its real price fell in the late
1950s.[571] This meant that for many years the main British user of oil remained
the RN; petrol for internal combustion engines was the other source of growth.

In 1919 two reports on motor fuel prices were produced by a sub-committee of
the Standing Committee on the Investigation of Prices. It included
representatives of the Petroleum Executive, the Automobile Association,
commercial vehicle users and motor vehicle workers' trade unions.[572] They
argued that the solution to high prices was to increase supply rather than to
control prices. The consuming countries should act jointly under the auspices of
the League of Nations. The manufacture of substitutes should be encouraged; it
was vital that these should not be controlled by monopolies. A minority on the

---

[570] G. G. Jones, 'The Oil-Fuel Market in Britain, 1900-14: A Lost Cause Revisited', *Business History* 20, no. 2 (1978), pp. 131-52.

[571] Ibid., p. 148.

[572] PP, *Profiteering Act, 1919. Report on Motor Fuel Prepared by a Sub-Committee Appointed by the Standing Committee on the Investigation of Prices*, HMSO 1920 [Cmd. 597]; *Profiteering Acts, 1919 and 1920. Second Report on Motor Fuel. Prepared by a Sub-Committee Appointed by the Standing Committee on the Investigation of Prices*, HMSO 1921 [Cmd. 1119].

committee further argued that it was necessary for there to be some government control over the production and distribution of substitutes. J. C. Clarke of the Petroleum Exchange dissented from the idea of any government control of prices, output or transport of oil products. This would discourage the rise in production that was the only way to bring down prices. The current situation resulted from temporary shortages of fuel and transport.[573]

The government made some efforts to encourage the production of oil from coal; these come to little. In 1925 the Department of Scientific and Industrial Research argued that a million coal miners and processing plant operators would be needed in order to meet Britain's war oil demand by low temperature carbonisation of coal. The development of the Bergius hydrogenation process, first patented in 1913, followed by the Fischer-Tropsch process in the 1920s, led to the idea being re-considered in the 1930s. Germany, with ample coal but little oil and vulnerable to naval blockade, built plants of both types, but Britain constructed only one. The 1937 Falmouth Committee calculated that a hydrogenation plant with an annual production of 150,000 tons of oil would cost the same as a fleet of tankers capable of importing 1,800,000 tons per annum. It would be easier for the enemy to bomb the plant than to sink all those tankers. Coal to oil plants were suggested as a means of alleviating unemployment. The Committee argued they were a very expensive means of doing so. The main advantage of hydrogenation was that it produced high quality petrol.[574]

6.6 Administrative Arrangements

In November 1919 Long argued that the vital nature and complexity of oil supplies meant that the Petroleum Executive should continue to exist. A Cabinet Committee had recommended giving the Board of Trade responsibility for oil. Long thought that this was a mistake; the Petroleum Executive could not have carried out its work as effectively had it been part of another department. He wanted it to be put under the auspices of a minister who could give it significant attention, and who was not responsible to a consuming department. He suggested the Chancellor of the Exchequer or a Cabinet minister without major

---

[573] PP, *Cmd. 1119.* pp. 8-9.

[574] Payton-Smith, *Oil*, pp. 19-24.

departmental duties such as the Chancellor of the Duchy of Lancaster.[575] The Cabinet decided that it would be put under the Secretary for Overseas Trade, a junior minister at the Board of Trade who was not a member of the Cabinet. This was then Greenwood, followed by Kellaway and then Lloyd-Greame. It would not become part of the Department of Overseas Trade.[576] The Petroleum Department, as the Executive became, remained independent until October 1922 when it was merged into the Board of Trade.[577] This was done on the recommendation of the Geddes Committee and was motivated by cost cutting. The Petroleum Department argued that its work was more complex than the Geddes Committee realised, and it needed to retain its independence; its arguments were ignored.[578] The cost saving was small, but this may have been due to an attitude that every penny counted rather than a downgrading of the importance of oil. The 19 staff of the separate Petroleum Department cost £9,000 per annum; the Board of Trade retained five staff, at an annual expense of £2,500.[579]

6.7 Renewed Oil Merger Proposals

The deal negotiated by Harcourt and Deterding to bring Shell under British control was never ratified, but further attempts were made in the early 1920s to merge APOC, Burmah and Shell into a single company. These were initiated by the companies rather than the government. Its holding in APOC meant that government consent was required. The proposal started in July 1921 with a plan by APOC and RDS to save money by rationalising and merging their British distribution networks. The industry was switching from selling petrol in cans to the use of roadside petrol pumps; a joint venture would reduce the cost of this modernisation programme. Burmah was keen on a full merger because it was concerned that its oil supplies might last no more than 20 years, and it wanted to diversify geographically away from India. RDS would also be short of oil if its supply contract with APOC was not renewed when it expired in 1922. Geoffrey

---

[575] CAB 24/93, C.P. 115 'Petroleum Executive', W. H. Long, 11 November 1919.

[576] CAB 24/93, C.P. 180 'Petroleum Committee', M. P. A. Hankey, 24 November 1919.

[577] Payton-Smith, *Oil*, p. 40.

[578] POWE 33/58, 'Petroleum Executive: Need for Permanent Petroleum Department', 1918-28. J. C. Clarke to Jenkins, 20 May 1922; J. C. Clarke to Mead Taylor, 14 February 1923.

[579] Ibid. Report of Select Committee on Expenditure, 13 June 1924.

Jones quotes internal RDS memoranda that show that it was dismissive of the idea that British oil supplies depended on British control of oil companies; Britain could obtain as much oil as it needed whilst it controlled the world's oceans. RDS was interested in profits and needed British diplomatic support in its attempts to recover its Russian oil interests that had been sequestrated by the Bolsheviks.[580]

In January 1922 Lloyd-Greame, the Secretary for Overseas Trade, wrote a Cabinet memorandum on the merger proposal. It would put all RDS oilfields except those in Dutch colonies under British control. Burmah would buy the government's holding in APOC. Royal Dutch, Shell and Burmah would continue to be independent holding companies; each would take stakes in the operating companies, giving a British majority in all except those operating in Dutch colonies. Under the current arrangements RDS could move control of all its operations, including its 500,000 tons of British registered tankers, to The Hague. It was unlikely that this would happen whilst Deterding remained in charge, but things could change after his retirement. The management of RDS was clearly superior to those of the solely British companies. The transaction would result in the group being 51 per cent British owned. Lloyd-Greame's recommendation that a Cabinet Committee should report on the issue was accepted. He suggested that the decision should not be announced until after the completion of the Washington Conference, which was then in progress, since it might be controversial and make other issues harder to resolve.[581]

The committee, chaired by Baldwin, the President of the Board of Trade, recommended that the government should retain its holding in APOC, which should not be allowed to participate in the merger. It would be in the interests of all three companies, which would reduce both capital and operating costs, but it was difficult to come up with any method by which consumers could be sure of benefitting from these savings. The concept of bringing Shell under British control was appealing, but it was unclear exactly what this meant. The proposal would not give definite and lasting British control of the foreign oilfields. The only way to be certain of controlling an oilfield in wartime was to

---

[580] Jones, *State*, pp. 222-23.

[581] CAB 24/132, C.P. 3637 'Proposed Amalgamation of the Royal Dutch, Shell, Burmah and Anglo-Persian Oil Companies', P. Lloyd-Greame, 6 January 1922.

control the territory where it was located. The merged group would be controlled by its most talented executive regardless of his nationality. The Committee agreed with the Admiralty's contention that the merger would put it in a worse position than its current long term contract with APOC. The new group could supply oil of the Admiralty's specification only from Persia, Borneo and Sarawak. The Admiralty would be faced with a monopoly supplier in the East, which might artificially limit output. This could not happen with APOC, which had financial and contractual obligations to the government. The merger would have a negative impact on the Empire, especially India. The new group would want to restrict output in expensive fields such as those in Burma. Small companies in Trinidad and India would find it hard to compete. The existing government holding in APOC created political problems for Britain, especially in the USA; it would have to be sold if the merger went through. Even then it was likely that the merger would produce diplomatic problems for Britain, which would be accused of creating a rival to Standard (NJ). Lord Inchcape and the chairman of APOC both argued that the government would receive a better price in the future.[582]

Baldwin told Cowdray in May 1923 that it was wrong for the government to hold shares in APOC because a state controlled company would never be as well managed as a privately owned one. Baldwin was by then Chancellor of the Exchequer; the Treasury was opposed to the government investment in APOC. Baldwin became Prime Minister just afterwards; in October Neville Chamberlain, the new Chancellor, argued that APOC should merge with other oil companies because it was poorly managed and would soon need new capital.[583] In January 1924 Leo Amery, the First Lord of the Admiralty, argued against disposal of the government's APOC stake. The share holding in APOC was acquired in order to provide secure oil supplies at a reasonable price. It succeeded in doing so since it supplied 40 per cent of the RN's oil at advantageous prices; the certainty of this supply put the Admiralty in a strong bargaining position when buying the balance of its needs. It had been argued that it was risky to place such reliance

---

[582] CAB 27/180, 'Oil Companies Amalgamation', 1922; POWE 34/1, 'Oil Concessions in Great Britain and the Empire', 1920-38; CAB 24/137, C.P. 4050 'Committee on the Proposed Amalgamation of the Royal Dutch, Shell, Burmah and Anglo-Persian Oil Companies', S. Baldwin, 23 June 1922.

[583] Jones, *State*, p. 229.

on a single oilfield; the high price that another company was willing to pay to obtain this field suggested that these fears were misplaced. Whilst the government remained the main shareholder in APOC, and thus the Persian oilfields, it possessed full knowledge and control of the depletion rate. Under the proposed transaction the new group would make up any shortfall in supplies from Persia from its other developments but at the market price. It would be in its interests to increase production in Persia so that this field was exhausted before the end of the Admiralty contract. The RN would continue to receive its oil but would have to pay a higher price for it. The new group's only other sources of oil of Admiralty specification were Borneo and Sarawak. The former was Dutch territory, and the Dutch Navy had preference over its supplies; neither was as well located for the RN as was Persia. The proposed merger would be acceptable to the Admiralty only if it provided all of the RN's oil, instead of the current 40 per cent, at a fixed price.

The scheme was claimed to have the following benefits:

1. Reduced costs as a result of the end of competition between the companies. This was in the interests of the companies, but might not benefit the public or the government.
2. Removal of the state interest in a commercial company. This was a benefit, unless there were special reasons otherwise; in this case, there were such reasons; the RN's oil supplies.
3. Removal of government support for a company that was claimed to be poorly managed and financed. These accusations were unjustified; APOC had short term problems, but a good future.
4. Ending state control over APOC would please foreign, especially US opinion. It was likely that the US would object even more to the government helping to form a rival to Standard Oil (NJ).
5. Bringing Shell under British control. This was desirable, but it was unlikely that the proposed scheme would achieve genuine British control of the group.

There were also a number of objections:

1. The oil price, and thus the price being obtained for the state's APOC shares, was depressed.

2. The merger was likely to lead to higher prices for oil products, which would be unpopular.

3. It would be bad for the domestic refining and shale oil industries.

The Labour Party, motorists and the Australian government had all objected to the transaction. The uncertainty had created problems for the management of APOC. The proposal should be blocked, and it should be made clear that, as far as possible, this decision was final.[584] The Conservative government could take no action since it fell within a few days. The new Labour Chancellor, Philip Snowden, quickly produced a report, which recommended that the proposal be rejected. He accepted the reasons put forward by Amery and added that the transaction would be likely to cause redundancies in the British refinery, shale oil and oil distribution industries.[585] The Conservatives were returned to power in the autumn 1924; in November they announced that the state holding in APOC would be retained.[586] Problems with the management of APOC were dealt with by changes in both its structure and personnel. In 1923, Slade, now APOC's vice chairman, produced a plan to re-organise it into a holding company structure. Cadman left government service to became an adviser to APOC in 1921; the government persuaded the company that they should promote him because of his knowledge of both government oil policy and the oil industry. He became a managing director in 1923, deputy chairman in 1925 and chairman in 1927.[587] The government continued to be the largest shareholder in British Petroleum, as APOC became, until 1987.

6.8 Chapter Summary

Civilian demand for oil rose, but not by as much as some forecast. The Admiralty had to put the technical advantages of oil over coal first; businesses had to compare this with the cost advantages of coal to a British consumer. This meant that most boilers and furnaces continued to be fired by coal, with civilian use of oil largely confined to internal combustion engines. Attempts to create a large,

---

[584] CAB 24/164, C.P. 20 (24) 'Admiralty Views on the Proposed Sale of the Government's Holdings in the Anglo-Persian Oil Company', L. S. Amery, 10 January 1924.

[585] CAB 24/164, C.P. 32 (24) 'Petroleum Committee', P. Snowden, 26 January 1924.

[586] Jones, *State*, p. 229.

[587] Ibid., pp. 224-25; Yergin, *Prize*, p. 262.

British controlled oil company failed. No scheme that guaranteed that the merged group would always act in British interests could be worked out. British control of the seas and of oil bearing territories was what mattered, not the shareholding structure of companies. The RN was able to buy oil cheaply because of the its long term contract with APOC. RDS and APOC obtained their objectives of maximising profit and shareholder value by co-operating with each other and with their American rivals.[588]

After the First World War Japan was seen as Britain's most likely opponent despite the Anglo-Japanese Alliance. The possibility of war with the USA was much less likely but could not be completely excluded because of tensions between the two countries. Britain could not afford to maintain a Far Eastern fleet large enough to defeat the IJN and keep the necessary force in home waters. The Admiralty saw mobility as the solution to this problem; this required large oil reserves, which were themselves expensive. Iraqi oil was well positioned to supply a fleet in the Far East and on transit there. Budgetary considerations were the main obstacle to the Admiralty's plans. A committee under Sir Eric Geddes had been established in August to look at ways of cutting government spending. In November the Washington Conference began. Its decisions would affect the Admiralty's plans significantly. At the same time moves would be towards allowing US oil companies a share of Iraqi oil. This would remove an obstruction to good Anglo-American relations, and was possible because of the realisation that control of oil bearing territory was more important than ownership of companies.

---

[588] Jones, *State*, pp. 229-40; Yergin, *Prize*, pp. 260-65.

7 Anglo-American Disputes over Oil and the Washington Naval Conference

Oil was a factor in the poor Anglo-American relations in the years immediately following the First World War, but there were other reasons for antagonism between the two countries. The USN's 1916 building programme meant that it might soon overtake the RN as the world's largest navy. The Americans were suspicious of Japanese intentions and did not want Britain to renew its alliance with Japan when it expired in 1922. The USA feared that its oil would soon run out and that Britain was attempting to corner the market in the rest of the world. Britain argued that it had very little oil, whilst the USA dominated the global industry.

The importance of oil to US relations with Britain is shown by the high proportion of the documents on Anglo-American Relations published in the 1920-23 volumes of *Foreign Relations of the United States* that deal with either oil or the related issue of economic rights in British mandated territories.[589] Geoffrey Jones points out that the government shareholding in APOC gave that company problems in South America, where the USA encouraged countries to refuse concessions to companies controlled by foreign governments. Foreign Office concern that the establishment of a big, entirely British oil company would worsen relations with the USA was one reason for the rejection of such plans; this applied even if the state was not a shareholder in the group.[590]

John DeNovo argues that in 1917 few Americans thought that overseas oil was of any significance to their country; US oil companies produced oil in only two foreign countries, Mexico and Romania. The lessons of the war, coupled with concerns that US oil would run out and that the British were taking control of the world's oil, meant that by 1920 obtaining overseas oil was one of the aims of US foreign policy. Later in the decade new discoveries in the USA reduced the need for overseas oil and an aggressive foreign oil policy; a number of US

---

[589] "FRUS". 1920 vol ii pp. 649-74, 1921 vol. ii pp. 71-118, 1922 vol. ii pp. 287-358, 1923 vol. ii pp. 218-71.

[590] Jones, 'British', pp. 225-26.

companies had by then established themselves in the Middle East.[591] Subsequent historians of the US oil industry who broadly agree with this analysis include Gerald Nash, Stephen Randall and Daniel Yergin.[592] Randall points out that not all supporters of a more aggressive overseas US oil policy were close to the industry. Some were, including Requa and Van H. Manning, director of research at the American Petroleum Institute. Others, such as Daniels, were more suspicious of oil companies. In 1920 the American Institute of Mining and Metallurgical Engineering called on the government to make strenuous efforts, including the use of reciprocal agreements, to gain access to foreign mineral resources, Its president, Herbert Hoover, became Secretary of Commerce when the Republican President Warren Harding took office in March 1921.[593]

7.1 US Suspicions of Britain

The USA became suspicious of British intentions towards oil as early as January 1916. During a House of Commons debate on economic warfare on 10 January, Walter Runciman, the President of the Board of Trade, commented that:

> we must carry further our investigation into the control of oil. We never seem to get to the bottom of that fact. We must see to it that the control of coal within this country, or within the Dominions, does not pass out of British hands.[594]

On 11 January, the *New York Times* reported the debate under the title 'British Planning World Oil Control.'[595] It quoted Runciman as saying that 'we must keep control of the world's coal; we must secure control of the supply of oil';[596] the first part was an accurate paraphrase of his comments on coal, but he did not make the comments on oil attributed to him by the newspaper. In 1920 David

---

[591] J. A. Denovo, 'The Movement for an Aggressive American Oil Policy Abroad, 1918-1920', *American Historical Review* 61, no. 4 (1956), pp. 854-76.

[592] Nash, *United States Oil Policy, 1890-1964. Business and Government in Twentieth Century America*, pp. 49-72; S. J. Randall, *United States Foreign Oil Policy since World War I: For Profits and Security*, 2nd ed. (Montreal: McGill-Queen's University Press, 2005), pp. 13-42; Yergin, *Prize*, pp. 194-206.

[593] Randall, *United States*, pp. 13-17.

[594] *Parliamentary Debates, Fifth Series, House of Commons*, vol. lxxvii, p. 1362.

[595] "New York Times Archive", New York Times <<http://www.nytimes.com/ref/membercenter/nytarchive.html>> (accessed 1 December 2010). 'British Planning World Oil Control', 11 January 1916

[596] Ibid.

White of the US Geological Survey published an article on 'The Petroleum Resources of the World'[597]. It included lengthy quotes from a 1919 article by Sir Edward Edgar Mackay in *Sperling's Journal*. Mackay claimed that US oil reserves would soon be exhausted, leaving the USA dependent on British oil. White thought that some allowances had to be made for bias towards Britain and hyperbole in Mackay's opinions, but they backed White's case that the USA would soon be dependent on foreign oil. White cited an editorial from the 24 February 1920 edition of the London *Financial News*, which claimed that Britain by then controlled at least 56 per cent of the world's oil, and perhaps 75 per cent if British owned fields in South America were added; this compared with only 2 per cent in 1914.[598]

In 1926 a book by John Ise, Professor of Economics at the University of Kansas, repeated the allegation that Runciman had in 1916 claimed that Britain planned to control the world's oil supplies, quoting the views of Mackay and of the *Financial News*. Mackay had repeated his views in 1923. Ise emphasised that Mackay stated that Britain had an intentional strategy of obtaining as much oil as possible, and then waiting until US supplies ran out. Ise cited Beeby Thompson, a pioneer of the Trinidad oil industry, as saying that this was the British policy. Thompson, unlike Mackay, opposed this strategy, as it was likely to lead to retaliation.[599] Ludwell Denny, writing in 1930, reported Mackay's views, which he said had been frequently quoted in the USA. He produced a statement allegedly made by Pretyman to *The Times* in May 1919, asserting that Britain by then controlled nearly half of the world's oil, compared with 2 per cent in 1914;[600] no such claim can be found in *The Times*' extensive digital archive.[601] Not only Americans re-produced Mackay's views; the French author Pierre L'Espagnol de la Tramerye and the Danish Professor Anton Mohr both quoted them.[602] Mohr pointed out that *Sperling's Journal* was the house publication of Sperling & Co., a bank of which Mackay was a director, but added that they had been re-printed

---

[597] D. White, 'The Petroleum Resources of the World', *Annals of the American Academy of Political and Social Science* 89 (1920).

[598] Ibid., p. 133.

[599] J. Ise, *The United States Oil Policy* (New Haven, CT: Yale University Press, 1926), pp. 460-62.

[600] Denny, *We Fight*, p. 30.

[601] "The Times Archive", The Times <<http://archive.timesonline.co.uk/tol/archive/>> (accessed 1 December 2010).

[602] L'Espagnol de la Tramerye, *World*, pp. 166-68; Mohr, *Oil*, pp. 196-99.

in the *Philadelphia Public Ledger*, making them well known in the USA. What none of the contemporary commentators mentioned was that Mackay was a private citizen expressing his personal opinion. He had no official position, and had not been participated in any of the several official British committees on oil policy as either a member or a witness. The wide circulation of his views encouraged American mistrust of Britain.

Walter Long did have an official and senior position; in March 1920 he made a speech to the British Institute of Petroleum Technologists that raised US fears about British oil policy. According to Stephen Roskill, Long's comments were little reported in the UK but were repeated in American newspapers, including the *New York Times*.[603] It pointed out that the day after Long's speech a Senate Foreign Relations sub-committee had called on the President to send a US warship and marines to Batum to protect US citizens and property there and along the railway to Baku. Long had claimed that Britain had an opportunity to take control of the world's oil supplies. Doing so would give it complete freedom of action. The British government would be heavily criticised if it failed to take advantage of this chance. The newspaper stated that oil was as important to the USA as it was to Britain.[604]

In March 1920 Sir Auckland Geddes, Eric's brother, was appointed British Ambassador to Washington. In June he wrote to the Prime Minister setting out his thoughts on the USA. There was a lot of agitation against Britain; it was most strongly supported by Irish-Americans and, via them, most Catholics. Britain had a significant number of friends, but the majority of the country was just to the anti-British side of indifference. Most felt somehow slighted by Britain's possession of a bigger navy than the USN but admired Britain. There was a belief that the League of Nations was a British plan to enlist the US armed forces in support of British aims. Oil had been causing particular problems with the US public's attitude towards Britain. Geddes claimed that a recent speech of his had calmed things:

> The real thing that has been angering them was the idea sedulously propagated by the Press that Great Britain had obtained a monopoly

---

[603] Roskill, *Naval*, p. 219.

[604] "N.Y.T. Archive". 'To Protect American Interests', 26 March 1920

of the Oil of the world and was proposing to hold them to ransom. Since my New York speech last week in which I dealt with oil fairly fully, this particular symptom has disappeared and the disappearance has undoubtedly been extremely helpful in getting the people to think more sanely.[605]

In November Geddes telegrammed the Foreign Office about US attitudes towards Japan and the Anglo-Japanese Alliance. Throughout the USA there was suspicion of Japan; the problems that it faced because of its growing population, restricted territory and shortages of raw materials were acknowledged. The US did not desire a conflict with Japan but wanted to stop Japanese immigration to the USA. Most Americans would like to see an end to the Anglo-Japanese Alliance and the USA, Japan and Britain agree to an open door policy in China. The Senate was unlikely to agree to an alliance between Britain and the USA. An agreement with the President that the two countries would maintain sufficient naval strength in the Pacific to outnumber Japan could be concluded; it would last for the balance of his term in office. Despite opposition to renewal of the Anglo-Japanese Alliance, extending it would not strengthen the oil, Irish and other anti-British lobbies. It restrained the more extreme of the anti-British factions; deciding now not to renew it would be correct only if British policy was to avoid any disputes with the USA. He wanted it renewed but modified to comply with the League of Nations Charter.[606]

7.2 The USA and Overseas Oil

The USA was concerned that it was being shut out of international markets. It was the world's largest oil producer, but Mexico was the only other country in which its oil companies had significant producing interests.[607] Rising demand and declining output were expected to soon make it a net importer. US plans for expansion of its merchant navy required international sources of oil. On 31 July 1919, his last day as Chairman of the US Shipping Board, Edward Nash wrote to President Wilson urging the establishment of a worldwide bunker network to

---

[605] PA, Lloyd George Papers, LG/F/60/4/1, 'Sir Auckland Geddes to the Prime Minister', 4 June 1920.

[606] NMM, Beatty Papers, BTY/13/28/5, 'British Naval Officers and Officials: Long, W H, 1st Viscount (1858-1924), Letters and Papers 25 Feb 1919-21 Jun 1922'. Telegram from Sir Auckland Geddes, 15 November 1920.

[607] Jones, *State*, p. 219.

supply US ships with fuel; this increasingly meant oil. Nash claimed that Britain had control over a wide range of oilfields throughout the world, with great future potential. These were mostly held by RDS but included APOC's Persian reserves. US merchant ships might not return to US ports for several years so would be dependent on foreign bunkering depots in two thirds of the world. Nash wanted the USA to set up its own chain of bunkering facilities to give its merchant fleet oil supplies around the world.[608]

In March 1920 US Senate Resolution 331 requested that the President inform it of any restrictions in foreign countries on oil development by US citizens and indicate what measures were being taken to guarantee equal treatment for US citizens. It singled out France, Britain, the Netherlands, Japan and Mexico.[609] A month later the State Department replied; US diplomats were well aware of the significance of oil, and produced timely reports on this issue, which were circulated to all relevant departments. They had been told to give all legitimate help to reputable US citizens and businesses attempting to obtain mineral concessions. They had been warned to be wary of US citizens acting for foreign interests and of US registered but foreign controlled companies. The State department had no means of encouraging overseas activity by US oil companies or restricting the actions of foreign ones.[610] A significant proportion of its report was devoted to restrictions on oil development by foreigners in British territory.[611]

Each territory of the British Empire had its own legislation on the oil industry. British strategy was to prevent foreigners from controlling any of the Empire's oil and to obtain oil supplies in other countries.[612] US citizens were kept out of the Persian oil industry by APOC's exclusive rights. In British occupied territories such as German East Africa and parts of the Ottoman Empire British policy appeared to be to prevent development of oilfields by maintaining the pre-war regulations. Palestine, then expected to be a rich oil province, was singled out.

---

[608] Link et al, eds, *Wilson*. vol. 62, Edward Nash Hurley to President, 31 July 1919, pp. 77-79.

[609] "FRUS". 1920, vol. i, 'The Acting Secretary of State to President Wilson', 14 May 1920, p. 351

[610] Ibid. 'The Secretary of State to Senator Wesley L. Jones', 15 April 1920, pp. 350-51

[611] Ibid. 'Report to the Senate in Response to Senate Resolution 331', pp 351-68. Comments specific to the British Empire, Palestine and Persia (pp. 354-61, 365) were greater than those on all other countries (pp. 353-54, 361-65).

[612] Ibid. p. 354.

Mesopotamia did not rate a separate mention, possibly because of the uncertain situation in the Ottoman Empire. Throughout the world restrictions on foreign involvement in the oil industry generally applied to all and did not single out Americans. The State Department regarded this as being inimical to good international relations but not illegal under international law. Foreigners were mostly excluded by governments and colonial administrations acting under discretionary powers. The use of these to discriminate against Americans was the soundest basis for US protests; the State Department was trying to obtain detailed information on specific cases of loss suffered by US oil interests overseas from the discriminatory application of executive powers. Future prospects for US investment in the overseas oil industry depended on reciprocal agreements with foreign governments.[613]

There was some confusion in the USA over the British government's relationship with RDS On 12 April 1921 Senator Henry Cabot Lodge claimed in a Senate speech that Austen Chamberlain had told Parliament that the British government controlled it. Avery Andrews wrote to Lodge on behalf of RDS explaining that this was not the case. Chamberlain, the Chancellor of the Exchequer, had stated that the British government retained its shareholding in APOC. A question was asked about this in the House of Commons about RDS' contract to buy oil from APOC. Greenwood declined to give any details as the government had agreed not to become involved in APOC's commercial activities. In April 1920 the government had been asked if it was in negotiations to purchase a controlling stake in RDS; it had replied that it was not.[614] Talks did take place over bringing Shell under British control; these did not involve the government buying a stake in it and could have resulted in the sale of the government shareholding in APOC.

Claims in the overseas press that foreign oil companies were excluded from the British Empire led to the Petroleum Department preparing a memorandum putting forward the British point of view, which was presented to Parliament and published. A covering note from Curzon to the Ambassador to the USA, inviting him to use it when dealing with enquiries on the subject, made it clear

---

[613] Ibid. pp. 365-66.

[614] ROSK 7/188. Avery Andrews to Senator Henry Cabot Lodge, 27 April 1921.

that it was the views of the US press that concerned the Foreign Office. Apart from Russia, whose demand had been reduced by the effects of the revolution on its economy, only the USA used more oil than Britain. World oil output in 1920 totalled 67,000,000 tons; the solitary well in Britain produced only one ton, with Scottish shale oil contributing another 165,000 tons. Britain imported 3,368,000 tons of oil; its annual imports had reached 5,160,000 tons during the war. British use per head of population was only a sixth of that of the USA, but British needs were high and had mostly to be imported. There was no policy to exclude foreign oil interests from the British Empire, but Britain's shortage of oil meant that such measure could be justifiable.[615] Table 7-1 shows that most British oil came from the USA:

Table 7-1 Sources of British oil, 1920

Source	Quantity	Value
USA	61%	68%
Other foreign	37%	30%
British Empire	2%	2%

Source: PP, *Miscellaneous No. 17 (1921). Despatch to His Majesty's Ambassador at Washington Enclosing a Memorandum on the Petroleum Situation*, 1921 [Cmd. 1351], p. 2.

The restrictions on foreigners developing oilfields in the United Kingdom were wartime measures that had now been repealed; these restrictions were rather academic since little oil had been found in the United Kingdom, but their existence was criticised by the Americans. There was no general policy to exclude foreigners, but there were local restrictions in some parts of the Empire. The largest producer in the Empire was India, but it was a net importer of oil; leases had been given only to British subjects or to companies controlled by British subjects. This was normally the case on Crown land in Trinidad, the second largest producer, but an exception had been made for a US company. Egypt and Sarawak were other significant producers without nationality restrictions. There were no restrictions in Egypt. In Canada and parts of Australia leases could be granted only to British registered companies. This did not exclude foreigners since the largest oil company in Canada was Imperial Oil, a British registered subsidiary of Standard (NJ). The regulations in British Guiana, British Honduras, Nigeria, Kenya and Brunei were similar to those in Trinidad. There were no restrictions in South Africa, New Zealand, Newfoundland,

---

[615] PP, *Miscellaneous No. 17 (1921). Despatch to His Majesty's Ambassador at Washington Enclosing a Memorandum on the Petroleum Situation*, HMSO 1921 [Cmd. 1351]. p. 2.

Jamaica, Barbados, Brunei or British North Borneo; little oil had been found in any of these places. The British Government had no say in the granting of an exclusive concession to APOC by Persia. Britain insisted that the claim sometimes made that it controlled half of the world's oil was based on poor data and assumptions. Britain had temporarily lost its investments in south Russia, and its stake in Romania was no greater than that of the USA, France or the Netherlands. The USA produced two thirds of the world's oil, held a large share of the Mexican oilfields and was well placed to participate in the development of South American oilfields. The questions of Iraq and Palestine had been dealt with in separate correspondence with the USA. Concessions granted before the war had to be considered.[616]

There were restrictions on foreign investment in parts of the British Empire, but Britain's main problem was that little oil had been found in its territory. There was a lot of oil in the British Empire, but most of it could not be developed with the technology of the 1920s. The British controlled oil province that mattered to both Britain and the US industry was Iraq. British control of Iraq, including the oil of Mosul, appeared to have been guaranteed by the Treaty of Sèvres and the Anglo-French San Remo Agreement. The resurgence of Turkey under Kemal and the Iraqi revolt meant that it was uncertain if Britain would retain control over Mosul. Before that was resolved, the Washington Conference would deal with some of the other issues affecting Anglo-American relation.

7.3 The Washington Conference and Oil

In July 1921 President Harding invited Britain, France, Italy and Japan to a conference in Washington to discuss both disarmament and Far Eastern matters. Britain was rumoured to be about to organise a conference on the Far East, and the US wanted to control the agenda. Harding's Secretary of State, Charles Hughes, desired parity between the USN and the RN but was happy if this could be achieved without completing the US 1916 programme. He saw Japan as the main threat to the USA and wanted to end the Anglo-Japanese Alliance. The British had accepted the principle of naval parity with the USN but thought that they would have to build eight expensive capital ships to maintain it; the RN

---

[616] Ibid., pp. 4-5.

would slip to third place if the USA and Japan completed their construction programmes and Britain did nothing. They realised that the Anglo-Japanese Alliance was an impediment to good relations with the USA; it would have to be at least heavily modified and probably ended.

Hughes opened the conference with an offer to scrap all the capital ships from the 1916 building programme. Other countries had to stop building capital ships and must scrap enough older ones to arrive at a ratio of 5 US, 5 British, 3 Japanese, 1.67 French and 1.67 Italian. The USN had argued that it needed to be twice the size of the IJN but was over-ruled by Hughes. It was agreed that one of the Japanese battleships and two of the US ones then building could be completed. Britain, whose battleships were older, was allowed to build two, but to the new limits of 35,000 tons displacement and 16 inch guns rather than the larger vessels that had been planned. The greater age of Britain's ships also meant that the RN was initially allowed a greater tonnage of capital ships than the USN; equality would be achieved as ships were scrapped and replaced according to an agreed timetable. All types of ship were restricted in armament and displacement; only capital ships and aircraft carriers had a limit placed on their total tonnage. The French rejected a British attempt to ban submarines, leading Britain to block US proposals to introduce a tonnage limit for cruisers and destroyers. Some in Britain, including Churchill, thought that the RN could maintain an advantage over the USN by superiority in cruisers. This would create friction between the two countries later in the decade. The French refused to discuss land disarmament without American and British security guarantees, which were not forthcoming. The Anglo-Japanese Alliance was replaced by a Four Power Treaty under which Britain, France, Japan and the USA agreed to respect each other's existing positions in the Pacific. The five naval powers plus Belgium, China, the Netherlands and Portugal signed the Nine Power Treaty, which was supposed to guarantee an open door policy in China but offered no means of enforcing it. The conference closed with the signing of the naval disarmament treaty on 6 February 1922.

Britain went to Washington accepting parity with the USA in capital ships and wanting a 50 per cent margin over Japan, but expecting to have to spend heavily on new construction to maintain these standards. It came away with equality with the USA, a 67 per cent superiority over Japan and better than a two power standard in Europe. It was able to considerably reduce its construction budget. The Washington Treaty banned the development of naval bases within a specified zone of the Pacific. The Japanese asked for this in return for accepting a ratio of 60 per cent of the strength of the RN and USN rather than the 70 per cent that they desired. This prevented the USN from basing its main Pacific fleet at the Philippines or Guam; Japan was not so inconvenienced but did have potential bases within this area. Britain had already decided to develop Singapore, which was outside the prohibited zone, rather than Hong Kong, which was inside it. The Admiralty was unhappy with the impact of the 10 year construction holiday on the shipbuilding industry, but Britain could have few complaints with the Treaty; it was left in a relatively stronger position than it could have achieved by trying to compete with US naval construction.[617]

Lord Lee wrote in his diary that he was delighted by Hughes's initial proposal, which removed the risk of Britain having to enter an expensive naval race with the USA.[618] Eric Grove argues that the Treaty was better for Britain than for any of the other participants. The main negative was that Japan was now a possible opponent rather than an ally.[619] France appeared to be the big loser of the Treaty. It had been the world's second naval power for much of the eighteenth and nineteenth centuries; it was now joint fourth with Italy, a potential enemy in the Mediterranean that did not have France's global empire. Joel Blatt contends that France came out of Washington better than is often argued, and that French access to Middle Eastern oil was a factor in this. Its naval strategy concentrated on the Mediterranean, where it had three missions; transporting colonial troops to France, protecting imperial communications and convoying Middle Eastern oil to France. The French were shocked that Hughes's proposals left them inferior to Japan but decided that capital ship equality with Italy was

---

[617] "FRUS". 1922, vol. i, pp. 1-383; G. W. Baer, *One Hundred Years of Sea Power : The U.S. Navy, 1890-1990* (Stanford, CA: Stanford University Press, 1994), pp. 94-103; CAB 24/133, C.P. 3738 'Treaty for the Limitation of Naval Armament. Washington Conference', M. P. A. Hankey, 17 February 1922; P. M. Kennedy, *The Rise and Fall of British Naval Mastery* (London: Allen Lane, 1976), pp. 273-79; O'Brien, *British*, pp. 157-74; Roskill, *Naval*, pp. 300-30; H. H. Sprout, M. Sprout, *Toward a New Order of Sea Power. American Naval Policy and the World Scene, 1918-1922* (Princeton, N.J; London,: 1943), pp. 283-96.

[618] A. Clark, ed. *A Good Innings: The Private Papers of Viscount Lee of Fareham* (London: J. Murray, 1974), pp. 217-18.

[619] Grove, *Royal Navy*, p. 148.

acceptable as they could obtain overall superiority by outbuilding Italy in oil fuelled cruisers, destroyers and submarines.[620]

Washington discouraged the move towards diesel engined battleships that had been expected by Fisher and others because it limited the standard displacement of warships, which excluded fuel. Steam turbines used three times as much fuel as diesel engines but were lighter. A ship with oil fired steam turbines would have a lower standard displacement than an otherwise equal vessel with diesel engines. Few surface warships were ever fitted with diesels as their main engines; the most famous exceptions were the German *Deutschland* class, popularly known as pocket battleships. Diesels were more common in merchant ships, which emphasised fuel economy over displacement, but British ship owners were relatively slow to adopt them.[621]

7.3.1 Oil and the Conference

The British did not want to discuss oil at the conference, but were afraid that the USA would bring it up. Long and Pretyman, both retired from office, wrote separately to Lloyd George on this subject. Long's letter of 29 September stated that he was worried that the US would attempt to add oil to the agenda. Standard (NJ) had realised that it needed oil supplies from outside the USA in order to protect its market position, but faced competition from British companies. Britain might then be forced to make a compromise on oil that was contrary to its interests in order to conclude an agreement on disarmament. If it was too late to exclude oil, Long recommended that Lloyd-Greame, the minister responsible for oil, be added to the British delegation.[622] Lloyd-George replied that oil was not relevant to the subject matter of the conference, and that he was not aware of it being added to the agenda. He would consider Long's views if this changed.[623]

---

[620] J. Blatt, 'The Parity That Meant Superiority: French Naval Policy Towards Italy at the Washington Conference, 1921-22, and Interwar French Foreign Policy', *French Historical Studies* 12, no. 2 (1981), pp. 223-48.

[621] Brown, 'Royal Navy', pp. 244-45.

[622] PA, Lloyd George Papers, LG/F/34/1/67, 'Long to the Prime Minister', 29 September 1921.

[623] PA, Lloyd George Papers, LG/F/34/1/68, 'Prime Minister to Long', 24 October 1921.

Pretyman brought an article published in *The Times* on 5 November 1921 to the Prime Minister's attention. It argued that the Anglo-American oil dispute was an obstacle to success at the conference. British oil policy was driven by the Admiralty, whilst Standard (NJ) had a major say in US foreign oil policy. The American oil industry thought that Britain was trying to control global oil supplies. The newspaper contended that this was untrue. It was understandable that the government stake in APOC, attempts to increase British influence over RDS and the San Remo Agreement with France concerned the Americans. The RN's need to ensure its oil supplies and the US industry's desire to maintain its profits and supplies created a conflict.

The Times suggested that the solution was that the government should sell its stake in APOC and cut its links to RDS. In wartime oil supplies were secured by control of the oceans and of oilfields rather than by ownership of oil companies. Government ownership had forced APOC into poor commercial decisions, such as drilling on British territory rather than on foreign lands more likely to yield oil. Britain should agree to the US desire to open the door to oilfields on its territories; this would produce greater supplies and would not harm national security.[624] The Petroleum Department thought that its author was well informed. It might be Sydney Brooks who had links to US oil companies. It could not have come from RDS as it wrongly claimed that the British Government had a financial interest in that group.[625] The article provoked replies from both companies. Each wished to correct a single point but made no criticism of the article's overall argument. Walter Samuel of Shell refuted the claim that the government had any involvement with his group.[626] Charles Greenway of APOC denied that the government had forced his company to make decisions on non-commercial grounds.[627]

Lloyd George replied to Pretyman thanking him for bringing the article to his attention; he had not seen it, suggesting that oil was not a high priority for him at that time. The Prime Minister stated that all involved worried that the USA

---

[624] 'Oil Power', *The Times*, 5 November 1921.

[625] POWE 33/93, 'Washington Conference on Disarmament: Correspondence on Amalgamation of Oil Companies', 1921. Petroleum Department to Lloyd-Greame, 9 November 1921

[626] W. H. Samuel, 'Oil Power', *The Times*, 8 November 1921.

[627] C. Greenway, 'Oil Power', *The Times*, 9 November 1921.

might bring up oil at Washington. There had been no suggestion that they would. They were very keen that the conference should succeed and would not want to risk failure by introducing a contentious issue. Balfour, the head of the British delegation, had been instructed that he should say that he had not been briefed on it and could not discuss it without consulting the government and bringing oil experts to Washington. Cadman would be in New York on APOC business, and could be called upon if necessary.[628] Pretyman told Lloyd-Greame that he was entirely satisfied with this reply.[629] Cadman's presence in the USA was very convenient, but there is nothing in Curzon's briefing letter to Balfour on the subject to suggest that it was anything other than a fortunate coincidence. Curzon wrote that:

> The possibility of the United States Government's adding "oil" as an item to the agenda of the Disarmament Conference has received the earnest consideration of His Majesty's Government, and as a result of discussions with the various Departments concerned it had been decided that the British Delegates should if possible resist any attempt to induce the Conference to deal with the question of oil.
>
> I should however state, for your information, that Sir John Cadman, K.C.M.G., late of the Petroleum Department and now a Director of the Anglo-Persian Oil Company, is proceeding on business of the Company to New York, where he will be available for consultation by the British Delegation in the event of a discussion of the oil question being forced upon the British Delegation to the Conference.[630]

The US oil industry press had anticipated that oil would be discussed at Washington. On 9 November the *Oil, Paint and Drug Reporter* argued that oil was certain to be discussed at the conference and claimed that the State Department had studied the issue in detail. It expected the US to propose that the nations represented agreed to treat each others' nationals equally when allocating oil concessions and to eliminate waste. A permanent international oil conference would be established.[631] The 5 December issue of the *National Petroleum News* argued that Hughes would not introduce it from the start but would do so at the appropriate moment. The State Department had gathered an

---

[628] POWE 33/93. Prime Minister to Pretyman, 25 November 1921

[629] Ibid. Pretyman to Lloyd Greame, 2 December 1921

[630] Balfour Papers Mss. 49734. Curzon to Balfour, 9 November 1921, f. 227-28,

[631] POWE 33/93. Oil, Paint and Drug Reporter, 9 November 1921

enormous amount of information on the issue.[632] These articles sounded well informed, but oil was not discussed at the conference. It may be that they were part of a lobbying campaign by the oil industry to put it on the agenda, and that Lloyd George was correct in thinking that the US government would not want to risk the conference failing by introducing a divisive issue. Another possibility is that they planned to do so but were dissuaded by the conciliatory interviews and speeches given by Cadman.

In the 7 December issue of the *National Petroleum News* the article immediately preceding the one on the forthcoming Washington Conference was an interview with Cadman; the Cadman article had a larger headline. He insisted that Britain did not have a policy of excluding US oil companies and realised that it needed their expertise and capital. Misunderstandings had arisen between Britain and the USA because of differences in the ways that both businessmen and politicians expressed themselves in the two countries. This was compounded by propaganda from newspapers and individuals who wanted to stir up distrust between them.[633]

The next day he gave a speech to the Annual Meeting of the American Petroleum Institute, entitled 'As John Bull Views It.'[634] He was in the USA to visit refineries and oilfields to learn about current practices ahead of taking up his new post with APOC and wanted to take the opportunity to correct some misunderstanding over British oil policy. The British government had no say in the management of APOC, despite its shareholding, and owned no shares in RDS. He opposed political interference in commercial operations but urged co-operation between governments and companies. Britain did not have a policy of excluding foreign oil companies from its Empire. Some restrictions had been introduced, for example in India when the industry was in its infancy; it was then necessary to encourage local companies and to prevent large ones from leaving fields undeveloped. The modern oil industry required so much capital and knowledge that it would be wrong to exclude any companies. Britain did not operate a closed door policy; the countries of the Empire made their own laws,

---

[632] Ibid. *National Petroleum News*, 7 December 1921

[633] Ibid. *National Petroleum News*, 7 December 1921

[634] Ibid. American Petroleum Institute, Press Release, 9 December 1921

but he did not think that any of them would block foreign investment in their oil industries. The oil of Mesopotamia would be developed for the benefit of Iraq. The San Remo Agreement was not directed against any country.

7.4 The Door Opens to the Americans

The conciliatory speeches and interviews given by Cadman in 1921-22 laid the basis for the door to Iraq to open to the Americans. Britain was keen to remove areas of Anglo-American tension. Negotiations were left to the companies, but the governments were kept informed. At the start of February 1922 Churchill replied to a letter sent to him by Curzon late the previous year. He agreed that keeping the Americans out of Iraqi oil would give Britain continued problems in the Middle East. TPC's concession was not certain to be approved if it went to international arbitration, as the Americans had suggested. An official invitation could suggest that the British were concerned that the TPC claim was weak. It would be better if the first move came from Standard (NJ). A proposal for co-operation between APOC and Standard (NJ) in north Persia might lead to the companies working together in Iraq.[635] The change of government did not affect the policy of opening the door to the Americans. In December 1922 the Admiralty wrote to the Colonial Office stressing the importance of British control of Mosul but indicating that the makeup of companies was less significant.[636]

7.4.1 North Persia

A precedent for Anglo-American oil co-operation was set in north Persia. D'Arcy had declined oil rights in five northern provinces because he thought that competition from Russian oil would make them unprofitable. In November 1921 Standard (NJ) was granted the concession in this area.[637]

On 12 January 1922 Lloyd-Graeme told Churchill that coming to an equitable deal with Standard (NJ) in Iraq was the only way to avoid continuing disputes with the USA there and in the rest of the world. Cadman had been negotiating

---

[635] NA, CO 730/27, 'Colonial Office: Iraq Correspondence', 1922. 3167: Curzon to Churchill, 1 February 1922.

[636] Ibid. 60792: Admiralty to Colonial Office, 7 December 1922.

[637] Ferrier, *History*, pp. 570-73.

with Standard (NJ) on behalf of APOC over an equal shares of its north Persian concession. Lloyd-Graeme was hopeful that this would lead to a settlement in Iraq but believed that it was essential that the first move should come from Standard (NJ); it was vital not to show any uncertainty over the solidity of the British position.[638] Three days later Sir Auckland Geddes reported from Washington that the two companies had reached agreement.[639] The Foreign Office was in favour of the combination but opposed the proposal that Standard (NJ) alone should give Persia a loan; it feared that this would make the Persians think that their policy of playing the Americans off against the British had succeeded.[640] Lloyd-Graeme thought that the agreement was vital; arguing about the loan would jeopardise negotiations that the British government had instigated.[641]

The loan issue was settled by financing it from the oil royalties, but the proposed alliance between Standard (NJ) and APOC in north Persia was never finalised. The Persians objected because Standard (NJ)'s concession was not transferable to foreigners. Standard (NJ) became concerned that oil might not be found and wanted to be able to exit within a year. The Persians offered the concession to Sinclair, another US company, but it withdrew after it was implicated in the bribery scandal over the US naval oil reserves at Teapot Dome in Wyoming. The significance of the abortive negotiations was that they brought Standard (NJ) and APOC closer together.[642]

7.4.2 Palestine

Standard (NJ) had been granted a concession in Palestine by the Ottoman Empire before the war. In early 1920 it asked for permission to explore for oil. Britain refused on the grounds that it was unwilling to permit such activities in occupied enemy territory until its future had been settled. An application in May 1919 by the Zionist Organization of America to send two geologists to Palestine had been accepted on condition that they were visiting in a private capacity and not on

---

[638] CO 730/27. 3167: Petroleum Department to Churchill, 12 January 1922.

[639] Ibid. 3167: Sir Auckland Geddes to Foreign Office, 15 January 1922.

[640] Ibid. 3167: Foreign Office to Sir Auckland Geddes, 15 January 1922.

[641] Ibid. 3167: Lloyd-Graeme to Churchill, 17 January 1922.

[642] Ferrier, *History*, pp. 573-80.

behalf of any company.[643] In September 1921 Standard (NJ) renewed its request via the US Ambassador to London; the Foreign Office forwarded it to the Colonial Office, pointing out that Curzon blamed the USA for the lack of progress in granting the mandate for Palestine.[644] Churchill agreed with Curzon over the delay to the mandate but did not want to use this to block the application unnecessarily or to miss a chance to remove a source of Anglo-American antagonism, however minor. It should be made clear that granting permission did not imply an acceptance of the validity of Standard (NJ)'s concession. The High Commissioner in Palestine should be consulted first.[645] Standard (NJ)'s request was accepted; the Foreign Office noted that the existence of the concession had been a factor in the decision but insisted that this did not prejudice its validity. Standard (NJ) would not be allowed to develop any discoveries until the terms of the mandate had been agreed and had to provide the Palestine government with full details of its discoveries.[646] Little oil was found in Palestine, but this shows the British desire to remove a relatively minor source of tension with the USA.

7.4.3 TPC and the USA

The British government wanted Iraqi oil to be developed by the TPC, with the revenue accruing to Iraq. Britain would have a secure source of supply and the oil rather than Britain would fund Iraq. In June 1921 Hankey asked Churchill on behalf of the prime minister whether Iraqi oil should be developed by the British government or a private company. Churchill replied out that the correspondence between the Foreign Office and the US Government said that the Anglo-French Petroleum Agreement was based on the TPC's claim. As other interests were to be excluded on the grounds that the TPC's claim was valid the oil could not be developed other than by private companies. If it were to be developed by a

---

[643] FO 608/97/17, 'Mines and Minerals: American Zionist Scientific Mission; Visit of F Julius Fohs and William H Foster to Palestine in Connection with Oil Prospecting', 1919.

[644] CO 733/11, 'Colonial Office: Palestine Original Correspondence Sept-Dec', 1921. 47206: Oliphant to Colonial Office, 20 September 1920.

[645] Ibid. 47206: Shuckburgh to Foreign Office, 29 September 1921.

[646] Ibid. 53515: Oliphant to Harvey, 26 October 1921.

government it would be the Iraqi, not the British one; it would be far better if the work was carried out by a British company.[647]

Two months later Churchill wrote that ministers had decided on 23 January 1920 that Iraqi oil revenue should go to the state rather than to private companies. This did not rule out operation of the fields by a private company, which would pay royalties to the government. An Arab government was now being formed, making it inconsistent for Britain to own or develop the fields. Whilst arguing in favour of the TPC's claim to the concession Curzon had stated that neither this nor San Remo would prevent the Arab State from receiving the benefits of ownership or deciding the terms of development. Churchill thought that development of the oilfields should not be further delayed.[648]

In March 1922 he told the cabinet that work had yet not started. The High Commissioner for Iraq wanted to expedite the exploitation of Iraqi oil. This would solve political and financial problems. Iraq, despite its unexploited oil reserves, was suffering from high fuel prices. The railways were making a loss, largely because of fuel costs. It might be uneconomic to run the irrigation pumps of the Baghdad region, which were vital for agriculture, unless kerosene prices fell. Iraqis could not understand why the British, who would benefit from the prosperity of Iraq, were holding up development of Iraq's most significant natural resource. The reasons for the delay were that work could not proceed until the issues of mandates and the TPC concession had been settled with the USA. Britain could give up the TPC claim; the problem with this was the vigour with which Britain had publicly defended it. It could be submitted to arbitration, but it was not certain that Britain would win, as the claim was based on diplomatic rather than legal considerations.

One option was that the TPC would carry out exploration across the country and choose a certain number of areas to develop. The Iraqi Government could then offer licences to other companies covering the rest of the country. The problem was that this would confirm the monopolistic nature of the TPC concession. An alternative was to offer Standard (NJ) a percentage of either the oil or the

---

[647] CAB 24/125, C.P. 3077 'Mesopotamian Oil', M. P. A. Hankey, 27 June 1921.

[648] CAB 24/127, C.P. 3271 'Mesopotamian Oil and the Turkish Petroleum Company', W. S. Churchill, 29 August 1921.

shares of the TPC. The Colonial Office and the Foreign Office agreed that the best course of action was to allow US oil companies into the TPC; the Petroleum Department and APOC were understood to concur. An informal committee had decided that if Britain made the first move it might seem that it doubted the legality of the TPC claim. Initial negotiations should take place on a commercial basis with Standard (NJ) being manoeuvred into making the initial move. This had already happened following the successful negotiations between APOC and Standard (NJ) over the North Persian oil concessions.[649]

In April a meeting took place between Bedford of Standard (NJ), who was representing a consortium of US oil companies, and Greenway and Cadman of APOC. Bedford said that he wanted British and US oil companies to co-operate and would prefer it if discussions proceeded on a purely commercial basis, without political considerations. Greenway agreed but pointed out that the British government had been involved in the TPC. Bedford wanted US companies to be allowed to take a stake in the TPC and thought that he could persuade the US government to agree to this. Greenway said that, before talks could begin with the US companies, the US government would have to accept the validity of the TPC concession or at least that any discussions would not prejudice the TPC's claims.[650] The US consortium, the Near East Development Corporation, initially comprised Standard (NJ), Standard (NY), Gulf, Atlantic Refining, Texas, Mexican and Sinclair.[651] In June 1922 the State Department informed Bedford that it insisted on the principle of the open door and did not recognise that the TPC concession was valid. It did not want to stop US companies from exploiting commercial opportunities and had no objections to negotiations between US and British companies on two conditions. All US companies that wanted to participate should be allowed to do so, and the US government would not accept the legality of the TPC concession without an impartial investigation of the issue. The concession could be confirmed or a new one issued if US companies

---

[649] CAB 24/134, C.P. 3832 'Iraq Oil', 13 March 1922.

[650] POWE 33/95, 'Mesopotamia: Turkish Petroleum Co Negotiations Regarding San Remo Agreement', 1921-23. Memorandum by Cadman of meeting on 9 April 1922.

[651] Longrigg, *Oil*. Note 1, p. 68. Texas dropped out in 1923 and Sinclair in 1927, when Pan American replaced Mexican.

reached agreement with the TPC. Bedford informed the State Department that the consortium comprised all the US companies interested in Iraq.[652]

Standard (NJ) took the lead. In July Walter Teagle, its President, came to London to negotiate a US stake in the TPC. The French and RDS had to be persuaded. Cadman told Clarke that the French regarded their stake in the TPC as an option, leaving them free to accept a better offer if one came along.[653] According to Clarke Deterding of Royal Dutch would agree to bring the Americans into the TPC only if it was necessary in order to proceed with development of Iraqi oil.[654] The French had not yet formed a company to take up their stake, and their delegates had limited powers. They had no objection to including the Americans providing that it was not at the expense of their stake.[655] They tried to use the negotiations to alter the San Remo Agreement.[656] Churchill thought that problems arose because the French were represented by government officials at what were supposed to be commercial negotiations. They asked for diplomatic concessions when only financial aspects were supposed to be discussed.[657] Most of their requests were rejected except that that the clause that France would contribute disproportionately to any Iraqi stake was changed to make it come proportionately from all shareholders.[658] By December APOC and RDS had agreed that each of them, the US consortium and the French would have 24 per cent of the TPC. Gulbenkian would have four per cent instead of the five per cent he had been given in 1914; his shares would be non-voting. This required agreement from the Americans and the French. Lancelot Oliphant of the Foreign Office feared that the slowness of the French in taking up their stake in the TPC suggested that they might see it as an option, and were awaiting a clear acceptance of the company's rights. He wanted future discussions with the French to be undertaken by the TPC on a commercial

---

[652] "FRUS". 1922 vol. ii, The Acting Secretary of State to the Ambassador in Great Britain (Harvey), 24 June 1922, pp. 337-38.

[653] POWE 33/95. Cadman to Clarke, 4 July 1922.

[654] Ibid. Clarke to Shuckburgh, 5 July 1922.

[655] Ibid. Clarke to Colonial Office, 28 July 1922.

[656] Ibid. Clarke to Lloyd-Greame, 4 August 1922.

[657] Ibid. Colonial Office to Foreign Office, 10 August 1922.

[658] Ibid. Clarke to TPC, 14 December 1922.

basis.[659] It took several years to finalise everything, but the participants were moving slowly towards agreement.

7.5 British Naval Strategy and Oil after Washington

The result of the Conference required some adjustments be made to RN planning. In August 1921 the Committee on National Expenditure, normally called the Geddes Committee after its chairman, Sir Eric Geddes, was established. It produced three interim reports between December 1921 and February 1922; the armed forces were dealt with in the first of these.[660] The Navy Estimates for 1922-23 were approximately £81,000,000, of which £11,800,000 was for the construction, currently suspended, of four new capital ships. The committee made no recommendations on this or on any cost savings that might arise from the Washington Conference.[661] It thought that it might be feasible to make major savings on oil fuel for the fleet but did not consider this because it was 'a matter of high policy.'[662] It should be possible to reduce the Naval Estimates to £60,000,000 in 1922-23 and lower levels in later years.[663] Substantial cuts were also proposed in the Army and Air Estimates; in neither case was oil and petrol mentioned as a separate item.[664] The third and final report concluded by saying that the specific cuts identified by the committee were £13,250,000 short of the £100,000,000 target. It was confident that the gap could be made up from three sources; reduced naval spending resulting from the Washington Conference; cuts in expenditure in naval oil stocks; and reduction in military garrisons abroad.[665] The Admiralty argued that it was not possible to make such drastic savings.[666] Beatty left the Washington Conference before it ended to defend the RN from Geddes. Eric Grove argues that he did a

---

[659] Ibid. Oliphant to Petroleum Department, 28 December 1922.

[660] PP, *Committee on National Expenditure. First Interim Report of Committee on National Expenditure*, HMSO 1922 [Cmd. 1581].

[661] Ibid., p. 9.

[662] Ibid., p. 28.

[663] Ibid., pp. 31-32.

[664] Ibid., pp. 53-101.

[665] *Committee on National Expenditure. Third Report of Committee on National Expenditure*, HMSO 1922 [Cmd. 1589]. p. 170.

[666] *Remarks of the Admiralty on the Interim Report of the Committee on National Expenditure*, HMSO 1922 [Cmd. 1587].

good job.[667] The Cabinet established a committee, chaired by Churchill, to examine Geddes's recommendations for cuts in defence expenditure. the Washington Conference had concluded by the time that it reported.[668]

Churchill's Committee pointed out that Geddes had ignored inflation when comparing 1914 and current defence spending. Churchill agreed with his recommendation that an body to co-ordinate the three armed forces was needed. A Ministry of Defence might eventually fill this role; for now the CID should do so. Geddes had come up with specific savings of £14,500,000 in the Naval Estimates of £81,000,000, and claimed that a total of £21,000,000 could be saved, before any potential reductions resulting from the Washington Conference. Churchill's committee had considered only the post-Washington position but could not see how £21,000,000 could have been saved without a successful Washington Conference. Failure at Washington would have brought the world close to war in the Pacific. There would have been a naval building race between the USA and Japan requiring major construction by Britain unless it was prepared to allow the RN to fall to second or third place. Britain had now accepted a one power standard, giving it equal naval strength with the USA, but its situation was inferior to that of the USA; Britain, unlike the USA, was dependent on food imports. Good relations with the USA had to be maintained; it was hoped that US naval strength might decline during a long peace. The RN had to be kept up to the standard of the USN, which did not mean equality of all factors. If the RN was regarded as weaker than the USN, Britain's place and influence in the world would be diminished. The Dominions would think that the centre of the Anglo-Saxon world had moved to the USA.

The most probable opponent was Japan; the CID should look at it as a matter of urgency. Before the introduction of oil the RN was far more mobile than any other fleet in the world because of Britain's network of global coaling stations. Beatty said that the USA could not oppose Japan across the Pacific. Britain could not hold Hong Kong against Japan, and could not hold Singapore unless it was adequately defended. A fleet able to fight Japan could not be based at

---

[667] Grove, *Royal Navy*, p. 149.

[668] CAB 24/132, C.P. 3692 'Report of Cabinet Committee Appointed to Examine Part I (Defence Departments) of the Report of the Geddes Committee on National Expenditure', W. S. Churchill, 4 February 1922.

Singapore until oil stocks were established there and on the route to it. The oil fuelling depots and the Singapore base should be discreetly built up.[669]

Naval Estimates of £62,000,000 after the savings resulting from the Washington Conference were recommended. This was £2,000,000 more than Geddes had proposed without considering Washington. Table 7-2 shows that the Churchill Committee suggested cuts in defence expenditure that, whilst substantial, were not as much as the Geddes Committee had wanted.

Table 7-2 Defence expenditure cuts: proposals of Geddes and Churchill Committees

Service	Estimates, 1921-22	Sketch Estimates, 1922-23	Geddes Committee, 1922-23	Churchill Committee, 1922-23	Savings proposed by Geddes	Savings proposed by Churchill
RN	£ 82,479,000	£ 81,183,800	£ 60,000,000	£ 61,883,800	£ 21,183,800	£ 19,300,000
Army	£ 118,000,000	£ 75,197,800	£ 55,000,000	£ 58,549,800	£ 20,197,800	£ 16,648,000
RAF	£ 18,411,000	£ 12,957,000	£ 7,457,000	£ 10,750,000	£ 5,500,000	£ 2,207,000
Iraq and Palestine (military)		£ 12,720,700		£ 8,000,000		£ 4,720,700
Total	£ 218,890,000	£ 182,059,300	£ 122,457,000	£ 139,183,600	£ 46,881,600	£ 42,875,700

Source: Source: CAB 24/132 CP 3692 'Report of Cabinet Committee appointed to examine Part I (Defence Departments) of the Report of the Geddes Committee on National Expenditure., Winston S. Churchill. 4 February 1922.

The Admiralty said that the Washington Conference meant that it could accept a slower rate of build up of oil stocks. It had asked for £2,000,000 to be included in the 1922-23 Sketch Estimate for oil stocks on the route to Singapore. The Treasury had stated that no more than £1,500,000 could be spent on storage and reserves. This was originally unacceptable to the Admiralty. The intended Pacific agreement meant that it could now accept this for one year only. Other savings, detailed in Table 7-3, meant that a total of £2,321,000 could be saved on fuel costs. This was the second largest contributor to a saving of £19,300,100 on the Naval Estimates, which were reduced to £61,750,000. The biggest cut was £9,839,700 in the capital ship programme. The Admiralty insisted that it was impossible to cut fuel costs any further. The RN's mobility required adequate stocks of oil; Britain was dependent on US oil until reserves could be built up.

---

[669] Ibid., pp. 4-7.

This was unacceptable as it gave the USA diplomatic power over Britain. It was suggested that global oil interests might combine, making Britain dependent on them. Building up a reserve by buying consistent amounts annually saved money because it allowed oil to be purchased on long term contracts and transport to be planned. British naval policy was to have a war reserve at home and abroad for both naval and commercial needs. The conversion of the fleet from coal to oil meant that oil bunkering facilities had to be set up at strategic ports. Coal bunkering had been easier to provide as coal could be stored in the open if necessary, and did not need specialist ships to transport it. [670]

Table 7-3 Fuel cost savings proposed by Admiralty to Churchill Committee

Item	Saving	Total
Fuel costs, 1921-22 Estimates		£ 10,044,000
Fuel costs, 1922-23 Sketch Estimates		£ 7,075,500
Saving from slower build up of stock on route to Singapore	£ 500,000	
Reduced sea time by Atlantic and Mediterranean Fleets	£ 180,000	
Laying up of Royal Fleet Auxiliaries	£ 285,000	
Abolition of 25,000 ton oil contingency reserve	£ 100,000	
Reduction in overseas freighters resulting from items above	£ 100,000	
Saving from lower prices	£ 1,156,000	
Savings in labour costs	£ 1,500	
Total saving on fuel costs from Sketch Estimates		£ 2,322,500
Fuel costs, proposed 1922-23 Naval Estimates		£ 4,753,000

Source: CAB 24/132 CP 3692A 'Appendices to Report of Cabinet Committee appointed to examine Part I (Defence Departments) of the Report of the Geddes Committee on National Expenditure', Secretary, 4 February 1922, pp. 9-10.

The most important part of the Admiralty's oil programme was establishing reserves in and on the route to the Far East; this would allow a large fleet to sail to Singapore to protect India, Australasia and Britain's Far East interests. The original plan was that it should have been possible to send a fleet to Singapore by 1925; the 10 year rule meant that oil stocks sufficient for a war with Japan would not have been built up until 1929. The reduction in capital ships and the Four Power Agreement agreed at the Washington Conference allowed savings to be made. Completion of the home and overseas oil reserves could be delayed

---

[670] CAB 24/132, C.P. 3692A 'Appendices to the Report of Cabinet Committee Appointed to Examine Part I (Defence Departments) of the Report of the Geddes Committee on National Expenditure', Secretary, 4 February 1922, pp. 9-10.

until 1929; the £500,000 reduction in expenditure on oil in 1922-23 assumed that subsequent estimates were adjusted upwards. The Admiralty insisted that these proposals should not prevent it from asking for greater storage and build up of reserves in the future if required by changes in the international political situation.[671] The eventual Naval Estimates for 1922-23 totalled £64,883,700, including £4,635,000 on fuel. The Admiralty had requested that the reduction in build up of stocks on the route to Singapore be delayed for only a year, but there was a further fall in fuel expenditure to £4,290,000 out of total Naval Estimates of £58,000,000 the next year.[672]

In July 1922 the naval staff submitted a paper on the impact of the Washington Conference on Imperial naval planning. It argued that the USN could not do anything to prevent Japanese aggression in the Western Pacific because of the prohibition on it developing any naval bases west of Hawaii. This would leave the British Empire to deal with such actions alone. The Four Power Treaty meant that a conference would be held in an attempt to resolve any disputes in the Pacific. This reduced the risk of war but would not allow much time for military preparation if diplomatic efforts failed. The chances of there being a war in the next 10 years were regarded as small but provision still had to be made for the defence of the Empire. The safety of the Empire, including the Dominions, depended on the maintenance of naval communications. The Admiralty continued to believe that the best solution was the formation of a single Imperial Navy, but this was opposed by the Dominions. The base at Singapore and global oil stocks were vital to the strategy to move the main fleet to Asia in the event of war. The Admiralty wanted the Dominions to contribute to the construction of Singapore, either financially or with materials. They, along with India and some colonies, should establish the oil reserves that had already been recommended.[673]

---

[671] Ibid. 'Statement VI: British Oil Fuel Policy as Affected by the Washington Conference', pp. 34-35.

[672] PP, *Navy Estimates for the Year 1922-23*, HMSO 1922 (74). See Appendix III for details of naval fuel expenditure from 1919-20 to 1923-24; *Navy Estimates for the Year 1923-24*, HMSO 1923 (23).

[673] CC, Roskill Papers, ROSK 7/60, 'Washington Conference 1921-22'. 'The Washington Conference and its Effect upon Empire Naval Policy and Co-operation', original reference ADM 116/1776, C.I.D. Paper 176-C.

Financial constraints prevented the Admiralty from building up its oil stocks as quickly as it would have wished. On 14 December 1922 Amery recorded in his diary that the Admiralty had agreed to postpone completion of the home oil reserve until 1937 provided that it could finish the Singapore one by 1931 and the stocks on the route to Singapore by 1935.[674] In August 1923 the Financial Secretary to the Treasury, William Joynson-Hicks, argued that the home reserve of 4,500,000 tons, equal to 12 months' consumption of the then planned fleet, was more than was needed. By March 1923 2,457,560 tons of storage had been completed. This was enough for more than six months' consumption at the rate assumed in 1919; the reduction in the size of the fleet after Washington should mean lower consumption. There would be no difficulty in buying oil except in the event of war with the USA, which Johnson-Hicks did not think was a feasible proposition. The existing home reserve should be enough for hostilities with any European Power or Turkey. Separate provision was being made for a conflict with Japan. The oil price would rise in wartime, but wartime purchases might still be cheaper than stock bought years before at peacetime prices once compound interest was factored in. When the stocks were complete, the annual interest bill on the cost of purchase would be £1,000,000. He wanted the home oil reserves to be set at six months.[675]

A flaw in his arguments was that the ships scrapped after Washington were older coal burners. The Washington Treaty required Britain to scrap 20 capital ships immediately, and another four once the two new battleships were completed; all burnt a mixture of coal and oil. Fifteen of the 20 to be retained would be entirely oil fired; two light battle cruisers would be converted into aircraft carriers, giving Britain five, all exclusively oil burning.[676] The Director of Plans wrote to the Deputy Chief of the Naval Staff proposing that the Naval Staff should again consider the oil position. If the RN's current demands for oil stocks were reasonable extending the time taken to establish them or reducing the

---

[674] J. Barnes, D. Nicholson, eds, *The Leo Amery Diaries* (London: Hutchinson, 1980). vol. i, entry for 14 December 1922 ,p. 312

[675] CAB 24/161, C.P. 384 (23) 'Home Reserve of Oil Fuel for the Navy', W. Joynson-Hicks, 4 August 1923.

[676] For technical details of warships see Chesneau, *Conway's 1922-1946*; Gray, *Conway's 1906-1921*; For the list of capital ships to be scrapped and those to be retained, see CAB 24/133 C.P. 3738, Hankey. 'Treaty for the Limitation of Armaments', p. 12.

amounts supplied would eventually create problems. If they were too great the country's economic position required that they were reduced.[677]

The paper reiterated that the reasons why the RN required large oil reserves. It depended on oil, very little of which was produced in the British Empire, making the mobility of the fleet and much of the Merchant Marine reliant upon foreign supplies. Special tankers and storage facilities were required. Britain had suffered an oil crisis in 1917; oil would be even more significant in a later war. The Admiralty concluded in 1919 that 12 months' war usage was the appropriate level of reserves. This was accepted by the Cabinet; the decision was reviewed and confirmed by the CID in 1921 and again in 1922. The latter review concluded that the oil reserves should total 8,139,000 tons. The Treasury now proposed home reserves of only six months' war expenditure. In the final year of the recent war, 24,000,000 tons of coal and 3,769,000 tons of oil had been used. This was for a war of relatively limited mobility. The fleet was now almost entirely oil burning, and the use of oil by merchant ships had risen since 1918. These factors suggested that the 1922 estimate was too low, especially for a war fought a long way from home waters. The new estimates are given in Table 7-4. These were thought to be conservative since they did not allow for losses of oil by attacks on tankers or storage facilities, any working margin or possible growth in oil usage by merchant ships; extrapolation of the growth rate of the last three years would take this to 4,000,000 tons, rather than the 2,000,000 estimated. Supplies from British controlled sources, such as Persia and Egypt were assumed to cover these risks, but these could be disrupted by enemy action or by technical or labour problems.[678]

---

[677] ADM 1/8673/234, 'Oil Fuel Reserves. Memorandum for the Committee of Imperial Defence', 1924. D. of P. to D.C.N.S. 28 August 1923, original reference Cabinet No. 384/23

[678] Ibid. NS1086.

Table 7-4 Naval oil reserves required and adopted, 1923

Usage	Tons
Fleet including armed merchant cruisers	4,767,000
Auxiliaries and transports directly concerned with operations	2,510,000
Merchant Marine	2,000,000
Total required	9,277,000
Reserves	
Home	4,500,000
Abroad	2,639,000
Not determined	1,000,000
Total currently adopted	8,139,000

Source: NA, ADM 1/8673/234, 'Oil Fuel Reserves. Memorandum for the Committee of Imperial Defence', 1924. NS1086, pp. 4-5.

The Treasury's desire to reduce the RN's planned oil reserves and the Admiralty's desire to increase them led to a lengthy correspondence between Amery and Neville Chamberlain.[679] The situation was still unresolved in February 1924 when a minority Labour Government took office. It was considered at two meetings of the CID that month. At the first the First Lord of the Admiralty, Lord Chelmsford, pointed out that the Admiralty wanted to add 500,000 tons to its oil reserve each year but had been allowed only 200,000 in 1921, 400,000 in 1922 and 220,000 in 1923 by the Treasury. Snowden agreed that an oil reserve was necessary and accepted that 12 months' supply might be the appropriate level. He could not see how the Admiralty had calculated its figures for its target reserve and pointed out the significance of public opinion; there were many other claims on government funds. He wanted to delay accumulation of the reserves and review the situation in two or three years time. He hoped for a second Washington Conference and perhaps better relations with Japan. He was unconvinced by the Admiralty's claim that it would be hard to obtain oil in wartime and pointed out that a war with Japan would probably not be global so would put less strain on British merchant shipping than the last one.[680]

At the second meeting Lord Haldane, the Chairman. pointed out that CID had decided in December 1922 to delay completion of the home reserve until 1937, subject to there being no worsening in the political situation; stocks on the route to the East had to be ready by 1931. The Admiralty had now been asked to

---

[679] Ibid.

[680] ADM 116/3102, 'Post-War Oil Storage Abroad', 1918-27. CID, 4 February 1924.

take their oil reserves as a whole, meaning neither the Home nor Eastern reserves would be completed until 1937. The Admiralty wanted 8,139,000 tons, the level agreed in 1922 rather than the higher one suggested in the 1923 Admiralty memorandum referred to above. This included 1,000,000 for merchant shipping; it was intended to look at this separately. Current reserves totalled 2,830,000 tons, leaving 4,309,000 to be provided. The CID confirmed the 1919 decision that the minimum level of oil fuel reserves should be 12 months' war consumption.[681]

7.6 Chapter Summary

Oil was one of a number of factors souring Anglo-American relations in the early 1920s. The Washington Conference eased the other areas of tension, at least for a while. The end of the risk of a new naval race and the government's desire to cut spending meant that the build up of the RN's oil reserves were delayed. The fleet was reduced in size, but the ships scrapped almost all burnt a mixture of coal and oil so oil demand did not fall commensurately. Oil was not discussed at Washington, to Britain's relief, but the improvement in Anglo-American relations that resulted was significant for Britain's oil strategy. Instead of having to allow for the possibility of US hostility in oil planning, Britain could adjust its oil policy to help improve Anglo-American relations. Japan was now Britain's most likely enemy, affecting naval planning, including the RN's oil needs. At the same time as the Conference, Cadman was in the USA, trying to explain Britain's oil position to the Americans. His speeches and interviews helped with Anglo-American reconciliation.

The British Empire had little oil so the main area of dispute concerned the potential oil of Mosul, where Britain claimed that the TPC had a valid concession. Britain realised that control of oil bearing territory was more important than ownership of companies, so giving US companies a stake in the TPC would not harm Britain's strategy of obtaining secure oil supplies from Mosul. This enabled Britain to attempt to remove this irritant to Anglo-American relations, but there were questions over the legality of the TPC's claim; a consortium led by Colby Chester, a retired American Admiral, was trying to

---

[681] Ibid. CID, 11 February 1924.

obtain a concession from the Turkish Republic. The US government insisted that it could not take sides between Chester and the US companies who were negotiating for a stake in the TPC.

8 The Bonar Law Government and Oil

The Bonar Law Government considered whether or not Britain should remain in Iraq. Turkey's revival under the leadership of Kemal Ataturk and its victory in the Greco-Turkish War required the peace treaty with it to be renegotiated at Lausanne. Mosul and its potential oil was a factor in both. The Turks argued that Mosul should be Turkish, while Britain wanted it to be part of Iraq. If Mosul was Iraqi the TPC could be confident of retaining its concession. US companies had been negotiating for a share in the TPC since the middle of 1922, but a US group, the Chester Concession, had been granted wide-ranging economic rights in Turkey by the new government. If Mosul became Turkish the concession could go to either Chester or the TPC. The TPC concession had not been formally ratified because of the outbreak of war in 1914, so it was not certain that it was legally binding on Turkey. At Lausanne the US observers insisted that the USA could not favour either Chester or the potential US shareholders in the TPC over the other.

The Chester Concession was officially named the Ottoman-American Exploration Company, but it is usually called after its head, Colby Chester, a retired USN admiral. It had been trying to win the rights to construct railways in the Ottoman Empire since 1908; the terms would allow it to exploit all mineral resources 20 kilometres either side of the line. This was awarded in 1910, but was never ratified by the Ottoman parliament. On 10 April 1923 Turkey granted it a concession, but this was cancelled on 13 December. [682]

8.1 The Treaty of Lausanne

The Lausanne Conference to negotiate a new peace treaty with Turkey started on 20 November 1922. The Turks were in a far stronger position than they had been at Sèvres; they were united and possessed the moral and actual advantages of recent military victories. Britain, France and Italy were disunited. Britain's main strength at the conference was the negotiating skill of Curzon, its chief delegate. He obtained the presidency of the conference and the chairmanship of

---

[682] Gruen, 'Oil,' pp. 117, 120.

the Territorial and Military Commission, the most significant of its three commissions. The first question of major importance to Britain, freedom of the Straits, was resolved to Britain's satisfaction. The other main issue for Britain was whether Mosul would be part of Turkey or of Iraq; it was harder to settle.[683] Before the conference, the War Office told the Foreign Office that it wanted Mosul and Kurdistan to be part of Iraq. The Turks would be further from Baghdad and would have to cross difficult territory to threaten it. Handing them over to Turkey would place the British garrison at Baghdad would be in a risky position.[684] The Admiralty opposed any change to the Iraqi frontier that would threaten the oilfields or pipeline.[685] During the conference the new British government was reviewing its Iraq policy.

8.1.1 The Bonar Law Government's Iraq Policy

On 16 November 1922, a month after Bonar Law became Prime Minister, the Duke of Devonshire, the Colonial Secretary, wrote a memorandum on Mosul. The Turks were going to demand its return; it was unclear if they meant the vilayet or just the town. The town was towards the north of the vilayet, so it would be possible to draw a frontier putting it into Turkey but leaving most of the vilayet in Iraq. This would be politically impracticable as Mosul town and the plains country were mostly Arab, whilst the hill country to the East was Kurdish; the towns of Erbil, Kirkuk and Kifri to the south were almost entirely Turcoman. If Mosul town became Turkish so would the vilayet; the Air Ministry believed that it would then be impossible to hold Baghdad. Cox argued that this would be a betrayal of Faisal. Devonshire thought that it was hard to disagree. Faisal's prestige would be destroyed, and the Iraqis would look to deal with the Turks whilst they could. The loss of Mosul vilayet would cost Iraq some of its most fertile land and the oilfields on which its future wealth depended. The 60,000 Christian inhabitants would be likely to be massacred so would retreat with the British. They included 20,000 Assyrians who had already been expelled from their homes and moved to Iraq because they had backed the Allies in the war. Departing now would be a humiliating blow to Britain that would destroy its

---

[683] Dockrill, Goold, *Peace*, pp. 236-40.

[684] FO 141/722/12, 'Papers Leading up to the Lausanne Peace Treaty of 24 July 1923', 1923. War Office to Foreign Office, 19 October 1922.

[685] Ibid. Admiralty to Foreign Office, 20 October 1922.

prestige in the East. The Foreign Office had suggested that Turkey might be compensated for giving up its claim. The Middle East Department argued that the claim was unjustified, and the Turks had no right to any compensation. Even if they were entitled to something there was a good argument that this should come from Iraq, not Britain, as Mosul was Iraqi, not British. One possibility was that Turkey might receive a share of Iraqi oil, but this would add more complexity to an already complex situation. Other options included economic rights for Turks in Iraq, Iraqi recognition of the spiritual suzerainty of the Caliph and reciprocal diplomatic representation.[686]

The Cabinet instructed Curzon that he should not discuss any Turkish proposal to include Mosul in Turkey since Mosul had already been allocated to Iraq. He should not do anything that would increase Britain's commitments to Iraq. A committee, chaired by Devonshire, was set up to consider Britain's position in Iraq.[687] Its starting point was a note prepared by the Colonial Office, stating that control of the oil was one of five advantages of staying; the others were the air route across the Middle East, grain and cotton, safety of Persian Gulf and maintenance of an Arab state between Turkey and Persia. Further reasons to stay were the various obligations to locals.[688] The Colonial Office expanded upon these points in another note. The protection of the Persian oilfields and pipeline was a separate issue from that of the oil of Mosul. Oil had yet to be found in Iraq, but it was certain that large quantities were present, especially in Mosul. Britain might receive the concession even if Mosul was returned to Turkey. What mattered was keeping one of the world's largest potential oilfields within the British sphere of influence. Britain had spent a huge amount of money in Iraq since 1914, but spending had now been reduced to a reasonable level. Leaving now would mean that the past expenditure had produced no returns, but staying a while longer could produce substantial rewards.[689]

---

[686] CAB 24/140, C.P. 4303 'The Question of Mosul', Devonshire, 10 November 1922.

[687] CAB 23/32, 'Cabinet Minutes and Papers 64(22) - 72(22)', 1 November - 29 December 1922. Cabinet 76(22), 16 November 1922.

[688] NA, AIR 8/57, 'Iraq Committee 1922-23: I.R.Q. Papers and Meetings', 1922-23. 1. Note prepared by the Middle East Department, Colonial Office, I.R.Q. 2

[689] Ibid. 2. Note prepared by the Middle East Department, Colonial Office, to implement the skeleton statement circulated as I.R.Q. 2.

At the committee's first meeting on 8 December 1922 Amery, the First Lord, said that the Admiralty thought that it was vital to physically control the actual and potential oilfields and pipelines. The nature of the concessions was less important.[690] Four days later the majority of the committee agreed that commitments entered into during and after the war, and the acceptance of the mandate, meant that Britain should ratify a treaty that had been agreed with Faisal to implement the mandate. Lord Novar, the Secretary of State for Scotland, Lloyd-Greame, the President of the Board of Trade and Ronald McNeill, the Parliamentary Under-Secretary at the Foreign Office, dissented. McNeill was representing the Foreign Office on the committee because Curzon was at the Lausanne Conference. He read out a letter stating that Curzon was in favour of the resolution.[691] Amery wrote in his diary that McNeill's view must be embarrassing for Curzon, who wanted Britain to remain in Iraq.[692]

Amery submitted a memorandum to the committee ahead of its next meeting, explaining that the Admiralty wanted to keep British influence over Iraq because of oil. If the Iraqi oilfields were proven control of them would significantly improve Britain's poor oil situation. Along with the Persian field they were well located to supply operations in the Far East. In the short term withdrawing from Iraq would put the Persian oilfield, which supplied over half the RN's needs, at risk.[693] Following a visit to Iraq Amery said that he hoped that the government would not succumb to press pressure to quit Iraq. Britain had spent a lot there, but costs had now been brought under control. The RAF could run it cheaply. Investment in irrigation would produce large quantities of cotton and grain. Faisal and his cabinet saw themselves as Iraqis and would fight for Mosul. They regarded the oil as a major Iraqi resource that should not be given away by Britain. They claimed that neither the Turks, the TPC nor Admiral Chester had a valid concession. Amery argued that 'this oil question is a very burning one in Iraq and should not be lightly settled over the head of the Arab government.'[694]

---

690 Ibid. 45. Committee on Iraq. First Conclusions, 8 December 1922.

691 Ibid. 46. Committee on Iraq. Second Conclusions, 12 December 1922.

692 Barnes, Nicholson, eds, *Amery.* vol. i: 1896-1929, entry for 12 December 1922, p. 311.

693 AIR 8/57. 10. Admiralty reasons for retaining Iraq within our general sphere of influence. Memorandum by the First Lord of the Admiralty. I.R.Q. 10, 16 December 1922.

694 Ibid. 13. Impressions in the new Kingdom of Iraq. Extracts from a letter. Note by the First Lord of the Admiralty. I.R.Q. 15, 26 December 1922.

Novar and Lloyd Greame argued that Britain should leave Iraq because of the cost of staying. They did not think that the oil justified substantial expenditure by Britain and rejected the other reasons for remaining. In January Novar wrote that:

> 'The one serious reason advanced for continued occupation is to guard existing and potential supplies of oil, and that not only for ourselves but for America and other countries. It is not apparent why we should bear the whole cost of protecting property in which so many other powers are interested, while if the safety of the wells can be secured by a trifling baksheesh to the tribes, it will be better to adopt these methods rather than those of costly occupation.[695]

The idea that Britain could rely on local tribes to defend the Mosul oilfields had been rejected by General Lord Cavan, the CIGS. He contended that British influence over these tribes would be limited if Britain withdrew from Mosul and Baghdad. Iraq would be a buffer between Turkey and Persia and Afghanistan.[696] Lloyd-Greame did not agree that Iraq would prove to be an effective buffer against Turkey and Russia, requiring further British military expenditure to defend Iraq. The oil would be developed whether Britain stayed or not.[697]

In March 1923 Devonshire's report recommended that Britain should stay. The argument of leaving because of the cost of remaining was outweighed by the promises made by Britain, its obligations under the mandate, the interests of Iraq and its people and of Britain and its Empire. Since the Committee was established Curzon had argued at Lausanne that Mosul had to be part of Iraq. The issue had yet to be settled; even if Britain wanted to withdraw it could not do so until it was resolved. British evacuation of Iraq would lead to Turkey taking over Mosul at once and the collapse of the Arab Kingdom of Iraq. Withdrawal would take two years unless reinforcements were sent to cover the evacuation. It would break promises made to the Arabs and to the League of Nations. The Turks would be unlikely to stop at Mosul and would take over Baghdad and Basra as well. This would affect British interests in the Persian Gulf and would put the RN's oil supplies at risk. The Turks would want to regain control over Syria and

---

[695] Ibid. 19. Objections to be considered before confirming the Treaty with Iraq. Memorandum by the Secretary of State for Scotland. I.R.Q. 21, 10 January 1923.

[696] Ibid. 47. Committee on Iraq. Third Conclusions, 19 December 1922.

[697] Ibid. 33. Submission that the Committee should boldly face the broad issues of withdrawal from Iraq. Memorandum by the President of the Board of Trade. I.R.Q. 33, February 1923.

Palestine. The result would be that Turkey would have be in a stronger position than before the war; Britain's position in the Middle East, and even in India, would be threatened. The Committee recommended that Britain should terminate its mandate within a maximum of four years from the conclusion of peace with Turkey. The mandate would in any case be ended when Iraq entered the League of Nations; this would require it to have secure frontiers and a stable government. During these four years Britain's only expenditure in Iraq should be military and air spending, which would be reduced over the period, and the costs of the High Commissioner and his staff.[698]

Devonshire's report was followed by another from Lord Salisbury, the Lord President of the Council, He agreed with its principal recommendations. Britain wanted to give up Iraq and the Iraqis wanted it to go. This could not be done until it was certain that the Turks would not take over Iraq once Britain left. He suggested agreeing to this policy but keeping it secret.[699] On 26 April the Cabinet approved the Committee's recommendations. A new agreement would be signed to look after British interests. This should be announced as soon as arrangement could be made for a simultaneous announcement in Iraq.[700] On 2 May it was decided to state the new policy to Parliament the next day.[701]

8.1.2 Mosul

In December Curzon informed the Cabinet that the Turks would concede every other point, sign the treaty and end their friendship with Soviet Russia if Britain would give them Mosul vilayet. The Colonial Office had persuaded Curzon that surrendering Mosul would lead to the loss of Baghdad, the end of the Iraqi kingdom, the return of the Turks and a diplomatic defeat for Britain. He suspected that the Turks did not actually want Mosul but desired to be able to claim victory in Asia. They might want to claim, perhaps inspired by Russia, that they had been willing to concede everything except Mosul, but Britain had

---

[698] CAB 24/159, C.P. 167 (23) 'Committee on Iraq', Devonshire, 23 March 1923.

[699] CAB 24/159, C.P. 182 (23) 'Report of Committee on Iraq', Salisbury, 5 April 1923.

[700] CAB 23/45, 'Cabinet Minutes and Papers 1(23) - 28(23)', 1 January - 16 May 1923. Cabinet 22(23), 26 April 1923.

[701] Ibid. Cabinet 23(23), 2 May 1923.

prevented peace by insisting on having Mosul and its oil.[702] The press, notably the *Daily Mail* and the *Daily Express*, were campaigning for Britain to exit the Middle East on cost grounds. Robert Blake argues that the Prime Minister did not pay much attention to press criticism, but in this case it coincided with his views. He wanted to exit Iraq and did not want there to be the slightest suggestion that Britain might go to war for oil. On 8 January he reminded Curzon that Britain must not go to war for Mosul or try to enforce Sèvres without French support, which would not be forthcoming.[703]

On 23 January 1923 the Lausanne Conference turned to the Mosul question. Curzon had been in correspondence with Ismet Pasha, the chief Turkish delegate, on this issue for the last two months. Each insisted that his argument was backed by ethnic, political, historic, geographic, economic, military and strategic reasons. One key area of dispute was whether or not the Kurds, who comprised nearly 60 per cent of the population of Mosul, were ethnic Turks. Ismet thought that they were. Curzon disagreed. Ismet pointed out that the Kurdish delegates at Ankara wanted Mosul to be part of Turkey. Curzon claimed that they were not representative of the Kurdish population. Ismet said that a quarter of the population of Mosul were Arabs; the balance were Turkish. Another argument was over whether Mosul was economically linked more closely to Anatolia or to Baghdad. The Turks claimed that the British should have returned Mosul to them because they had no right to have occupied it in 1918 after the armistice was signed.[704] Ismet made no mention of oil. Curzon said that he wanted to deny the claims made by the global press that Britain was motivated by oil in its desire to control Mosul. He said that:

> The question of the oil of the Mosul Vilayet has nothing to do with my argument. I have presented the British case on its own merits quite independently of any natural resources there may be in the country. I do not know how much oil there may be in the neighbourhood or Mosul, or whether it can be worked at a profit, or whether it may turn out after all to be a fraud. During the time I have been connected with the foreign affairs of my country I have never spoken to or interviewed an oil magnate. I have never spoken to or negotiated with

---

[702] CAB 23/32. Cabinet 69(22), 7 December 1922.

[703] R. Blake, *The Unknown Prime Minister. The Life and Times of Andrew Bonar Law, 1858-1923.* (London: Eyre & Spottiswoode, 1955), pp. 487-88.

[704] PP, *Lausanne Conference on near Eastern Affairs 1922-1923. Records of Proceedings and Draft Terms of Peace.*, HMSO 1923 Cmd. 1814. pp. 339-93.

a single concessionaire or would-be concessionaire for the Mosul oil or any other oil.[705]

He went on to accuse the Turks of offering concessions in Mosul and Baghdad vilayets to British businessmen. Britain believed that the TPC had a valid concession but did not want there to be a monopoly. Negotiations were under way to bring other countries into the TPC. If oil was found and developed Iraq would be the main beneficiary, but the world, including Anatolia, would also benefit.[706]

Peter Sluglett notes that Curzon must have been aware of the high probability that Mosul contained large oil deposits.[707] He would had access to the report written by the naval staff ahead of the Paris Peace Conference arguing that the Britain needed oil and that Persia and Iraq were the best potential sources.[708] Curzon had participated in discussions on Mesopotamian oil even before 1919. Balfour said at the 13 August 1918 meeting of the War Cabinet that Britain needed the Mesopotamian oilfields. Curzon was present and commented that if Britain lost Baku then these were the only other significant ones available.[709] Curzon may have thought that Mosul should be part of Iraq regardless of the oil, and he may not have met any oil tycoons. His claim that he did not have any idea if there was oil in Mosul was false.

Ismet insisted that the issue was one of territory, but he had to comment on oil. Once Mosul was returned to Turkey the oil would be developed for the benefit of the world. A judicial enquiry was needed to discover the validity of the concession said to have been granted to the TPC in 1914. The Turks had received approaches from several potential concessionaires and had sent experts to London in order to find out about the resources of these groups. He wanted a plebiscite to be held. Curzon argued that it would be impossible with a nomadic and largely illiterate population; nobody was willing to supply the troops that would be needed to keep order. Curzon said that the matter should be referred

---

[705] Ibid., p. 360.

[706] Ibid., pp. 360-61.

[707] Sluglett, *Britain*, p. 72.

[708] FO 608/97/15.

[709] CAB 23/43, p. 10.

to the League of Nations if agreement could not be reached; Ismet argued that Mosul was part of Turkey so Turkey could not consent to having its fate determined by arbitration.[710] Andrew Mango, Kemal's most recent English language biographer, believes that the principal Turkish motive was a desire to have all the Kurds in Turkey, not the oil. Dividing the Kurds between Turkey and Iraq would encourage separatists.[711] Mosul provided an issue on which the Turks could attempt to split the Allies.[712]

The USA had not been at war with the Ottoman Empire but argued successfully that its contribution to the Allied victory meant that it had an interest in the outcome and was represented by observers. Fiona Venn notes that they were particularly interested in obtaining access to oil.[713] On 23 January 1923 they said that they were pleased that Curzon had said that major natural resources should not be developed by monopolies, and that Britain would not link concessions to diplomatic interests or the continuance of its mandate over Iraq. They reiterated that the USA continued to insist on the principle of the open door. All US interest had to be treated equally with conflicts being determined by judicial review. This indicated that bringing US companies into the TPC would not mean the removal of US support from Chester.[714]

A draft treaty was put to the Turks on 31 January. Britain referred the Mosul question to the League of Nations for arbitration because the conference had been unable to solve it.[715] Ismet stated that Turkey had no claims on the territories of the Ottoman Empire where the majority of the population were Arabs. He wanted eight days to consider the treaty. Curzon stated that he had been summoned home and had to leave in two days time.[716] The British were already concerned that the conference would break down. The French had recently occupied the Ruhr in retaliation for German defaults on reparation

---

[710] PP, *Cmd. 1814.* pp. 397-402.

[711] A. Mango, *Atatürk* (London: John Murray, 2001), pp. 366-67.

[712] Ibid., p. 378.

[713] F. Venn, 'Oleaginous Diplomacy: Oil, Anglo–American Relations and the Lausanne Conference, 1922–23', *Diplomacy & Statecraft* 20, no. 3 (2009), p. 418.

[714] PP, *Cmd. 1814.* p. 405.

[715] Ibid., p. 433.

[716] Ibid., pp. 444-46.

payments. Lord Derby, the War Secretary, thought that their reluctance to risk conflict with the Turks as well was understandable.[717] Michael Dockrill and Douglas Goold argue that the French view that the treaty was only a basis for talks encouraged the Turkish refusal to sign it. The conference was suspended after the British delegation left on 4 February. Dockrill and Goold contend that this benefitted the outcome since the treaty would have been ineffective if Turkey had been forced to sign it. The conference resumed in late April. The British delegation was headed by Sir Horace Rumbold, the Ambassador to Constantinople, and the treaty was finally signed on 24 July.[718]

The treaty did not included any specific mention of the TPC and its concession, but correspondence between Rumbold and the Foreign Office shows that this was an important issue for Britain. On 9 July he told the Foreign Office that the latest draft of the treaty would state that the pre-war TPC concession was valid and remains in existence. It was hoped that to avoid US objections by not making any statement of general principle.[719] Three days later Joseph Grew of the US delegation said that the USA would not agree to validating the 1914 TPC concession in the treaty because not all of its legal requirements had been fulfilled. He argued that the British, by trying to validate it, were attempting to obtain an unfair benefit from their military victory in the east, which would not have been possible without the US intervention in the west. He claimed that the US opposition to the concessions protocol was not directed against any one company; Rumbold replied that the US actions were aimed at the TPC.[720] By 17 July all references to the TPC and its concession have been removed from the treaty; the British delegation told the Petroleum Department that this was mainly, if not wholly, due to co-operation between the USA and the Turks. The oil rights would go to the Iraqi government.[721] The Turks insisted that the TPC concession could not be included in the treaty because of their obligations towards the Chester Concessions. Ismet said that it had been granted when the

---

[717] CAB 21/270, 'Notes of Informal Meeting of Ministers, 24 January 1923 - Includes Lausanne Conference', 1923. Derby to Hankey, 23 January 1923

[718] Dockrill, Goold, *Peace*, pp. 243-44.

[719] POWE 33/201, 'Iraq: Turkish and Italian Claims for Participation in Oil Resources', 1923. Rumbold to Foreign Office, 9 July 1923.

[720] Ibid. Rumbold to Curzon, 12 July 1923.

[721] Ibid. Payne to Clarke, 17 July 1923.

Turks had no communications with the rest of the world and had to give the concession to the first suitable applicant. Rumbold stated on 17 July that:

> I stated categorically that His Majesty's Government regarded all the obligations undertaken by the Ottoman Government in 1914 as binding on the Turkish Government in any territory which might remain to Turkey as a result of the Peace Treaty. They did not, I said, recognise any rights, whether within or without such territory, which might be alleged to have been granted by the Turkish Government to any third party and which would conflict the rights of the Turkish Petroleum Company. I affirmed the strong intentions of His Majesty's Government to hold the Turkish Government responsible for any failure to fulfil the obligations contracted in 1914.[722]

Ismet claimed that it was a legal issue that should be settled by arbitration. Grew said that the US opinion of the TPC remained unchanged. Rumbold argued that the British government had a responsibility towards the TPC. Turkey could not use arbitration to solve a conflict between two companies that had been created by its actions. He could not see how the USA had the right to intervene in a dispute over the rights of a British company in Turkey.[723]

The next day Curzon sent a very urgent telegram to Rumbold, showing that he was concerned about Britain's oil rights in Mosul:

> I am most uneasy at learning that you jettisoned case of Turkish Petroleum Company whose claim I repeatedly emphasised in discussion when at Lausanne regarding Mosul...it appears to me that mere unilateral reservation, however strongly couched by you cannot but prejudice materially our position in forthcoming negotiations about Mosul and will also weaken most seriously company's claims to rights under 1914 concession.
>
> Unless you are convinced that my apprehensions are not fully justified, you should insist on putting back the Turkish Petroleum Company into the protocol.
>
> I object very strongly to additional validity given to Chester Concession by our surrender.[724]

---

[722] Ibid. Rumbold to Foreign Office, 17 July 1923.

[723] Ibid. Rumbold to Foreign Office 17 July 1923.

[724] Ibid. Curzon to Rumbold, 18 July 1923.

It was not feasible to put the TPC clause back into the Lausanne Treaty. The company protested, but this was a matter of formality.[725] It entered into talks with the Iraqi government over a concession. Even if Mosul was granted to Turkey the TPC might still obtain the concession. In January 1925 the League of Nations Boundary Commission visited Iraq. Gertrude Bell, the Oriental Secretary to the High Commissioner, wrote that one of the Commissioners had told her that the Turks had informed them that the TPC would receive the concession regardless of the fate of Mosul. Another Commissioner had said the same thing to Sir Henry Dobbs, the British High Commissioner. Bell thought that this increased the chances of Mosul going to Iraq since it meant that Commission would not think that Britain was motivated by oil.[726] In late 1921 she had complained about the way in which the administration of Iraq was being hampered by the US refusal to recognise the mandate. She wrote that 'Oil is the trouble, of course - detestable stuff!'[727]

8.2 TPC - Final Structure and Concession

It took six years from the first talks between the US consortium and the TPC before everything was finalised. Negotiations with the USA, France, Iraq and Gulbenkian had to be concluded. The League of Nations had to decide the fate of Mosul. The existence of the oil had to be confirmed.

8.2.1 France and the TPC

Pineau, the head of the French delegation to the 1922 negotiations, could not understand how the British government could claim that the talks were purely commercial when it held a large stake in APOC. He was unable to persuade the Americans and British to allow France into their oil projects outside Iraq or to negotiate at a government level. He persuaded Raymond Poincaré, the French prime minister, that France would do better if it had its own national oil company to deal with the Anglo-American companies. In 1924 the Compagnie Française des Pétroles was established to hold the French stake in the TPC. It

---

[725] Ibid. Clarke to Oliphant, 25 July 1923.

[726] "Gertrude Bell Archive", University of Newcastle <<http://www.gerty.ncl.ac.uk/index.php>> (accessed 27 October 2008). Bell to her mother, 28 January 1925.

[727] Ibid. Bell to her father, 4 December 1921.

was owned by French companies and banks involved in the oil industry, including the French subsidiaries of foreign oil companies, but the government had a close involvement. It appointed two directors and could veto others, and had the right to purchase up to 80 per cent of its oil.[728] In 1929 the government took a 25 per cent stake.[729]

8.2.2 The USA and the TPC

Gerald Nash says that Secretary of State Hughes gave unclear advice to the US mission at Lausanne. He stuck to the principle of the open door for all US interests, refusing a request by Standard (NJ) to treat it specially. The Turks were keen to work with the USA as they thought that the Americans, unlike the British and French, would not exploit economic concessions for political gains. Hughes missed this opportunity.[730] In December 1922 he reminded Teagle that the State Department believed that the TPC concession was invalid until confirmed by the government concerned. It could not favour one US group over another in the case of a dispute.[731]

By late 1923 Hughes had adopted a more pragmatic approach towards the TPC. Stephen Randall quotes him as telling President Calvin Coolidge that the agreement was the best that could be achieved to help US companies. It did not fully accord with the principles of the open door. Hughes thought that the US government should promote co-operation rather than competition between US and foreign companies; Coolidge agreed. Randall quotes Wesley Frost, the Acting Foreign Trade Adviser, as saying that the open door principle did not work in the case of oil. The first few companies would take all the oil, leaving nothing for later entrants.[732]

---

[728] Melby, *France*, pp. 70-79.

[729] Ibid., pp. 103-4.

[730] Nash, *United States Oil Policy, 1890-1964. Business and Government in Twentieth Century America*, pp. 58-60.

[731] "FRUS". 1922, vol. ii, Correspondence between Secretary of State and President of Standard Oil of New Jersey, 15-30 December 1922, pp. 349-52.

[732] Randall, *United States*, pp. 36-37.

8.2.3 Italy and the TPC

At Lausanne, Benito Mussolini, the new Italian Prime Minister, renewed Italian efforts to obtain a share of Iraqi oil. Italy now had a bargaining chip; co-operation at the conference. On 16 December 1922 Curzon told the Italians that they would receive a share of the oil, either shares in the TPC or guaranteed oil supplies, once the Mosul issue had been decided in Britain's favour. [733] The company objected to this and a proposal to allow Turkey a stake in the TPC; introducing US companies created problems but brought in industry expertise. Italy and Turkey would bring difficulties without any benefits.[734] Delays over the resolution of the Mosul issue and the admission of US companies to the TPC meant that the question of Italian participation in Iraqi oil was not settled by the end of the Conference. The Italians ceased to press the issue, and Britain had less reason to offer them anything. Marian Kent argues that Britain treated Italy poorly, but the Italians created problems for themselves by the opportunistic manner in which they approached the issue of economic participation in the former Ottoman Empire.[735] Italy, unlike France and the USA, had nothing to offer Britain in return for a share of Iraqi oil so did not receive anything.

8.2.4 Iraq and the TPC

Negotiations between the TPC and the Iraqi government over a concession lasted from October 1923 until March 1925. The first meeting of the TPC with the CFP represented was held in London on 22 July 1924. Most issues regarding the concession were agreed, but Gulbenkian declined the shareholding that was offered to him. By the end of February 1925 agreement had been reached on all points except that the company was reluctant to allow the Iraqis the shareholding that they had been promised by the San Remo Agreement. On 4 March the TPC admitted to the Colonial Office that it could not avoid giving the Iraqis a shareholding, but the Iraqis dropped their demand for a shareholding and the concession was granted on 14 March. Ronald Ferrier suggests a number of

---

[733] M. Kent, 'Guarding the Bandwagon: Great Britain, Italy, and Middle Eastern Oil, 1920-1923,' in *National and International Politics in the Middle East: Essays in Honour of Elie Kedourie*, ed. E. Ingram (London: Cass, 1986), pp. 157-58.

[734] POWE 33/201. H. A. Nichols, Managing Director, TPC, to Petroleum Department, 24 January 1923.

[735] Kent, 'Guarding,' pp. 158-59.

possible reasons for the Iraqis change of stance; a desire for royalties now rather than dividends later; pressure by the British government; internal political reasons; or concern that failure to agree might result in the League of Nations not awarding them Mosul.[736] The Iraqis did succeed in having their royalties paid in gold rather than sterling and on a sliding scale that increased their share as output rose.[737]

The League of Nations Boundary Commission reported on 17 July 1925 that Mosul should awarded to Iraq. The Turks tried to have the decision reversed, but all involved had accepted by it by 18 July 1926.[738] Whilst all the geological evidence persuaded everybody involved that there was oil in Mosul, commercial quantities were not found until a major discovery was made at Baba Gurgur, near Kirkuk, on 15 October 1927. Gulbenkian's stake was not settled until 31 July 1928. He insisted on his right to 5 per cent and to be paid in cash, not oil. He agreed to take oil, which he could sell immediately to the CFP. The TPC shares were divided 5 per cent to Gulbenkian and 23.75 per cent to each of APOC, RDS, the CFP and the Near East Development Corporation, the US consortium. The partners signed the self-denying ordinance, or Red Line Agreement, in which they agreed to co-operate in the former Ottoman Empire, meaning all the oilfields of the Middle East except Kuwait and Persia.[739] The other members of the Near East Development Corporation were bought out by Standard (NJ) and Standard (NY) in the 1930s.[740]

8.3 Chapter Summary

Britain had a number of reasons to want to control Iraq. It wanted to protect its traditional position in the Persian Gulf, and the route to India. Both these could have been met by control of just the Basra vilayet. It wished to fulfil promises made to the local population and felt an obligation to install a new administration to replace the Ottoman one that it had removed. These required

---

[736] Ferrier, *History*, pp. 583-85.

[737] Sluglett, *Britain*, pp. 74-75.

[738] Ibid., pp. 85-86.

[739] Yergin, *Prize*, pp. 202-6.

[740] Gruen, 'Oil,' p. 122.

at least the Baghdad vilayet to also be held and probably Mosul, because it provided a more defensible frontier. Oil came into the equation in two ways. Britain wanted secure supplies, and it provided revenue that would finance the administration of Iraq, which Britain was unwilling to subsidise. Without the oil and its revenue it is unlikely that Britain would have retained more than Basra, regardless of its any obligations to the population. The TPC might still have won the concession if Mosul had been awarded to Turkey, but Iraq would not then have had the oil revenue. A British controlled concession in Turkey was not as good for Britain as oil in Iraq. It was more important that oil should be in territory controlled by or friendly to Britain than that concessions should belong to British companies. Archival evidence shows that oil motivated Britain's desire that Mosul should remain part of Iraq.

Other parties were treated according to their value to Britain. Faisal was expelled from Syria by the French because they thought that he was obstructing their plans for the country. Britain offered him the Iraqi throne and continued to support him because he could govern Iraq cheaply, with military support provided by the RAF. The French and the Americans both received stakes in the TPC because they had something to offer in return. The French had to agree to change the Sykes-Picot Agreement and to allow oil pipelines across their territory. Britain was keen to have good relations with the USA. The Americans accepted a deal that did not really fulfil the principles of the open door, but which benefitted US companies and was the best that could have been achieved. Italian attempts to obtain a share of Iraqi oil were initially unsuccessful as they had nothing to offer in return. At Lausanne it appeared that they would receive a share as Britain then needed their support. They did not as their interest had waned by the time that the TPC concession, its structure and the award of Mosul to Iraq had been concluded. The Kurds did not receive autonomy within Iraq as the Arab government, which Britain needed, did not want to give it to them. Turkey failed to obtain Mosul but was otherwise successful at Lausanne. Britain now controlled a potentially very large oil province. Obtaining this had affected its policy towards the Middle East and relations with France, Italy, Turkey and the USA.

Conclusion

Britain's oil strategy affected relations with France, Italy, Turkey and the USA, Middle Eastern policy, relations with oil companies and naval strategy during 1914 to 1923. Previous analyses of British oil strategy have concentrated on one of these parts, so have not brought all the aspects together. By 1914 the RN's increasing use of oil meant that Britain had to consider oil's strategic significance. The Admiralty invested in APOC to enable it to develop its Persian oilfields and gave it a long term supply contract. Protection of the oilfields, the pipeline to the Persian Gulf and the refinery at Abadan were amongst the reasons why IEF D was sent to Basra in November 1914. Winston Churchill, who was responsible for the decision to put Admiralty funds into APOC, did not want troops to be sent to the Gulf; he argued that they should be used at a more decisive point. This shows that the motivation behind the APOC transaction was to provide regular and cheap oil supplies in peacetime; it was assumed that oil could be bought in the market during wartime, a point made by Arthur Balfour, Churchill's successor as First Lord. IEF D secured the oilfields, pipeline and refinery by early 1915. There are better explanations for the subsequent expansion of the Mesopotamian campaign than oil. These are over confidence after early victories, an insistence that a further advance was needed to secure each conquest and a desire for a victory somewhere. Britain had no war aims in the Ottoman Empire before the de Bunsen Committee was established in 1915. The de Bunsen Committee included protection of the existing oilfields in Persia and obtaining control of the potential ones in the Mosul vilayet of the Ottoman Empire in its list of British desiderata, but these were only part of a lengthy list of British interests in the region. In 1916 the Sykes-Picot Agreement gave France much, but not all, of the Mosul vilayet and its potential oil. The establishment of a French controlled buffer zone between British and Russian territory was then regarded as being more important than British control of all of the oil.

The policy of business as usual continued until April 1917. Most Allied oil came from the USA even before it entered the war. It dominated the global oil industry and had adopted a policy of selling goods and materials to whoever could pay for and transport them. Rising demand for oil and tanker losses then meant that there was a risk that Britain would run out of oil. Walter Long was put in charge of oil matters. He had the necessary administrative skill and political stature to solve the problems and the sense to delegate technical matters to John Cadman. The Petroleum Executive was set up to manage Britain's oil requirements. Supplies were allocated and rationed with the armed forces being prioritised. Oil was deemed to be more important than food, as food could not be imported without control of the seas and protection of merchant ships from U-boat attack, which depended on oil fired warships. The 1917 oil crisis affected all the Allies; they set up the Inter-Allied Petroleum Conference to co-ordinate their oil needs. They never had quite enough, but they always had more than the Central Powers who had fewer trucks and tanks and had to restrict sorties by their aircraft. The oil crisis made Britain, France and Italy realise the need to secure their future oil supplies. In the USA it brought the companies closer to the government.

In July 1918 Admiral Sir Edmond Slade produced a paper arguing that Britain needed to secure reserves of oil and that the best place to do so was in Mosul. Slade was a director of APOC, and his paper led to a dispute with Long because it appeared to be written from APOC's point of view. It contained unsubstantiated allegations against the Petroleum Executive and RDS. The Admiralty had to retract the parts of it relating to oil company politics, but Slade's arguments on the strategic importance of oil in general and Mosul in particular were accepted. Subsequent papers by the Petroleum Executive and the Admiralty repeated his opinion that Britain needed to control its oil supplies and that Mosul was the best available source. He argued that Britain's control of the seas depended on its global dominance of coal bunkering. The world's merchant fleets were switching to oil, so Britain had to develop a similar position in oil bunkering in order to maintain its naval power. This view was accepted and reiterated in later papers. In October 1918 British forces in Mesopotamia, which had been a quiet theatre for some time, advanced to capture the town of Mosul. This was later controversial, as Britain at best bent the terms of the armistice with the Ottoman Empire to do so. In December Georges Clemenceau agreed with David Lloyd George's request that Britain should control all of the Mosul vilayet. The two prime ministers were not accompanied by any aides at the time; the only written record of what was discussed is a note made by Maurice Hankey in his diary relating Lloyd George's account of the meeting. Clemenceau was criticised in France for handing over Mosul, but Sykes-Picot gave France only about half of the potential oilfields. France had no company capable of exploiting them. Exchanging its part of Mosul for a share in British operated fields was an attractive option for France, especially if it could in return obtain British support for its other aims. Britain had objectives other than oil in Mesopotamia, but most of them could be met by control of the Basra vilayet. Only its oil, and perhaps irrigation schemes, required the Mosul vilayet.

Despite the agreement between the two prime ministers it took some time until Britain and France concluded an oil agreement. Long and Henry Bérenger signed one in April 1919, but Lloyd George cancelled it. The very similar Greenwood-Bérenger agreement of December 1919 was never ratified. An Anglo-French oil agreement was signed at San Remo in April 1920 and ratified. This was followed by the Treaty of Sèvres, which imposed very harsh terms on the Ottoman Empire. It appeared to give Britain all that it wanted in the Middle East, including the League of Nations mandate over Iraq, comprising the vilayets of Basra, Baghdad and Mosul. The similarity between the three oil agreements indicates that the first two were victims of other Anglo-French disputes during the peace conferences. Sèvres did not last thanks to the revival of Turkey under Mustafa Kemal, and disputes amongst the Allies. San Remo offended the Americans, who saw it as excluding them from the Iraqi oilfields of Mesopotamia. It was widely, albeit wrongly, believed that US oil production would soon peak.

Oil was one of a number of factors souring Anglo-American relations; others included Ireland, and the risk of a naval race between Britain, the USA and Japan. By 1919 the Admiralty had accepted that the RN would have to be based on a one power standard versus the USN, but feared that it would have to embark on a major construction programme in order to maintain parity with the USN. The US proposals at the Washington Conference meant that the RN had to build only two new ships to maintain equality with the USN in battleships. Britain hoped that it could maintain naval supremacy via cruisers and smaller ships. It might have been unable to maintain even a one power standard with the USN in a building race. Washington avoided such a race and gave the RN better than a two power standard excluding the USN. Some planning for a war with the USA took place, but the most likely future opponent was Japan. The fleet was smaller than in 1914, but the threat was now more widely spread geographically. This meant that British naval planning had to emphasise mobility, meaning that reserves of oil were needed at home, in the Far East and on the route to the Far East. Slade's view that British security depended on control of the world's fuel bunkering was accepted, resulting in plans being made to provide oil stocks for merchant shipping. The location of Middle Eastern oil made control of it particularly attractive. Plans for the build up of large reserves were devised, but the need to cut government spending meant that the completion date for these was continually pushed out. Government economies also meant that wartime administrative arrangements were not retained. The amounts saved were low, but this is probably an example of assuming that every penny counted rather than an indication of a downgrading of the importance of oil.

Reconciliation with the USA over oil began around the same time as the Washington Conference. Cadman, who had recently left government service to take up a senior post at APOC, was then in the USA and gave a series of conciliatory speeches and interviews. The archival evidence shows that his presence in the USA at that time was a fortuitous coincidence. His efforts led to negotiations to allow US oil companies a share of Iraqi oil. It was realised that the US companies could offer valuable technical expertise and capital; control of oil bearing territory was more important than the nationality of companies. From 1916 to 1924 several attempts were made to merge APOC, Burmah and Shell into a single company with a British majority. No scheme that suited all parties, or which guaranteed British control, could be devised. RDS supported the Allied war effort during the war. The British management of Shell behaved patriotically; those who distrusted Royal Dutch never explained why it would act against the interests of a country whose navy controlled the world's oceans and was the world's biggest consumer of oil.

On more than one occasion during the early 1920s Britain considered leaving Iraq, or at least vacating the Mosul and Baghdad vilayets and holding onto the Basra vilayet. The Iraqi Revolt of 1920 raised questions over the cost of remaining in Iraq. The solution to this was to place Faisal, who had fought with Britain during the war, on the throne and to govern through an Arab government; the RAF and local troops would provide most of the military strength. The reasons to hold onto Mosul and Baghdad were prestige, the need for a defensible frontier, promises to the Arabs and oil. Oil was important both because Britain needed secure supplies and because it provided Iraq with revenue. This system proved to be long lasting, but it was thrown into question in late 1922 by Turkey's victory in its war with Greece. The Treaty of Sèvres had to be renegotiated, raising the possibility that Turkey would regain Mosul. The fall of the Lloyd George Coalition meant that British policy might change.

The new Bonar Law Government formed a committee to examine whether or not Britain should remain in Iraq. It decided to stay; even those of its members who wanted to leave thought that oil was the only reason to stay. Whilst it was deliberating, negotiations with Turkey were taking place in Lausanne. One of the most problematic questions was whether Mosul should be part of Turkey or of Iraq. The Turks stated that they wanted to control only those parts of the Ottoman Empire where ethnic Turks comprised the majority of the population; they claimed that the Kurds of Mosul were Turkish so Mosul should be Turkish. Curzon argued that Mosul should be Iraqi, contending that the Kurds were not Turkish. He insisted that oil had nothing to do with his views, claiming that he did not know if there was even oil in Mosul. Regardless of what he thought of the ethnicity of the Kurds and of the need for Iraq to have defensible frontiers, he certainly knew that Mosul was highly likely to contain oil. He had discussed Mosul and its oil at Cabinet meetings and had access to reports describing the great potential of the Mosul oilfields. The conference was unable to resolve the future of Mosul and left the decision to arbitration by the League of Nations, which awarded it to Iraq in 1926.

If Mosul had become Turkish the oil concession might still have been awarded to a British company, but it could also have gone to another group, such as the American Chester Concession. A British owned concession in a foreign country did not provide as much security of supply as an oilfield in British controlled territory. BP was British and RDS partly British, but this did not help Britain when the USA threatened to cut off oil supplies after the Anglo-French invasion of Suez in 1956.[741] In 1973, following the Yom Kippur War, the Arab countries cut

---

[741] T. A. B. Corley, 'Oil Companies and the Role of Government: The Case of Britain, 1900-75,' in *Competitiveness and the State: Government and Business in Twentieth-Century Britain*, ed. G.

back exports and embargoed some consumer countries. The British government tried to make BP and RDS favour Britain, but both refused as doing so would be in breach of contracts with other consumers and contrary to the interests of their shareholders.[742] The award of Mosul to Iraq rather than the grant of the concession to the TPC gave Britain control over its oil.

By 1923 Britain had laid down an oil policy, which was to ensure supplies of oil, principally for naval use, by controlling oil bearing territory. Mosul was the largest available potential oilfield. Attempts to explore for oil at home failed to find significant quantities. Conversion of coal to oil was considered, but the necessary plants were expensive and vulnerable to aerial bombing. Building tankers to import overseas oil was cheaper. Britain obtained the mandate for Iraq and ensured that Mosul was part of Iraq. It did have other interests in the region, but most of them required control of only Basra of the three vilayets that comprised Iraq. Iraqi oil was well located for a navy that based much of its fleet in the Mediterranean, but might have to move it to the Far East in wartime. Development of Iraqi oil was initially slow, and it was 1927 before a large strike at Baba Gurgur confirmed that there was oil in Mosul. This led Britain to look at Venezuela as an alternative source of supply.[743] Iraq output was only around 100,000 tons in 1933, but reached 4,020,000 tons in 1936.[744] It fell in the early years of the Second World War. Most British oil came from the USA, whose production had risen rather than declined. Italian entry into the war closed the Mediterranean, whilst the RN played a relatively small role in the war with Japan. Iraqi and Iranian oil was used mainly to supply forces in the Middle East and India.[745] Iraqi output fell from 4,040,000 tons in 1939 to 1,610,000 in 1941, before rising to 4,620,000 in 1945. Iranian production was higher; 10,190,000 tons in 1939, 6,600,000 in 1941 and 16,840,000 in 1945.[746] The output of both countries then rose quickly.

Jones, M. W. Kirby (Manchester: Manchester University Press, 1991), p. 169; Yergin, *Prize*, pp. 489-93.

[742] Corley, 'Oil,' pp. 175-76; Yergin, *Prize*, pp. 623-24.

[743] See McBeth, *British*.

[744] Longrigg, *Oil*, pp. 478-79.

[745] See Payton-Smith, *Oil*. for British oil policy in the Second World War.

[746] Longrigg, *Oil*, pp. 478-79.